Robidoux's Town
A Nineteenth-Century History
of
St. Joseph, Missouri

by
Robert J. Willoughby
M.A. - Ph.D.

Robert Willoughby

Published by Platte Purchase Publishers
A Division of The St. Joseph Museums Inc.
Editor
Alberto C. Meloni
Production Managers and Editorial Assistants
Sarah Elder and Jacqueline Lewin

Library of Congress Control Number (LCCN): 2006901086
Willoughby, Robert J.
    *Robidoux's Town: A Nineteenth-Century History of
    St. Joseph, Missouri*/by Robert J. Willoughby, M.A., Ph.D.-
    Paperback Edition (A Platte Purchase Publishers Saint Joseph
    Series) Summary: It is the nineteenth-century biography of
    St. Joseph, Missouri; its potential, its successes, its competition
    for population, for economic stature, for transporation links,
    and for cultural distinction.

International Standard Book Number (ISBN): 0972535373
    [1. Platte Purchase Publishers (MO) – Adult History
    2. St. Joseph Museums Inc. – History/Local
    3. American Urban History – History/Urban
    4. Economic – History/Urban
    5. Cultural – History/Urban
    6. Missouri – History/Urban]
Originally published in Hardcover by Westphalia Publishing, 1997
ISBN 1-882935-31-4

Printed in USA by
BookMasters, Inc.
Mansfield, Ohio 44905

Front Cover: "St. Joseph 1850" by Harry Wright, From the Collections of the
            St. Joseph Museum
Back Cover: Joseph Robidoux, Founder of St. Joseph, Missouri, From the
            Collections of the St. Joseph Museum
Illustrations: From the Collections of the St. Joseph Museum or as they appeared in
            the *Museum Graphic* of the St. Joseph Museum (out of print)
Cover Concept: Alberto C. Meloni   Cover Design: Sarah Elder

Published by Platte Purchase Publishers

St. Joseph Series

On the Winds of Destiny by Jacqueline Lewin and Marilyn Taylor

Old Saint Jo by Sheridan Logan

Rare and Scarce Saint Joseph Books, Pamphlets and Music by J. Marshall White

Robidoux's Town by Robert J. Willoughby

Children's Discovery Series
The Elephant Way by Joyce Rochambeau

Civil War Series
A Darkness Ablaze by Joseph K. Houts, Jr.

As the Mockingbird Sang by Suzanne S. Lehr

Others
Midland Empire Studies: An Interdisciplinary Review of The St. Joseph Museums Inc.

Joseph Robidoux. *Courtesy of the Boder Collection*

TABLE OF CONTENTS

ILLUSTRATIONS

ACKNOWLEDGMENTS

Writing an urban biography of a city so rich in history as St. Joseph presented a real challenge. I could not have completed the work without the help of many people. Foremost, I wish to thank Dr. Lawrence Larsen, the chairman of my doctoral committee at the University of Missouri-Kansas City. He continually provided me with encouragement, guided me with patience, and gave constructive criticism of my work all along the way. I may never hope to be his peer as a historian, but I would be honored to be considered a protégé. My thanks go to other members of the faculty of UMKC; Dr. Louis Potts and Dr. William Worley of the History Department, and Dr. Dale Neuman and Dr. David Atkinson of the Political Science Department. Each provided excellent guidance, comment, and critique of this work. Likewise, my appreciation to Dr. Frederick Spletstoser for his excellent course, The Rise of the City in United States History, which greatly expanded my understanding of many urban topics.

I extend my gratitude to the reference library staff at the River Bluffs Regional Library in St. Joseph, for their help with local research materials and microfilm. Thanks to the staff at the Benedictine College Library in Atchison, Kansas, for processing many interlibrary loans, and especially to Mrs. Miriam O'Hare for help locating government documents. A debt is owed to Mrs. Carolyn Nuchols, a friend who patiently helped me master computer skills over a number of years. Thanks to Mr. Stan Hall of the St. Joseph Chamber of Commerce for allowing me access to the Boder Manuscript Collection and thanks also to archivist Clara Gallant who did such an excellent job cataloging the collection.

Last, but not least, thank you to my wife, Christine, who put up with my piles of research materials lying all over the house and for her encouragement. Further appreciation goes to my family, friends, and the staff at the University of Missouri-Kansas City who encouraged me to continue moving ahead and to never stop learning.

PREFACE

Urban historian, Charles N. Glaab, discussed in his book, *Kansas City and the Railroads*, the importance of what he called the "bridge legend" in the development of that city as the regional metropolis of the Great Plains. His belief was that by securing the first railroad bridge over the Missouri River, Kansas City took the lead over other regional cities in extending its own transportation and economic domain and therefore grew to greater urban influence than any of its neighbors. Glaab also pointed out that securing the bridge was not the only reason Kansas City grew to regional hegemony, but that the bridge legend had in fact some strong historical grounding.[1]

Of course, this work is not about Kansas City. It studies the development of nineteenth-century St. Joseph, Missouri. There is a link in that Kansas City stood as one of St. Joseph's major urban rivals during the decade, 1860-1870, when events were taking a crucial turn for both cities. Those opening comments about Kansas City are also significant to the study of St. Joseph in that as a competitor for urban dominance in the region, St. Joseph developed no "bridge legend" of its own. Despite early economic and transportation advantages, St. Joseph's turning point did not hinge on a single great event, like a bridge opening, but rested on its seeming failure to create either a large a sustained body of urban supporters willing to dedicate their time, energy, and money at critical points in time.

Those familiar with urban history often associate the rise of a great city with some singular event or economic trend. Even a disaster becomes a positive event if the city rebuilds and improved because of it, such as in the case of the Great Fire of Chicago, or the San Francisco Earthquake. Economic successes, like Pittsburgh, home to the nation's steel industry, or Detroit with the auto industry, are other examples of developments that changed the course of a city's history. But, as Glaab said, while the event may be a significant contributing factor, it cannot tell the whole story of a city's rise to urban greatness, nor is it necessarily the only cause of a city's failure to fulfill its potential.

Cities, like the human beings who build them, are immensely complex living organisms. As individuals we are distinct from all others and our life stories reflect that complexity. So too, the life stories of cities reflect the impact of an array of interacting forces that have shaped the past, present, and future destiny of urban settings, great or small. The rise and fall of noted persons, powerful or infamous, pious or flamboyant, good or evil, create life stories that greatly influence others. As such they warrant the inquiry of the biographer, the historian, and the social scientist. Cities, have no less effect on society and warrant similar attention. Just as with individuals, whom we generally measure in stature by their successes or failures, the success or failure of a city to attain a position of national or regional stature becomes the ultimate point of focus for much historical inquiry.

Competition between cities to assume dominance of a region has existed since the beginning of this nation and represents an underlying theme throughout urban history. While the country was still in its infancy, consisting of only thirteen states, and ninety percent of its inhabitants lived in rural communities, eastern seaboard cities like New York, Boston, and

Philadelphia, competed for dominate positions in trade, political influence, and social stature. As the nation expanded westward, new outposts that eventually became towns and cities sprouted along the frontier line. Their ultimate success often depended on the ability of their economic and political leaders and promoters to compete for and seize a position of influence, and then dominate their regions.

Within this nineteenth-century biography of the city of St. Joseph, Missouri, I examine the city's potential, its successes, how it competed for population, for economic stature, for important transportation links, and for cultural distinction, and how its initial promise to win regional hegemony over other cities of the Great Plains region went unfulfilled. Thus the story of St. Joseph, Missouri, holds an important place in the development of the American West as well as being a part of the nation's urban history.

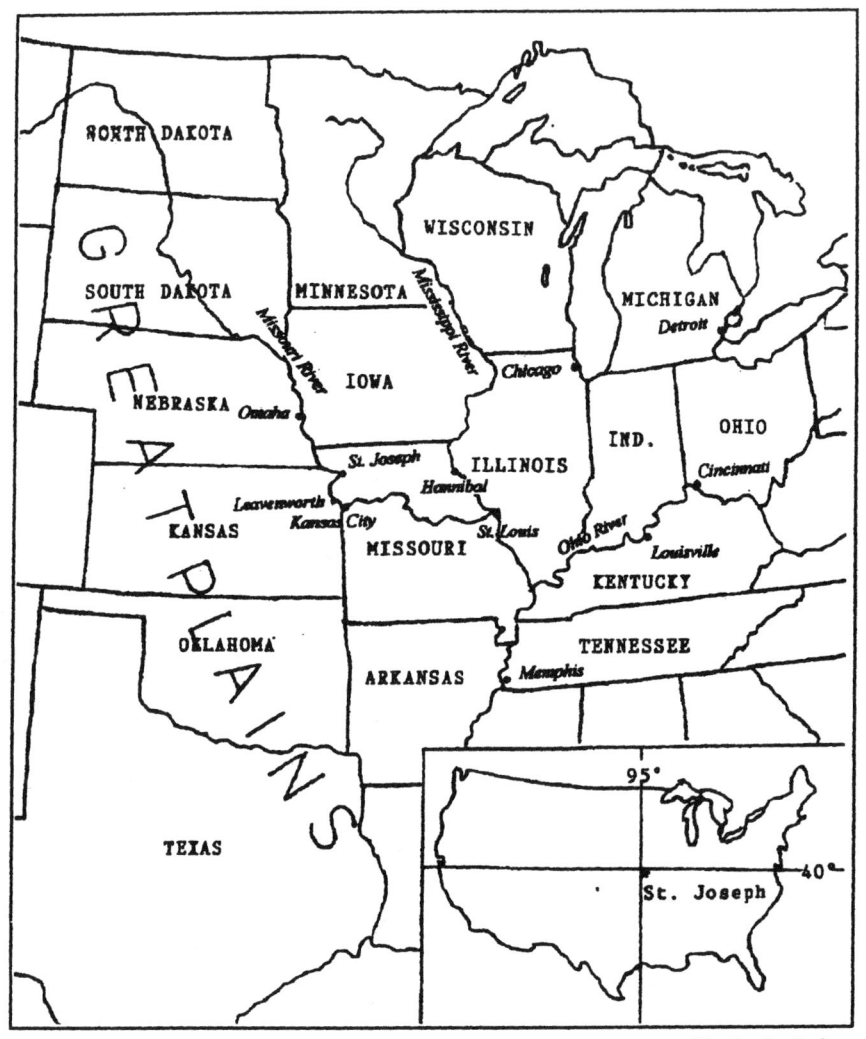

Map by the Author

viii

CHAPTER 1

Location, Location, Location
1800-1845

"St. Joseph occupies so important a geographic position with reference to all parts of this Continent, and is surrounded by such extraordinary natural advantages, that it requires no uncommon degree of sagacity to foresee the influence she is one day destined to wield, and the consequences she will assuredly attain in the future chronicles of the West."[1]

Colonel M. F. Tiernan

May 6, 1850

Those powerful words of endorsement, spoken by a soldier and a railroad surveyor, a man who had traveled often across the West, carried an element of truth in 1850, even if Colonel Tiernan may have been an overly zealous promoter of the city's future. Only seven years after a weathered old Indian trader founded *1843* the town, it stood on the verge of urban greatness. Within the next decade that claim to fame increased and, as the colonel stated, St. Joseph did leave major historical tracks on the "chronicles of the West." It is also said fame is fleeting. Within another decade, the fortunes of the city would be battered, although not completely destroyed: First by the effects of the Civil War; and then through the strenuous and often bitter competition among St. Joseph and its urban rivals to the north and south. Recovery and substantial economic growth occurred through the rest of the nineteenth century, but the luster of the town's initial promise would never again shine as intensely as it had in 1850.

Why was the future of St. Joseph viewed in such glowing terms by men like Colonel Tiernan, and so many others who either resided in, or visited the place in the mid-nineteenth century? Primarily, the town's geographic location made it ideally situated to be a springboard for the nation's advance into the American West. Its position is almost dead center on the map of the continental United States. A nineteenth century gazetteer of Missouri described it like this, "St. Joseph has all the advantages of a *central location*. It is midway between the Atlantic and the Pacific, British America and the Gulf."[2] In terms of simple geography, that meant that it could serve as a natural hub for transportation, communication, and commerce. The town sits on the banks of the Missouri River, on the edge of the Great Plains. In 1850 it provided the right location to serve as both a point of departure for crossing the great prairie as well as a base of economic conquest and settlement for that immense region.

In the minds of the city's promoters during the town's first two decades, there was much to be proud of and boast about. St. Joseph held the potential to develop into a great city and dominate the region, just as had other great cities of the nation's heartland St. Louis, New Orleans, and Chicago. Open enthusiasm abounded during the 1850s. St. Joseph had grown into the largest town west of the Mississippi between St. Louis and San Francisco. It became a recognized jumping off point [point of departure] for both the Oregon and California Trails. By 1859, it was the westernmost terminal of the American railroad and telegraph system and St. Joseph had developed into the second most active river port on the Missouri above St. Louis. Its combination of transportation facilities and growing mercantile base made it worthy of the most halcyon descriptions from newspaper editors, politicians, visitors, and urban promoters. Supporters of the other regional towns along the edge of the Great Plains--Independence, Kansas City, Atchison, and Leavenworth to the south, and Omaha to the north--competed with St. Joseph for regional dominance during that period. Town promoters often fought it out in the region's newspapers and jockeyed for favorable positions with state and national legislatures and potential investors in transportation and industry.

So why, by the end of the nineteenth century, had the city of so much early potential and promise failed to win regional dominance? St. Joseph's twentieth century history reflects that earlier failure. The city has at times stood dormant and not been able to compete with other growing communities, not just in the region, but within the state of Missouri.

The course of St. Joseph's history can provide some answers. The narrative of town building is an elemental part to understanding the influence of urbanization on the history of the United States. Regionally, St. Joseph's contribution to the development of the American West, is a prime example of urban influence which is, just as important as understanding the role of the cattlemen, the miners, the wagon masters, the cavalry, and the Indians. Further, the influence of geography, spelled out in the nineteenth century theories of natural advantages, and the relation between geography and transportation, and transportation and economic growth, are

2

indispensable parts in telling St. Joseph's story.[3]

What variables or events make a city grow or decline? Attaining economic prowess is important because people need services and places to work. Some argue that a low crime rate, good schools and affordable housing, parks and recreation and a cultural life also make a city livable and attract growth. If one reads the promotional literature from St. Joseph's beginning and then studies the statistics on where it has come in the last 150 years, one might be moved to ask, what happened? The city has not only fallen short of its initial promise to become a great regional metropolis, but within the state of Missouri it has also shown dramatic decline when compared to other urban centers. It is fair to say that much of that early literature reflected a certain amount of boosterism, or even wishful thinking, that flowed from the mouthes and pens of local promoters and newspaper editors, not unlike dozens of other aspiring towns during the early nineteenth century. But, hard statistics on population, trade, or the number of steamboat or train arrivals then can not be denied any more than modern census reports which paint a gloomy picture today.

Within the state, the town has fallen from its early nineteenth century second place position in population to sixth. Its 1990 metropolitan statistical area [MSA] population of 83,083, lags substantially behind St. Louis, Kansas City, Springfield, Joplin, and Columbia. Of the six major metropolitan statistical areas, it has by proportion the largest population over age 65 and the fifth oldest median age. It ranks fifth out of the six in median income, in the value of its housing, and in the numbers of citizens living below the poverty level. Also, St. Joseph is last of the six in statistical measures of educational levels for its citizens and has the highest unemployment rate.[4]

Some will argue that statistics can be made to show or say anything one wants. It could just as well be said, that the numbers show St. Joseph has the least murders and other violent crime, the largest area of parks per capita, and the most churches for a city of its size. By the modern standards of urban measurement, St. Joseph might be considered an old, declining city, rich in history with an early promise, that just did not fully develop. Some might challenge the accuracy of that statement, so it is left to an examination of the city's history to find the most plausible answers.

Often individuals or groups make the key decisions in a community's history that determine its destiny. Whether or not to promote a certain industry,

3

Joseph Robidoux as the elder statesman. *Courtesy of the Boder Collection*

develop a new transportation technology, or attract a viable labor pool are examples. Sometimes those decisions were made by persons outside the community, in a distant center of business or government. Just as important as "who" in the decision making process is the "when." Sometimes the timing of even a single decision can cause a city's historical direction to change course. In the case of St. Joseph, nearly all the major decisions regarding its future occured in the nineteenth century.

The first great decision in the history of St. Joseph had to do with its location. Two important elements figure into the reason behind this. First, someone initially saw economic value in the site, which in turn attracted others, and second, the geographic factors of its location, generally described as its natural advantages, became a drawing point. In the early nineteenth century natural advantages were considered the most important factor in the location of towns and cities. Having a good natural harbor on the ocean, like New York City; or on a large lake, like Chicago or Cleveland; or a river port, like New Orleans, St. Louis, or Cincinnati; or being situated at the crossroads of major interior transportation routes, like Atlanta or Buffalo on the Erie Canal, all represent examples of a site having natural advantages. St. Joseph's location on a bend of one of America's great rivers, the Missouri, would have been considered, in the nineteenth century, a clear advantage. What made that particular bend better than any other of the million bends on the river poses a difficult question. The location of St. Joseph combined the personal preference of a founding figure with particular features of topography that were not found anywhere else. In the nineteenth century natural advantages generally equated to economic advantages, because the potential for economic prowess, not just the topography of the area, built towns into cities.

Any visitor who arrives in the city today, and asks a native, "Why is St. Joseph located here?" would likely get the simple answer that a man named Joseph Robidoux picked the site, for a fur trading post, sometime in the early 1800s. That response is supported by the popular tourist image, promoted in St. Joseph, that adorns billboards, the sides of buses, and tourist flyers, and has reigned in portraiture over hotel lobbies, bars, and city hall for a number of years. It is the image of an old gentleman, dressed in the most unassumingly plain clothes, with a pleasantly smiling, weathered old face, shielded by a wide brimmed slouch hat, reclining in a chair, with his walking cane in hand. At first glance he is not overly

5

imposing, but after longer observation and thought, one may notice there is a certain regality to him. That is the popular image of "Father Joseph" or "Old Joe" Robidoux, who, in all the local folklore, presided over the birth of the city that bears the name of his patron saint. It is a simple, neat, grandfatherly package of local history, firmly grounded in reality. Joe Robidoux was the first white man to live in the area, and it was his name, and his name alone, that appears on the document creating the city in 1843. Obviously, one man, even as a sole proprietor, does not make a town or city. But he is also that identifiable person in history whose initial economic activities attracted others who did build a town.

ROBIDOUX AND THE BLACKSNAKE HILLS

Stepping out of the pirogue (a dug out canoe) onto the embankment of the muddy, swirling, great Missouri River, young Joseph Robidoux first set foot on the site of his town sometime during the summer of 1800. No more than seventeen at the time, handsome and swarthy with dark brown, nearly black hair, he already had the experience along with the physical and mental frame of a frontiersman. Robidoux and his traveling companions were there to make contact with local Indians and start a trading relationship. Born in St. Louis in 1783 of French-Canadian descent, he traveled upriver to carry on his father's business as one of the important outfitters and traders on the upper Missouri River. Area Indian tribes—the Missouri, Joway, Otoe, and Iowa—had valuable furs which he hoped to exchange for trade goods, like knives, mirrors, pots and pans, cloth, and liquor. Their landing site was a creek that flowed into the Missouri. He and his French speaking compatriots called it *Le Serpent Noir,*[5] "the blacksnake." Because of the sharply rising river bluffs, the area became known as the Blacksnake Hills. Why it was called blacksnake might be attributed to a number of sources. A band of the Missouri tribe called the Blacksnake Indians lived in the area. The dark, shaded, winding creek that flowed through the area reminded them of the black serpents. Or it may have been the fact that there were black snakes, indigenous to the area, crawling all over the place when they arrived. No one really knows if one or all of the explanations are correct. The name Blacksnake Hills took, and the site retained that name until it officially became St. Joseph in 1843.

Local historians, who like to assign a town's beginning to its first building, claim that Robidoux built a cabin there around 1803, but there is no concrete evidence to support this belief.[6] Lewis and Clark, who explored the Missouri River after the United States acquired the Louisiana Purchase from France in 1803, did not record seeing a cabin there when they poled and roped their way upstream during the summer of 1804. On July 7, 1804, they wrote: "In the morning the rapidity of the water obliged us to draw the boat along with ropes. At six and three quarter miles, we came to a sandbar, at a point opposite a fine rich prairie on the north, called St. Michael's. The prairies of this neighborhood have the appearance of distinct farms, divided by narrow strips of woodland, which follow the borders of the small runs leading to the river. Above this, about a mile, is a cliff of yellow clay on the north."[7]

The reference to the name, "St. Michael's" in describing the prairie, is ascribed to the idea that Robidoux had named the area in honor of his little brother Michel [French variation of Michael], born in 1798. Apparently one of the members of the expedition had either been to the area with Robidoux earlier or knew first hand of his family in order to pass that information on to Lewis and Clark. Whether or not that was true, one can only speculate. Based on calculations of time and distance, the Ju'y 7 entry in the Lewis and Clark journals does describe the site of the future St. Joseph.[8] As far as confirming any type of structure at that site, Lewis and Clark did record seeing other trading posts along the Missouri River during that same stretch of time and did make note of them.

At that time Robidoux had not committed to anything like building a town at Blacksnake Hills nor did he even use it as a permanent trading base or attempt to acquire ownership. He was a young, freewheeling fur trader who traveled extensively throughout the Mississippi-Missouri river valleys, while keeping a family, consisting of his wife and eventually eight children, comfortably ensconced in St. Louis. By all accounts he had a friendly, engaging personality, was hospitable and generous to family and stranger alike, and ambitious in his youth. Apparently the subject of business could produce a caustic, irritating side of his personality. Shrewd and self-serving, by all accounts of his contemporaries, he openly admitted to his ambition and the drive to succeed at what he did.[9] The handling of his business affairs, particularly his role in the development of the southwestern fur trade, eventually positioned him to come into possession of the

7

site of St. Joseph. But from the time he first saw the area, until he settled there permanently, thirty years elapsed. During the interim, no one gave the Blacksnake Hills much attention. The question arises as to why Robidoux ever came back to the area.

In 1809, Robidoux's father died and he assumed the management of the family businesses. With younger brothers Francois and Antoine, he expanded the family fur trading empire. As the eldest brother, he became the "chief executive officer" of the venture while they provided the leg work. The base of his far flung western operation lay not at the Blacksnake, but further up the Missouri River, near the junction with the Platte at Council Bluffs, near present day Omaha. What happened to Robidoux at Council Bluffs had as much bearing on his eventual establishment of the town site at Blacksnake Hills as did anything else. His success as a trader there could not be questioned. His penchant for rubbing the people he worked with the wrong way can also not be questioned. He once locked his competitor, Manuel Lisa, in a cellar so he could trade with neighboring Indians by himself.[10] That kind of behavior and other incidents eventually led to his departure from Council Bluffs and his decision to settle at his eventual destination, St. Joseph.

The fur trade on the upper Missouri had been a wide-open market. There were big companies involved, like the Canadian firms, the Northwest Fur Company, and the Hudson Bay Company. Large American companies included Manuel Lisa's Missouri Fur Company, William Ashley's Rocky Mountain Fur Company, and John Jacob Astor's American Fur Company. They competed with a number of regional companies like the one Robidoux worked for. It was known as the French Company, later called B. Pratte & Company. A St. Louis consortium controlled by the Chouteau brothers, a powerful St. Louis family with trade interests all along the lower Missouri River, owned the firm. Beyond the control of the companies were hundreds of independents, mountainmen who trapped and skinned the animals, and freelance traders who owned no allegiance to anybody. Though technically employed by the French Company, Robidoux's freelancing got him into trouble, and eventually exiled from Council Bluffs. As a result of these problems he settled at the Blacksnake Hills site.[11]

At the Council Bluffs post in the early 1820s, Robidoux continued to work closely with his brothers Antoine and Francois, and two others, still younger, Michel and Isadore. As William Ashley's newly formed Rocky Mountain Fur

8

Company pushed into the northern and central Rocky Mountain region, particularly the Green River region, Joe Robidoux supplied and sent his younger brothers, often in teams, into the field. They not only shadowed Ashley's operation, but also went off in other directions, deep into the Southwest, to Santa Fe and Taos, New Mexico. Those freelance activities with his brothers came to the attention of the people he worked for, Berthold, Pratte, and the Chouteaus in St. Louis. The duty of reporting his activities fell to his field partner, J.P. Cabanne, who had a strong personal dislike for Robidoux. Cabanne claimed Robidoux used company money, supplies, men, and horses for his private ventures, or as Robidoux said, "hunting two hares at the same time." Robidoux claimed he did not. Robidoux might work for the company at Council Bluffs, but as far as the Rocky Mountain region and the Southwest trade, they were competitors. He complained about his treatment by the company in a letter to the Chouteaus written in his fractious English: "Employee I never wanted to be, & still less, last year, despite your telling me that I was like a 'maneuvering snake' in order to be hired. I could very well see that I could do better, & I see still more distinctly now that I have not done well." Robidoux blamed the confining business practices of the company for his discontent. He chided the company bosses with, "It's your turn to say your 'mea culpa'."[12]

Complaints against Robidoux's tactics continued, flowing primarily from the lips and pen of Cabanne. Besides calling him a snake, he referred to Robidoux as a "rascal" and reported that the men at the Council Bluffs post responded to Robidoux with "great repugnance." The situation came to a head in 1826 when Robidoux acquired a separate license from the government to trade on the Missouri between Bellevue and Niobrara, south of the Bluffs post. The following year, 1827, he went into a private partnership with a fellow trader of French stock, Baptiste Roy.[13] Along the way, B. Pratte & Company had become a subsidiary of the Western Department of the American Fur Company. The new parent company, at Cabanne's urging or insistence, relented and bought Robidoux off, getting him out of the Council Bluffs area altogether. Sometime in 1828, or early 1829, the company gave him $3,500 for his stock of goods and paid a bribe of $1,000 per annum for two years to get Robidoux to stay out of the Indian trade completely.[14] It was an important decision by the company and a significant event for the eventual location and development of St. Joseph. The Blacksnake Hills site must have lain fallow in the back of Robidoux's mind, and he recalled it for his eventual return to the trading business.

9

Painting of Pottawatomies at mouth of Black Snake Creek by R. F. Kurz
- 1845. *Courtesy of the Boder Collection*

THE BLACKSNAKE HILLS POST

Joseph Robidoux retired, if only temporarily, to St. Louis, and operated what remained of the family businesses located there, primarily a bakery. He apparently was neither very happy nor very good at doing it. His brothers continued to use the area around the Blacksnake Hills, particularly the landing spots on the riverbank at Roy's Branch (a creek that flowed into the Missouri River named for Baptiste Roy) or Blacksnake Creek, as trading bases with the neighboring Indian tribes. A government Indian agency, planted just a few miles southeast of the Blacksnake Hills in 1825, increased the number of Indians passing through the area. The potentially viable Indian trade contributed to Robidoux's decision to leave St. Louis and make the Blacksnake Hills his home. His enjoyment of the wilderness life style, the challenge of barter and conversing with the Indians in their own dialects in which he was fluent, and the inability to adjust to the civility of the city led him back to the wilderness.

10

When exactly Joseph Robidoux returned to permanently stay in the area is still a matter of contention. Many articles of early St. Joseph history, including the first history of the area published in 1881, put him at the Blacksnake Hills in the year 1826. The problem with the 1826 date is that it does not coincide with events taking place at Council Bluffs and the resulting bribe to stay out of the trade for two years. If a trading post existed at Blacksnake Hills in 1826, it may have been built by or belonged to one of his brothers, possibly Francois or Michel, who had a license to trade in that area.[15]

From the Blacksnake Hills site, Robidoux believed he could quickly establish a lucrative Indian trade and continue operations in the West with his brothers and sons, who traveled far afield. A ready transportation highway in the form of the Missouri River provided relatively easy access to markets. Keelboats, and the early steamers brought trade goods upriver; mackinaws, wide, flat-bottomed trading boats propelled by oars or rafts, could be used to float the furs and hides down to St. Louis. Having made amends with the Chouteaus, and probably no earlier than 1831, Robidoux again ascended the river with a stock of goods and the understanding that he would settle at Blacksnake Hills. The Chouteaus paid him a salary, a substantial $1,800 per annum, and he agreed not to interfere with the trade at Council Bluffs nor to further torment old Cabanne. The initial site of his post at Roy's Branch did not prove suitable and he moved to the mouth of Blacksnake Creek, two miles to the south. There he chose a site near the base of the bluffs that rose two or three hundred feet above the flood plain. Clean, fresh water flowed in Blacksnake Creek, and he built a cabin close to the river embankment.

Robidoux settled in at Blacksnake Hills permanently, but that is not when the town began. The cabin of varying reported dimensions for a time stood alone inside a rudimentary log stockade as the seed of the future city. Reportedly Robidoux spent much time alone there. He was isolated in that he was probably the only white man at the post on any given day, but definitely not alone in any other sense. He owned a French speaking black slave named Poulite whose basic duty was to keep house. Some contemporary accounts say that Indian wives and children abounded.[16]

Robidoux showed no interest in developing a town at that time. Besides, he could not have legally done so even if he wanted to, because the Blacksnake Hills were not yet part of the state of Missouri. When Missouri became a state in

11

1821, its western boundary, drawn along a straight north/south line, followed approximately. west longitude, 94 degrees, 40 minutes. Northwest Missouri, from that line west to the natural course of the Missouri River, remained Indian country. Robidoux, a federally licensed trader, jealously guarded his territory. By the early 1830s, new tribes from the East, such as the Sac and Fox and eastern Iowa Indians moved into the area. They had been displaced from the Mississippi valley by warfare and the Treaty of Prairie du Chien in 1830. The move brought them into land conflict with other tribes, like the Otoe and Missouri bands who already lived there. However, more Indians in the region meant potentially more trade for Robidoux.

By the early 1830s, the Blacksnake Hills post began developing a hinterland. A hinterland is an outlying region around a town or city that usually is based on a mutually beneficial economic relationship. The town, or initially the post in this case, provides a central collecting point for the area's produce, furs or lumber, and later crops and livestock. In return, the hinterland receives finished or manufactured goods and services to which it would not otherwise have access. A town or city is tied to its hinterland through its transportation links. Decisions to aggressively pursue or expand hinterland were key to the eventual development and prosperity of many cities in the United States. For the Blacksnake Hills post, the first hinterland comprised the area of Robidoux's Indian trade operation and was fairly extensive. Robidoux employed around twenty *engages* [French for employee] to develop the trade throughout the area, extending east to the Grand River valley and west into what is now Kansas at least 50 miles. When his traveling traders were not making contact, the Indians from both sides of the Missouri River traveled directly to the Blacksnake Hills post to do business.[17]

As an initial transportation link, Robidoux operated a rudimentary ferry that connected his post with the west bank of the river. Steamboats, involved in government operations such as ferrying troops or supplies or those active in the upriver fur trade, plied past the post during the spring and summer months, gradually replacing the keelboats and mackinaws as primary cargo haulers. Robidoux got his supplies from St. Louis, so he benefited from the slowly increasing steamboat traffic link, though he still sent furs downriver on mackinaws. Passengers were still of a limited number during the 1830s. Only those with specific interest in the wilderness, the fur trade, or missionary work went very far up the Missouri. The Blacksnake Hills site gradually became a recognized stopping point on the way upstream for taking on a load of fuel and for crewmen to stretch their legs. Robidoux's post offered a visible and relatively safe place to rest.

In April 1833, one early visitor stopped at the site and wrote one of the first published descriptions of what was to become St. Joseph. His name was Maxmillian, Prince of Wied, and his travels took him upriver on the steamboat *Yellowstone*, in the company of the Swiss artist, Karl Bodmer. They explored parts of the American wilderness and kept an invaluable journal and notebook of sketches. On the 24th, Maxmillian began his journal entry thus: "We saw the chain of the Blacksnake Hills, but we met with so many obstacles in the river that we did not reach them till towards the evening. They are moderate eminences, with many singular forms, with an alternation of wooded and open green spots. Near to the steep bank a trading house has been built, which was occupied by a man named Roubedoux [sic] an agent of the Fur Company." Maxmillian described Robidoux's house as white and "surrounded by the bright green prairies" with a "very neat appearance."[18]

In the same entry, Maxmillian reported about the still very apparent wildness of the territory: "When the steamboat lay to, between 500 and 600 paces from the trading house, some of the engages of the company came on board, and reported that the Joway Indians, whose village was about five or six miles distant, had made an incursion into the neighboring territory of the Omahas, and killed six of these Indians."

On his return trip a year later, from the upper Missouri area around Fort Union, he commented again on the future site of St. Joseph. In his journal entry for May 16, 1834, he reported an appealing scene that might be described a modern travel brochure: "Towards four o'clock in the afternoon we reached the beautiful chain of the Black Snake Hills, and not long after, Roubedoux's [sic] trading house in the neighborhood of the Joways and Saukies, or Sac. The forest covered hills, as well as the prairie stretched at their foot, were now adorned with the most lovely verdure. The two houses at this spot were painted white, which when seen from the river, gave them a very picturesque appearance amid the surrounding green. Behind the dwelling houses were extensive fields of maize, protected by fences, and a very fine cattle were grazing in the plain."[19] Descriptions of the rich landscapes of northwest Missouri were factors in drawing settlers to the area. Many began to move into the region that Robidoux had until that time occupied as a private fiefdom.

By 1834, immigrants from the East began pushing across the legal state boundary into Indian territory. To the white settlers, the arbitrary invisible line of longitude that drew the northwest boundary of the state was not as logical as simply allowing the boundary to follow the natural course of the Missouri River. The reality of the squatters' argument became the basis for a major political decision within the state, and became an important step toward making the Blacksnake Hills into a viable town site. An amendment to the Missouri constitution in 1834 stated as much: "That the boundary of the State be so altered and extended, as to include the tract of land lying on the north side of the Missouri River, and west of the present boundary of this State."[20]

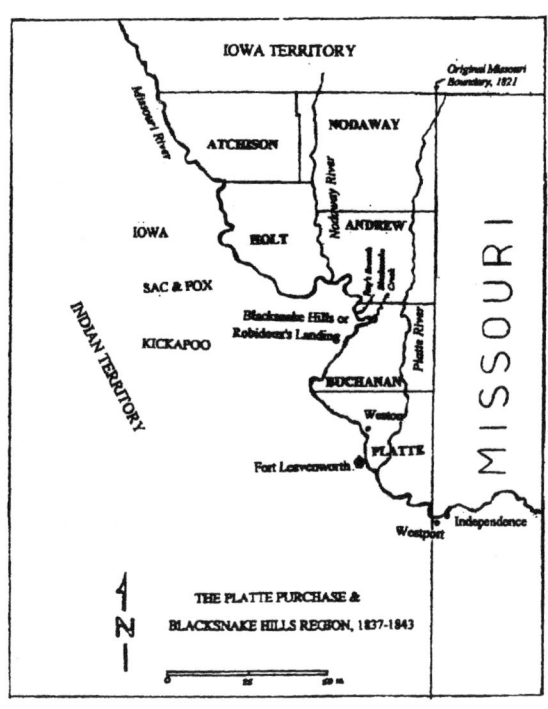

Map by Author

14

Squatters invaded the area first. Not concerned with obtaining legal title, their presence helped exert pressure on the Indian population to give up the territory. The squatters drew the attention of the army, which legally had a duty to rout them out, and Robidoux, whose Indian trade appeared threatened. As a licensed trader, he and his operatives should have been, legally, the only white men in the area. But that was not the reality. By 1835, there may have been 200 or more families living illegally in the southern part of the Indian territory. General Andrew Hughes, in charge of the agency near Blacksnake Hills, loathed to take action against the whites. Nonetheless, the Indian superintendent at Fort Leavenworth proposed in 1835 to use federal troops to get the squatters out of the region. At that same time, members of Missouri's congressional delegation, headed by Senators Lewis F. Linn and Thomas Hart Benton, proceeded with their efforts to get support to annex the area. In August 1835, Linn wrote to John Forsyth, Secretary of State, to discuss the issue of possible military intervention to remove the squatters. He hoped to head off trouble from such an action and reinforce the impetus to acquire the area: "I hear an order has come from the War Department to remove the families who have settled on the Indian lands lying between our western boundary and the Missouri River, by military force. You know the independent and daring character of our frontier population, and knowing, you will easily believe that this step is not to be accomplished without violence and much distress, as the families are two or three hundred in number." Linn went on to point out "the utter uselessness of this portion of country for Indian purposes."[21]

In September 1835, Superintendent of Indian Affairs William Clark called a meeting of the Iowa and Missouri bands of the Sac and Fox Indians at Fort Leavenworth for the purpose of signing a treaty. In the document they gave up lands totaling about two million acres. This allowed the northwest Missouri border to extend to the river. Known as the Platte Purchase, the area included the counties of Platte, Buchanan [including the Blacksnake Hills], Andrew, Nodaway, Atchison, and Holt. In exchange the Indians received $7,500 in cash, reservation lands in Kansas, the promise of a school, livestock, and miscellaneous other incentives to include a ferryboat. One of the signatory witnesses of the treaty was H. Robidou, Jr.(sic), Joseph's oldest son.[22]

Robidoux's wilderness outpost, once beyond the leading edge of the frontier line, suddenly sat directly on top of it. People began to flood in and he

15

had to secure his claims. Robidoux hoped to receive two sections of land encompassing his post from the government for his help in dealing with and promoting a peaceful settlement with the Indians, particularly his friend and trade partner, the Sac chief, White Cloud. That help, was apparently quickly forgotten by the government, for Robidoux got no reward. Even support from Missouri Senator Benton failed to do Robidoux any good.[23]

NATURAL ADVANTAGES HELP ATTRACT SETTLERS

In 1839, the state legislature politically organized Buchanan County and set its boundaries. Robidoux filed claim to two quarter sections, 320 acres, in the northwest corner of Washington Township, itself in the northwest corner of the county. Robidoux's post, for the first time, came to the attention of others as a property with great economic potential. They knew a viable, profitable trading post already operated there. That along with the natural advantages of the area proved attractive, based on the number of people who flocked to its immediate vicinity. There were the bluffs and rolling hills, built on a base of ample limestone, to provide safety from flooding, yet close enough to the embankment for easy access to a boat landing. Those limestone deposits also provided an abundant supply of natural building material. To the south lay the flood plain or river bottom composed of rich, brown loess soil and sugar clay deposited by centuries of flooding. The river made a great curve at the site, forming a huge backward C with the combination of hills and plain forming an amphitheater-like site facing the river, as if it were the stage. A flat prairie, running from the opposite bank of the river west, served as a backdrop against the opposite bluffs, three or four miles in the distance. Nearby lay ample grassland for grazing and yet plenty of standing timber. Numerous creeks, like the Blacksnake, drained the area so it was not marshy or excessively wet. The river, as it made its big bend, cut its deepest channel against the eastern bank, freeing it from the shallow sandbars of the Kansas side.[25]

The natural advantages of the Blacksnake Hills clearly made the site superior to the other little towns and trading posts that had popped up in the region. Due to the topography of the rest of the county, the Blacksnake Hills site acted as the mouth of a funnel through which all produce had to pass on its way

16

to the river. On two occasions, in 1838 and 1840, Robidoux confronted claim jumpers, who saw the potential and had visions of laying out a town; and on another occasion, he turned down a lucrative offer to purchase his site by investors from Independence, Missouri.

Early in 1839 Warren Samuels and two other land speculators, gave the Blacksnake Hills a serious look as a potentially profitable town site. In the fall of 1839, they approached Robidoux with an offer of $1,600 for his property. Robidoux invited them to dinner, and after pleasant negotiations the parties agreed to terms. Samuels and his partners intended to pay him the money the next day. But then Robidoux brought out the cards for a friendly game to pass the rest of the evening. As the hour grew late, an argument erupted, supposedly involving the game. Robidoux suddenly called off the deal. The men from Independence went home the next morning empty handed. Robidoux may have suddenly had second thoughts about the price that was offered, and used the argument as a way to back out. Or maybe he was just an inveterate poker player; as several contemporary sources say, "he had a passion for card playing" and felt he had been cheated.[25] What we can conclude with certainty was Robidoux retained control of the prime Blacksnake Hills site.

He controlled it only for a while though, and apparently with no intent to build a settlement. Others began to arrive in the area. Their presence and numbers forced Robidoux's hand in the decision to plant a town. By the hundreds they moved into Buchanan County and right up to the edge of Robidoux's Blacksnake Hills property. They envisioned a town and were willing to show it to old Joe Robidoux as well. Buchanan County was divided into eleven townships. Those to the south, bordering Platte County and neighboring Clay County, began to fill first. Most of the people moving in had migrated from Kentucky and Tennessee following a pattern that had developed early in Missouri history.[26] Besides the attraction of both abundant and fertile farmland, Missouri's admission into the Union as a slave state attracted a large number of immigrants from slave states and brought their slaves with them; no questions asked.

Within two years of the Platte Purchase, a steady stream of land purchasing settlers and an indeterminate number of squatters, pressed toward the Blacksnake Hills. Robidoux had allowed his operatives and clerks to settle near the trading post on the river, by then also referred to as Robidoux's Landing. Thomas Sollers, Joseph Gladden, and Isadore Poulin brought their families there

17

when they went to work for Robidoux. In 1837 John and William Whitehead settled two miles southeast of Robidoux's. Shortly thereafter, within a mile of the post were families named Hanson, Cochran, Pough, and Waymire. Frederick W. Smith, a surveyor, arrived in 1838, and another surveyor, named Simeon Kemper in 1839. Dr. Daniel Keedy, one of the first physicians in Buchanan County, arrived in Washington Township in 1839, settling just south of Robidoux's store. He was soon joined by Dr. Silas McDonald, also a medical doctor, who moved into the area from Platte County. More families, with names like Fudge, Kaufman, James, Cox, and McCorkle, were Robidoux's neighbors by 1839.[27]

Robidoux began to shift his business away from the Indian trade to the supplying of the growing influx of farmers. Although the old weather-beaten trader still personally preferred the Indian trade, the next generation of newly arrived merchants saw the coming market for farm supply more clearly. While the Indian trade hinterland quickly shrank, general stores began popping up at nearly every crossroads. Farmers needed a place to trade their produce, establish credit, buy tools, and just socialize. Besides the economic necessities, the newly arriving settlers had political needs to be met. Buchanan County needed a county seat and many viewed the Blacksnake Hills post as the logical choice.

Beginning in early 1839, the county court, consisting of three judges elected to take care of the growing list of settler's needs, convened literally in Robidoux's living room. County records show him being paid for the room and fuel for several months. Not only the county court, but the circuit court as well met at his house, which also served as a polling place.[28] What relationship existed between Robidoux and the judges is not certain. There may have been a misunderstanding between them at some point because for some reason, despite the popularity of Robidoux's post, the court voted, somewhat abruptly, to establish the county seat elsewhere. The spot they chose, in August 1840, was then an unplotted site in the middle of the county, called Sparta. Sparta could only claim the advantage of being centrally located.[29]

The Blacksnake Hills post clung to its last moments of isolation. In 1840 Richard L. McDonald wrote of a visit to an uncle, Dr. Silas McDonald, one of the first physicians in Buchanan County. In his letter he described what he saw at the Blacksnake Hills: "The only occupant and owner of a business house was a Frenchman named Robadoux [sic] who lived there a number of years as an Indian trader, and who was at that time still engaged in the occupation. He was moving

18

around dressed in an old, red flannel shirt, his trousers strapped around the waist, on his head a slouched hat, and so tanned and weather beaten that it was difficult to tell whether he was a white man, a mulatto, or an Indian. His establishment consisted of three log cabins, one or more of which were filled with furs of otter, beaver, buffalo, deer, bear, and other skins; in the other buildings were stored provisions, trinkets, and supplies for the Indians, the latter chiefly in whiskey, tobacco and liquors. The old man seemed to be a very energetic, enterprising, shrewd business manager. He was familiar with several dialects of the Indian language and was highly respected by all the natives who dealt with him."[30]

But the burgeoning population of the county and Washington Township saw a stream of improvements that made Robidoux's outpost the foundation of a town, in fact, if not in legal title. The growing agricultural market in the region created a self- generating economic impetus, attracting more settlers, who planted more crops and in turn created more demands for goods and services. Besides livestock of all kinds, the river bottoms and hillsides flowered with vast fields of corn and wheat. Some farmers raised tobacco while hemp was popular with many more. The surrounding farmers needed a place to conduct business, and clearly the natural advantages of Robidoux's Landing topped all other towns in the region. By 1840 the river landing, saw more frequent stops by river steamers. That became an important drawing point. Robidoux opened a flour mill on the west side of Blacksnake Creek in 1841 to meet the demand to process local grain. Later that same year a sawmill, constructed by Dr. Daniel Keedy just south of the post, began operation. The county court began the process of "viewing" or laying out roads throughout the county, but despite what Sparta had hoped, Blacksnake Hills became the real center of the area transportation web.

Craftsmen of all descriptions moved into the immediate area to fill the demands created by the growing population. Other millers arrived, harnessing power from the creeks and small rivers, north, east, and south of Robidoux's. Louis Picard, a professional carpenter, and William Langston, a plasterer, arrived in 1842, along with the Belcher brothers, who were brickmakers. Dozens of new homes needed building and craftsmen found steady work. Jacob Mitchell, one of the early independent blacksmiths, earned a reputation as "a worthy son of Vulcan," the ancient god of iron. David Heaton, a cabinet maker, arrived, but when the cabinet business slowed, or the need arose, he made coffins. John Patee came to the area to manufacture and sell harvesting machines, but wound up dealing in

19

patent medicines. He bought a substantial tract of land just south of Robidoux's holdings that eventually became a major addition to the town.[31]

By 1840, a post office had opened at the Blacksnake Hills, with Robidoux's son, Julius C. Robidoux, its first postmaster. In February 1842, the county court asked Robidoux to build a tobacco warehouse at his landing on the Missouri River. The entry in the county record book read: "ordered by the court that Joseph Robidoux be authorized to erect a warehouse for the reception and inspection of tobacco at Robidoux's Landing on the Missouri River of the following dimensions: to wit 32 feet square with an offset of 12 feet by 16 feet thereunto 'anneseed' framed and well-weathered boarded 7 feet high and therein from the said Joseph Robidoux enters into bond with security to the satisfaction of the court in the sum of $2,000."[32] Tobacco had been a popular crop with those migrating from Kentucky and Tennessee into the area. The soil in the region seemed well suited for the growth of burley tobacco, which is still produced around the town of Weston, some twenty-five miles south of St. Joseph.

Besides the structure for tobacco, Robidoux built a warehouse for hemp. Dr. Silas McDonald had introduced the first hemp crops into the area in 1840. It remained the staple crop until after the Civil War and helped the state of Missouri maintain a second place ranking in the nation for hemp production between 1840 and 1860.[33] Hemp seed, purchased for around $80 per ton, required a low initial investment. With little or no cultivation, an acre could produce as much as 1,000 pounds of fiber which sold for around $3-4 per hundredweight. After cutting, hemp breaking, the practice of thrashing the stalks to separate the fibers, called for the greatest expenditure of labor. Beating the stalks against a wooden beam was hard physical work. Generally, farmers who owned slaves, assigned them that part of the process. Others might temporarily hire slaves from a master for the right price.[34] The warehouse at Robidoux's Landing became a major trans-shipment point for crops heading downriver to St. Louis and New Orleans.

A TOWN IS BORN

In November 1842, the county court appropriated $6,000 for a new courthouse to be built at Sparta. This touched off a public discussion among farmers and merchants in the county who clearly preferred and recognized the potential of the Blacksnake Hills, despite the Robidoux's reluctance to lay out a town. People began to agitate, especially the nearly two hundred residents who were by then either on Robidoux's property or its periphery. Only a small minority within the county supported the Sparta site. Despite the county court's attempts to make Sparta a viable county seat, little had been built there. Black-snake Hills appealed to those with an eye to setting up business houses next to the river with its superior transportation link, and to area craftsmen wanting to settle into shops with fixed addresses.

In the spring of 1843, two surveyors, Frederick W. Smith and Simeon Kemper, approached Robidoux about laying out a town. At that time, a hemp crop covered the hillside field. As recounted in family stories, old Robidoux finally agreed to a friendly competition between the two surveyors to draw up plans. Both agreed to survey and plat the site. Then Robidoux would pick whichever of the plans he liked best. There exists no evidence that he paid either of them for their work. But Smith, who held a plot of land directly east of Robidoux's, clearly benefited when the site became a town. His holding turned out to be one of the town's first additions. In early July 1843, the two surveyors presented their plans to Robidoux.[35]

Like most nineteenth century American town plans, both plats copied the popular grid pattern, streets crisscrossing at right angles and forming square blocks. The town sat hard against the Missouri River on the west and extended east about seven blocks. The north and south dimension extended ten blocks. Both surveyors numbered the north-south streets and named the east-west streets. Smith used the names of Robidoux's children, beginning with Faraon and continuing south; Jules, Francis, Felix, Edmond, Charles, Sylvanie, Angelique, and Messanie. Kemper named his town plan "Robidoux," appealing directly to the sense of proprietorship, while Smith named his "St. Joseph" after Robidoux's patron saint. Old Robidoux chose Smith's plan. One might conclude he did so out of some modesty, but Robidoux later told family members, he intended "to sell my land in lots, not give it away in streets."[36] Smith's plan had narrower streets, 60 feet wide as opposed to Kemper's 100 feet. This proved to be a key factor in the decision. Being an astute businessman, Robidoux saw the potential to squeeze a few more town lots from the 160 acres of his quarter section.[37]

In July 1843, Robidoux took the Smith plat and the legal description to

St. Louis where he recorded it before the state court. While there he also settled the issue of the mortgage. He owed Pierre Chouteau II $6,372.57, held as a lien against the town lots. The deed does not specify the basis of the debt. Robidoux may have borrowed money over some period of time to originally acquire the property or to consolidate old debts from his trading operations. The debt, and the need to pay it, may very well have provided the final impetus for Robidoux to start laying off lots. Robidoux signed and attested to the town plan, the note, and his statement as proprietor on July 25, 1843. The next day, July 26, Nathaniel Paschall, clerk of the St. Louis Court of Common Pleas, witnessed and accepted the documents. With a plan, and a business deal between old family friends consummated, and no doubt at the urging of a large number of people back at the Blacksnake Hills, or Robidoux's Landing, the town of St. Joseph came into being. The "birth certificate" began with the statement: "I, Joseph Robidoux, of the County of Buchanan and the State of Missouri, do hereby declare that I am the proprietor and owner of a certain town named St. Joseph."[38]

So, the place where so many saw promise became a town. Its location, as in nearly all good real estate deals, was a prime factor in attracting buyers for the lots. Merchants, tradesmen, promoters, and speculators moved in and bought hundreds of lots, at $150 for a corner and $100 for an interior space. Robidoux paid off his note to Chouteau within a year. Others recognized the value of the location and snapped up adjoining properties as fast as they could. Those tracts would one day comprise most of the city's major additions. Within three years, residents of Buchanan County abandoned the county seat at Sparta. By nearly unanimous vote they proclaimed St. Joseph their new seat of government. The editor of St. Joseph's first newspaper made the case for St. Joseph perfectly clear when he wrote: "St. Joseph is not the centre of the territory of the county, but she may be considered the centre of business, for she is the point at which almost every farmer in the county deals. She is to use a figure, the heart whence commenses [sic] the life giving principles of trade."[39] The prospects for immediate growth, in population and economic importance, and as a mercantile center for the whole of northwest Missouri seemed bright.

22

CHAPTER 2

Wagon Trails and Steamboats
1845-1860

In the ancient world it was said that all roads led to Rome. Due to its position in northwest Missouri during the 1840s and 1850s it could be truly said metaphorically that all roads and other transportation links led to St. Joseph. And not just local transportation either. There were connections with places as far and as diverse as Chicago, St. Louis, the Oregon Country, Salt Lake City, and San Francisco. The common thread could be found in the growing economic prowess of the town and its merchant houses. In the years immediately before the Civil War, St. Joseph established itself as the premiere mercantile center, not only west of the Mississippi River valley, but well beyond the front range of the Rocky Mountains. For a brief period, the town could claim to be the "Queen City" of the West.

It all goes back to the concept of hinterland. If a city prospered, it had to have an area, a hinterland, that provided the raw materials for its industry, markets for its production, a population base from which to draw its inhabitants, a social and cultural life to hold those inhabitants once they arrived, and the necessary transportation links to move people, materials, and products. In other words, without hinterland, growing towns and cities could not exist or develop for very long. The greater the area of hinterland, the greater the city would become. Hinterland was not something a town or city applied for, or received from the state. It had to be acquired, you might even say earned, by the business community within the city, by their hard work and sweat, and sometimes luck. Occasionally hinterland could be a geographic gift, or predetermined because of a natural transportation route that deposited people and materials near a river, or lake, or mountain pass. Most of the time, towns earned it by openly competing for it. Every community that had a vision of growing into something larger and greater wanted a region to dominate. The economic decision by the town's business leaders to aggressively pursue and expand hinterland often proved the most important early decision after determining location. How they secured that hinterland through transportation links was critical.

For St. Joseph, the decision to concentrate on the development of wagon

23

road connections became the basis for the town's early economic success An immediate hinterland developed in a concentric manner, expanding outward from the river port as the number of farmers needing supplies steadily increased in Northwest Missouri, and Northeast Kansas territory. They produced more agricultural raw material, grain and livestock, which in turn had to be marketed and brought in from ever increasing distances. Those agricultural products arrived in St. Joseph primarily on wagons. After sale or processing, the products were then shipped by river to more distant markets downstream, primarily St. Louis. In return, the supply of finished goods came by wagon overland, or as with the bulk of products, upriver by boat from St. Louis. Later, by the end of the 1850s, the arrival of the railroad would begin to change the pattern of shipping and receiving and forever change the scope and shape of St. Joseph's hinterland.[1]

For St. Joseph's business houses, the hinterland did not just expand in concentric rings. The area of mutual economic dependence soon took on more of the characteristics of tentacles extending from the body of an octopus. At first, the tentacles followed the undulations of the natural transportation routes, sometimes to great distances from the body. The Missouri River tentacle extended well to the north, into the Dakotas and even Montana, where military outposts and some Indian trade bases stood. The Oregon and California Trails became major western tentacles along which St. Joseph businessmen spread their wares, eventually pushing their market hinterland all the way to the Salt Lake Valley and beyond. Later, the railroads, arriving from the east, made St. Joseph the tip of a tentacle extending out from the great metropolis, Chicago.

In the 1840s, overland transportation routes were primitive. Wagon roads leading into St. Joseph, were simply dirt paths, following the line of least natural resistance. The roads had little or no grading, no paving of any kind, not even gravel. Tree stumps dotted the grade where it passed through a timbered area. During the winter months, when covered with heavy snow, they were impassable. The same was true in the spring when the thaw and rains turned them into rutted quagmires. During the hot summers, they swirled with dust, and in the autumn the rains turned them to mud again until the first hard freeze turned the surface to the consistency of iron. Roads were primitive but important. Early on, the merchants of the new town, including old Robidoux, understood the necessity of transportation links to their immediate hinterland, the smaller farm

24

communities throughout Northwest Missouri. In March 1850, they petitioned the county court to insure that all major roads in the area led to the town. In part, the court record read: "On the petition of Joseph Robidoux and others the court appoints David J. Heaton, John S. Pickett, and John Rode to view a change in the state roads from St. Joseph to Gallatin and from St. Joseph to Plattsburg and also from St. Joseph to Savannah so that said roads shall meet the termini of streets at the corporate limits of the town of St. Joseph."[2]

Besides meeting the need to haul produce and supplies to and from the area's farms and other small towns, the wagon roads were used for regular coach service between St. Joseph and outlying communities. Small companies like that operated by Samuel Wade were typical. He ran a stagecoach service between Weston in Platte County and St. Joseph, with departures every other day. The distance was about 30 miles the way the crow flies. Wade advertised that it took just eight hours via his coach. John Frink offered tri-weekly stagecoach service to places like Liberty and Glasgow on the Missouri River, and even Hannibal on the Mississippi.[3]

Securing the local hinterland over area roads proved important to the town's economy, but even greater economic opportunity was realized with the opening of the great western wagon trails. During the decade of the 1840s and 1850, those wagon trails carried tens of thousands of emigrants from the East to the rich farmlands of Oregon and the gold fields of California. In competition with other western towns establishing themselves on the edge of the Great Plains, St. Joseph vied not only for a share of the economic pie, but also for the largest portion. In direct competition for the emigrant's dollars stood Independence, Missouri, sixty miles to the south. It was an established town, twenty years older than St. Joseph. It had garnered the position as the jumping-off point for the main trails leading into the Southwest. Premier among them was the Santa Fe Trail, which opened in 1821. Between Independence and St. Joseph stood Westport, the Town of Kansas (Kansas City as it was called in the early 1840s), Weston was on the Missouri side of the river, and Leavenworth on the Kansas side.

Emigration to Oregon began as a trickle during the late 1830s, with Independence outfitters, experienced from the Santa Fe trade, providing an established jumping-off point and a ready stock of supplies. By 1844, political troubles with Mexico began to cut deeply into the Southwest trade just as

25

migration to Oregon began to steadily increase. Independence merchants and suppliers assumed the new trail would replace business lost from the old. By that time St. Joseph had been born and stood ready to compete directly. not only with Independence. but with St. Louis as well, as the primary supply and jumping-off point for the trip across the Great Plains. The advantage St. Joseph possessed lay in that it sat further upriver than either St. Louis or Independence. Two extra days on the steamboats brought them further along, thus reducing for the emigrant the time and distance involved in the more arduous overland travel by two weeks. By beginning at St. Joseph and supplying for their trip there, the emigrants could avoid the trek from St. Louis, via the St. Charles wagon road, to St. Joseph. Even by bypassing Independence, angling across northwestern Missouri directly to St. Joseph, they could save 100 miles.[4]

At St. Joseph, emigrants took the ferryboat across to the Kansas bank, then traveling due west, connected with the main overland trail as it headed north and west toward the Platte river in Nebraska. The complete route to Oregon took them nearly 2,100 miles, across Nebraska, into Wyoming, where they took a welcome pause at Fort Laramie. They then traveled on through the South Pass in the Rocky Mountains, into the Salt Lake valley of northern Utah. From there, the emigrants crossed the interior ranges of the Rockies, following the Snake River to its confluence with the Columbia River, and finally reaching their destination in Oregon's Willamette River valley, four or five months after departing St. Joseph.[5]

As early as 1844, the first large emigrant wagon trains formed near St. Joseph. Cornelius Gilliam organized several trains, totaling 200 wagons with 800 people in the spring of 1844. They crossed the Missouri River on Capler's Ferry, a few miles northwest of the town, and after the grass came on they proceeded west. Among those accompanying one of the wagon trains was a young carpenter named James W. Marshall, whose name became known worldwide when he discovered gold at Sutter's Mill in California four years later.[6]

The opening of the feeder trail from St. Joseph presented immediate economic opportunity and attraction. New merchant houses and the shops of craftsmen had converted Robidoux's hemp field into a sizable town within those first eighteen months. Political organization quickly came in the form of articles of incorporation. granted by the state legislature, on February 26, 1845.[7] Joseph Robidoux sat as the town's first president of the board of trustees. Six others,

26

businessmen and lawyers, filled the board. Their stated purpose called for them to maintain civil order and peace in the new town, but unofficially they assumed the role of urban and economic promoters to the benefit of their own businesses and practices.

The town fathers, meeting as a political body for the first time in early April 1845, made decisions to insure St. Joseph's position as the jumping-off point across the plains. First, they licensed adequate ferrying facilities and oversaw proper operation of them from the town's own levee. In August 1845, Jeremiah Lewis became the first to be licensed by the town to keep a ferry operating from the town's levee, although other ferries operated earlier near St. Joseph, licensed by Buchanan County.[8] At the same time, the town's board of trustees passed an ordinance stating that there would be no more than two ferries operated from the city levee. They did not want too many ferries inhibiting the landing and departure of steamboats bringing passengers and goods to and from the town. The fine for operating an unlicensed ferry was set at $20. They also set ferry rates for the year 1846, as follows:[9]

Wagons with four horses or oxen	$1.00 +
Wagons with three horses or oxen	.87 1/2
Wagons with two horses or oxen	.75
Carriages or buggy	.65
Wheeled vehicles	.50
A mule or horse	.25
A man	.12 1/2
A cow, bull, steer, pack mule	.06 1/4

The rates compared closely to those charged by ferry operators in the county.

HITTING THE TRAIL

After organizing a city government, what the town needed next was a first class business and civic promoter, someone to help get the word out about St. Joseph as a major jumping-off point even more effectively than word of mouth or normal correspondence. The town needed a newspaper. They got both the promoter and the newspaper with the arrival of William Ridenbaugh in early 1845. Born in Pennsylvania in 1821, Ridenbaugh became an apprentice printer at an early age, and as a young man of 22 years, moved to Liberty, Missouri in 1843. There he opened his own printing shop and newspaper with a partner named George Leader. Ridenbaugh acquired his printing press from of all places, the Missouri River. A printing press belonging to the Mormons had been tossed into the river during the repression of that religious group during the 1830s. Ridenbaugh and his partner subsequently recovered and repaired it. In early 1845, the young printer saw greener pastures in St. Joseph, a growing town with no newspaper, and made a personal decision that would affect the entire town's history. Shortly

William Ridenbaugh, the town's first editor and primary promoter. *Courtesy St. Joseph Museum*

after his arrival he opened a printing shop there and established the *Gazette*. The first edition of the weekly paper appeared on April 25, 1845. Its first local editor was a lawyer, Lawrence Archer. They charged a subscription rate of $3 per year, or $2 in advance. Ridenbaugh, being a staunch Democrat, saw that the paper endorsed those candidates and issues from the beginning. But more importantly, he made it an immediate instrument to boost the town of St. Joseph.[10]

One of the *Gazette's* first editorials, published on May 9, 1845, represented a classic piece of promotional literature: "In consideration that the town of St. Joseph is yet quite young, that very little has been written concerning it, that comparatively few persons have visited it, and that this is the first newspaper published here, we will be indulged in writing an article whose object is to let people know what kind of place is our town and what are

28

its prospects. This article is intended for persons at a distance, and we will suppose that the reader knows nothing whatever of St. Joseph." Ridenbaugh then wrote probably the best, most accurate, and honest description of the new town in the following words:

"St. Joseph is situated on the east bank of the Missouri river, about 575 miles above St. Louis, and about 75 miles by the river from Fort Leavenworth. It is now about twenty months since this place was laid off into town lots: it contains 682 inhabitants: the original proprietor, Joseph Robidoux, has sold 316 lots to private individuals: there are twelve large mercantile establishments, three hotels, with a host of mechanics of all trades. Improvement is now rapidly going on in St. Joseph, and the mechanics all seem engaged. Much, very much trade is done by our merchants, we presume each one does a good business now, notwithstanding several potent causes have operated to curtail trade. Most of the ready money of the farmers has been taken for the last few years to pay for their land, the country is very new, and sufficiently large farms are not yet open, and for the last two years the crops have failed almost entirely."

It seems likely, based on his writing, Ridenbaugh had read or knew of the important theories of natural advantages, espoused and often published by a number of well-known nineteenth-century urban promoters. As his article continued, he masterfully applied those principles to promoting the town: "There are many circumstances connected with St. Joseph which conspire to make it not only a large but important place. This town is the farthest up on the Missouri river, which is a fact of some importance; it is true that two or three towns have be laid off above us, but it is agreed that all things considered there is not a good town site between this and the Council Bluffs, on this side of the river. The river at this place makes quite a bend; it runs as it were far into the country and turning short round runs back: we are situated on a point of this kind, and the consequence is that a much larger portion of land lies immediately contiguous to us than is generally the case with river towns. For these reasons an extensive scope of country must trade at this point. St. Joseph being the nearest and most convenient, and further the quality of the soil is good, so that the amount of produce of the country, when its resources shall be fully tested is incalculable."[11]

Ridenbaugh knew that supplying the overland emigrant could make St. Joseph grow. He had to tell those emigrants why his town should be their starting point. The number of emigrants going to Oregon steadily increased after

29

1844, due to the treaty with Britain, which in 1846 settled the boundary line dispute between Oregon country and Canada at the 49th parallel. Subsequently, the formation of a territory there in 1848 attracted even more people. The Mexican War, 1846-1848, caused western migration to dip somewhat during those years. St. Joseph actively competed to achieve hegemony among the towns on the edge of the Great Plains, with William Ridenbaugh and the *Gazette* as its voice. Constantly full of news about the West, letters from Oregon and California, information for emigrants who wished to organize near St. Joseph, and news of the war with Mexico, the little weekly paper actively promoted the town's merchant houses as the best suppliers in the region.

Emigrants apparently read the paper, or by other means heard of St. Joseph, and responded. An article in the May 2, 1845, edition of the *Gazette* described one of the large trains that had formed near St. Joseph: "Wm G. Tvault, Esq. is the elected Captain of the company, with whom we had some conversation, and thereby gained the following information. It is estimated that the company when made up and organized fully, will consist of above one thousand persons, one hundred wagons, and about two thousand cattle. It was ascertained by examination that each family had a full supply of provisions, and the whole wealth of the company is near one hundred and thirty thousand dollars. We visited their camping ground on the morning of the day when they started and accompanied them a short distance. Most of the families were comfortably prepared for traveling, and believed themselves as comfortable as if in a dwelling house. All seemed full of resolution, and we were surprised to see such cheerfulness, with the women as well as men."[12]

The season for departures over the trail lasted only a short time. It began in early April, dependent on how soon the grass came on, and generally ended by the middle of June. Most of the departures took place in May. Waiting any longer could mean running into trouble in the high mountain passes of the western Rockies, where snows often began in September. As a result, mercantile activity and high profits lasted for a brief but frenzied period, which the town's businessmen looked on with all the anticipation that modern retailers apply to the Christmas season. As the next season of migration approached, the *Gazette* ran regular announcements of organizational meetings for the emigrants, ads for the supply houses, and promotional articles with headlines like: "HO! FOR OREGON OR CALIFORNIA! The season of the year is approaching when all those who are desirous of emigrating to Oregon or California, will naturally turn their attention to the western boundary of Missouri, to select some favorable point at which to rendezvous, and where all their necessary outfits can be procured, at the least possible expense."[13]

By 1846 Ridenbaugh's paper reported that St. Joseph had a population of about 1,000 persons and had 13 large mercantile establishments "which are capable of furnishing every article in the *Grocery and Drygoods* line that may be required for an outfit, at prices as cheap, as the emigrant can bring them from St. Louis." Continuing his inducement for emigrants to use St. Joseph, Ridenbaugh appealed with a little name dropping: "Intelligent gentlemen (with previous Oregon companies), have written, from there, advising their friends and those desirous of profiting by *their experience*, to make St. Joseph the point, whence to take their departure for Oregon, being much the *nearest* and *best* route, and where all necessary supplies can be furnished. Mr. Clarke (well acquainted with the country between St. Joseph and Ft. Laramie) acted in the capacity of Pilot for the last Oregon company that left St. Joseph, and pronounces it to be the best and nearest route, having an abundance of grass, timber and water, for the use of the emigrants, and at regular intervals for camping."[14]

St. Joseph could really provide everything the emigrant needed. It had flour mills, pork slaughtering houses, which processed, according to the *Gazette*, an astonishing 5,000 hogs the previous winter. The town also had a large number of blacksmiths, wagon makers and saddlers. Draft animals for the wagons and thousands of head of cattle on the hoof were available from farms and ranches in Northwest Missouri. Nearly 36,000 head of cattle, mostly bound for Oregon, funneled through St. Joseph in 1846 alone.[15] Ridenbaugh also made sure the emigrants knew about the ferry service at the town. If they were convinced by then to make St. Joseph their jumping-off point, the *Gazette* and the town's merchants stood ready and eager to supply the emigrant with a shopping list of everything one needed to make the journey. Of course, the merchants offered to sell every item. This is what they said every emigrant needed: "The wagons should be new, made of thoroughly seasoned timber, and well ironed and not to heavy; with good light beds, strong bows, and large double sheets. There should be at least four yoke of good oxen to each wagon—one yoke to be considered as extra, and to be used only in case of emergency. Every family should have at least two good milch cows, as milk is a great luxury on the road."

31

The article suggested the following provisions for each person except infants: "200 lbs of bread stuff (flour and crackers), 100 lbs of Bacon, 12 lbs of Coffee, and 12 lbs of Sugar." They also recommended each family take the following articles in proportion to their number: "1 to 5 lbs. Tea, 10 to 50 lbs. Rice, 1 to 2 bushels Beans, 1 to 2 bushels dried fruit, 1 to 5 lbs. Salaratus, [salt] 5 to 50 lbs. Soap. Cheese, Dried Pumpkins, Onions and Corn meal may be taken by those who desire them. I would suggest to each family the propriety of taking a small sheet-iron cooking stove with fixtures, as the wind and rain often times render it almost impossible to cook without them, they are light and cost but little. All the foregoing articles may be purchased on good terms in this place."[16]

FIERCE COMPETITION FOR TRAIL BUSINESS

Halcyon newspaper articles were not only designed to sell St. Joseph to the emigrants, but also to lure them away from the other supply towns and jumping-off points for the trail—Independence, Westport, and Weston. The printed promotional voice of the town doubled in May 1848, when the *Adventure*, a weekly newspaper like the *Gazette*, began publication. Emery Livermore published and edited the paper. He made no bones about the fact that "the leading characteristic of the *Adventure* will be a fair, manly, and zealous support of the cardinal principles of the Whig party."[17] This surprised no one, considering the *Gazette* was just as zealously Democratic. Otherwise, Livermore demonstrated every bit as much excitement about the prospects of St. Joseph as Ridenbaugh. He had been one of the first merchants to establish a grocery and dry goods store in the town, and had been one of Ridenbaugh's first and best advertisement customers. One thing that both papers immediately agreed on was the unabashed promotion of St. Joseph at the expense of Independence. Besides the fight over being the best jumping-off point for the overland trails, the matter of securing whatever else they could from the state legislature or national congress became paramount in their editorials. Securing the overland mail route to Oregon, provided an example of the competition and gave the editors grounds to take pot shots at Independence: "Independence and St. Joseph are the only places so far as we are now informed, that have been spoken of as the depot of the Oregon mail, and in the rivalry for this honor Independence has much

32

advantage. Independence has been long known as the starting point for Santa Fe, California and Oregon and most of those who would most likely give intelligence upon this subject to Congress knew Independence before St. Joseph became a town. We say that those most likely to speak upon the subject and who recommend Independence are unacquainted with the road from St. Joseph; and those acquainted with both roads concur in saying that the St. Joseph road is nearer, better and safer. . .We are fully convinced by the lights that shine upon us, that the route from St. Joseph has much superior claims if rightly understood."[18]

It is obvious that the merchants and editors in Independence were quite aware of the economic importance of the wagon trail business and did everything they could to sell their town over St. Joseph. Their jabs and responses, published in the Independence *Expositor* and reprinted in both the *Gazette* and *Adventure*, no doubt to raise the public ire and promote readership, produced indignation and sometimes outrage in St. Joseph. "If the emigration from that place has been as great as it has been here," wrote the *Expositor* editor, "we pity their condition, as they must launch out on the plains with a scarcity of every thing, unless they made their outfit at St. Louis, or prior to their getting to St. Joseph. It is not reasonable to suppose that at that point they could begin to get all the necessaries for a long journey, because it is a new place, a new country, and has no surplus to spare."[19]

During the emigrant season of 1847, St. Joseph surpassed Independence as the main jumping-off point for the Oregon Trail. Of the 1,300 wagons that left that year for the Northwest, 867 departed from the St. Joseph area, 433 from the Independence area. The size of individual wagon trains leaving St. Joseph varied from as few as 23 wagons to as many as 109. The number of people in each wagon varied, depending on the size of the families, but four to six people was normal. Once across on the ferries, the individual trains set off at intervals of a day or two, spacing out about ten to fifteen miles apart along the trail. The spacing assured that the grass, needed to graze the horse and oxen, would remain ample. At least fifteen trains left St. Joseph in May of that year.[20] The *Gazette* seized the opportunity to further deride Independence: "The large number that have made this their starting point, proves conclusively that they consider this the best route, and the cry of 'high prices' and 'bad roads' falls harmless to the ground. The citizens of Independence may 'brag and boast' as much as they please, but rest assured that in two more seasons, the entire emigration for

33

Oregon and California will make St. Joseph the starting point."[21]

During the season of 1848, trail business fell off by nearly half. The *Gazette* reported in May that only 210 wagons had crossed as of the fifth day of that month and at most they expected only 500 wagons total for Oregon that year. However, the event that brought St. Joseph to preeminence as a jumping-off point to the western wagon trails had started to unfold. It began on January 24, 1848, when James Marshall, a foreman in the employ of John Sutter, found traces of gold in the tailrace of a sawmill being constructed on the American River in California's central valley. Though Sutter and Marshall swore each other to secrecy, the story leaked out within weeks. By early autumn of 1848, the news reached the East coast, touching off a frenzy of travel activities there. The people of St. Joseph probably had not heard about the discovery of gold in California, until they read it in one of their weekly papers in December of 1848. The *Adventure* reported the news under the modest headline: "Late from California and Oregon." If the headline was modest, the first descriptions of the gold field were not. "The whole valley of Sacramento may be said to be one vast deposit of gold, the metal lying in more or less abundance, from the crags of the Sierra Nevada to the emboucheres of that river and its many tributaries. People were completely engrossed in collecting it, to the abandonment of almost every other occupation." The article also reported prices and wages had gone sky high, that sailors were jumping ship as soon as they reached harbor, and that the whole Sacramento valley swelled with, "the multitude of golddiggers."[22]

Travelers could get to California by ship from any of the east coast ports, by going around Cape Horn, but that took four months at best and proved a brutal time for the typical landlubber. They could take a ship down to Panama, hike across the Isthmus and then sail up the west coast of Mexico. Or like most, they could take to the road or a river steamer, as far west as the edge of the Plains, and there join a wagon train bound for the gold fields. The overland wagon trail to California basically followed the early route of the Oregon Trail as far as Fort Hall in southern Idaho. After that, it diverted southwest to follow the Humbolt River as far as the eastern slope of the High Sierras. There one had to cross through, at any of a number of different passes, but always before the snows began to fall. Since St. Joseph already had a fine feeder trail connecting to the main trail coming up from Independence, and because it had regular steamboat service from St. Louis that deposited emigrants further along the trail, the town became "the" point of departure.[23]

People began to arrive in St. Joseph in late 1848, for two major reasons. First, there were those who hoped to get an early handle on supplies, wagons, and draft animals for the trip west to the gold fields. Secondly, there were those who were inclined to go into business, supplying the needs of others. In one way or the other both groups intended to get rich from the California Gold Rush. Only some would never have to leave St. Joseph to do so. As a result of the influx, the town's population doubled from what it had been only two years earlier. New merchant houses formed and opened on nearly every street. The newspapers filled with ads for everything the emigrant needed. The town's stores and warehouses became cornucopias of dry goods, ranging from foodstuffs to hardware to hats and boots to patent medicines. When emigrants were not being outfitted, then those same dry goods merchants either sold directly to area farmers or did wholesale business over a hinterland that stretched north to Council Bluffs, east to Chillicothe, south to the edge of Kansas City and Independence, and west to Salt Lake City.

Patrick McLeod, a forty-niner from Maryland, left a brief impression of the booming town in his diary in November 1848: "St. Joseph is situated on the east bank of the river in the county of Buchanan. The first house was erected in 1843. It is known on the map as Robedoux's [sic] Landing. The town contains about two thousand inhabitants and is rapidly increasing. Houses are being built in every direction, wages are high, capital scarce. There are in my opinion few places on the Missouri which offer greater inducements to the emigrant than St. Joseph."[24]

The St. Joseph *Gazette* echoed those sentiments in an article published in February 1849 under the caption, "Important to California Emigrants," as thousands of eager gold seekers began to crowd along the Missouri River waiting for the spring thaw, the grass to come on, and the trails to open. The editor attempted to encourage emigrants to use St. Joseph as their supply base and tried to lure them away from other jumping-off points further south. The article pointed out that St. Joseph had nineteen stores, of which three were newly opened, two steam flour mills, two steam saw mills, nine blacksmith shops, four wagon factories, two tin and sheet iron manufactories, and two saddle and harness making establishments.[25] The *Adventure* published a stream of advice for the expected emigrants, hoping to steer them away from Independence. One

35

editorial writer suggested: "From St. Louis to St. Joseph, by land, in the spring of the year is a task, and a *worse one* by far to Independence. On the south side of the Missouri, it is almost impassable." The writer encouraged people to take a steamboat from St. Louis, up to Hannibal, then across the state, thereby missing any chance of stopping in Independence at all.[26]

Besides being touted in the town's own newspapers, the feeder trail from St. Joseph received some impressive endorsements from noted military men coming back from the Mexican War via overland trails from California. They included Commodore Robert F. Stockton, naval hero of the war, who reported "the St. Joseph road was nearer and better than the one leading from Independence." A Major Harris, also known as "Black Harris," a military scout and well-known pathfinder for a number of wagon companies, said the St. Joseph route was "the best and nearest by upwards of one hundred miles." Still another wagon train leader, Captain Miles Goodyear, encouraged those wishing to sign on with him to come to St. Joseph. "The Captain is now in the place, and will leave for California early in the spring. Notwithstanding the extraordinary exertions that have been made to induce emigrants to avoid St. Joseph as a starting point, it has sprung up to be a town unparalleled in the history of the west and occupies a position beyond the reach of any successful competition as a starting point to Oregon and California."[27] The spring of 1849, saw a full scale war of words declared. Both St. Joseph and Independence claimed the status as the number one starting point for the emigrant going West.

Following the appearance of so many inflammatory articles, merchants and editors in both towns made a clear attempt to grab every emigrant dollar available for their own. However the battle did not seem to include price cutting. Emigrants still paid top dollar for everything from a team of mules to pots and pans. St. Joseph businessmen formed a committee and appointed a spokesman to further herald the glorious prospects of St. Joseph and bash the competition. The spokesman, identified in the paper as M. Thompson, was most likely Merriweather Thompson, who preferred using his nickname Jeff. Thompson, at that time an ambitious young clerk for one of the town's larger mercantile houses, would later be elected mayor. In an article published in the *Gazette* on February 23, 1849, Thompson did not spare any of St. Joseph's competition, calling Westport "but a village," and Leavenworth "just a military post," unworthy of consideration by emigrants. However, he leveled his main broadside at Independence saying: "Independence is what is called in the west an *old* town. It is indebted to, and still depends entirely upon the Santa Fe trade for its prosperity and support. There is no country back of it; there is no trade for it except the Santa Fe. While St. Joseph is a new town, not yet six years old. Its situation is far superior to any town on the river, and its unprecedented growth has depended entirely upon its natural advantages and resources, and it is indebted to no foreign cause for its increase. Its bone and muscle are within itself, and its blood is furnished by a vast tract of country to the north and east. The whole Platte Purchase, with exception of one county, centers its trade in St. Joseph."[28]

Independence counter-punched with anti-St. Joseph propaganda, including articles written by William Gilpin and published not only in the Independence and St. Louis papers but in East coast papers as well. Gilpin, a former soldier and newspaperman, by 1849 had become a noted writer and promoter of the urbanization of the West. He was a powerful advocate of geographic determinism and had predicted the rise of great cities, connected by railroads from the Mississippi Valley to the Pacific Coast, stretching along a band of latitude known as the "zone of intensity" of the "isothermal zodiac."[29] Gilpin predicted that a great city of a million people would one day occupy the area just north and east of Independence. He even invested in land there, creating Gilpintown. Gilpintown served as a river landing on the Missouri for Independence. Unfortunately for Gilpin, the land on the *west* side of Independence, now Kansas City, eventually became a metropolis of 1.5 million people. Gilpin had a powerful political ally in the person of Missouri Senator Thomas Hart Benton, who also promoted urbanization in the state. Both men strongly believed in the potential of Kansas City to dominate the western trade.

The *Adventure* responded in the battle of the newspapers by taking the *Expositor* and the St. Louis papers to task for blatantly misleading emigrants about St. Joseph. The editor expounded: "It is very amusing to observe the wineing [sic] and wimpering of our neighbor at Independence in the *Expositor* of the 7th last . . .and finding that the large posters and circulars distributed in St. Louis and on steam boats, together with Col. Gilpin's letter, published in the St. Louis, Louisville, Washington City and many other papers throughout the nation did not produce the desired effect—turn all emigrants to Independence. We are at a loss to know how the good people of St. Louis find it in their interest to humbug the emigrants in this matter of a starting point. Perhaps it would be too much to expect our friends of St. Joseph to tell in plain, unvarnished tale of the advantages and disadvantages of their town. We are afraid that they have been interested in holding out the great endorsement of St. Joseph as a starting point. We feel it is our duty, however, to warn all travelers to California, that there is more romance than reality in these vain pretensions of our little rival and their interested pufers [sic] in St. Louis."[30]

TRAILS WEST

The newspaper articles, and word-of-mouth recommendations, brought the emigrants for California spilling into the area around St. Joseph by the thousands. The merchant houses, wagon factories, and mechanics, particularly blacksmiths, were swamped with business. Area farmers sold every draft animal, horse, mule, or ox for premium prices and likewise every ear of corn or bit of hay. Mules sold for $40 to $60 each and oxen for $30 to $40 per yoke.[71] Ferries taking the emigrants across the river were so busy that several day delays were common. Between April 1 and June 15 of 1849, 1,508 wagons crossed the ferries from St. Joseph. At Duncan's Ferry, just four miles north of the city, another 685 wagons crossed. The numbers from other smaller ferries operating in Buchanan County approached another 500 wagons. Those figures do not include foot or horse traffic across the wide Missouri either.[32]

A traveler named Tate left his impressions of St. Joseph and its ferrying operations in his diary from 1849: "Tuesday, 24. [April] St. Joseph is a Flourishin place situated on the Mo. river where it makes a great bend to the east. We went this evening 16 miles to Mr. Fauts and stopped for the night, the Choerae [cholera] and small Pox prevail considerable at St. Joseph and the emigrants are crossing the river in to the bottom and some are going to fort Carney. [Kearney] Corn is very scarce."

"Thursday, 3rd. [May] Went into St. Jo and took our place at the ferry. About 40 teams ahead at each boat. They cross about 35 teams per day, Each boat, and some times there is a great contention about these rights, and at a landing 5 or 6 miles above this there was two men killed in a conflict for their rights. This is the finest place I have seen on the river for crossing, an eddy on both sides, and very narrow and good landings on both sides. St. Jo is beautiful situated and improving very fast. It now has a population of 14 hundred, three

38

churches, Presbyterian, Methodist and Catholic. I have found many old acquaintances who treated me with much kindness especially Doc. Cook and Lady. We have had a very disagreeable time here for three days. A heavy rain fell on us the first night and made it very muddy. Our teams we had to send several miles out to the country and grassed them on the Prairai as corn could not be had. The third day we crossed late in the evening."[33]

The following year, 1850, saw nearly 100,000 Americans migrate to California and Oregon, with St. Joseph newspapers estimating nearly half of them leaving from the city's feeder trail matching all the other jumping-off points combined.[34] The war with the town of Independence continued with the competing newspapers embroiled in mutual bashing. The St. Joseph *Adventure* took its opening shot early in January: "TO CALIFORNIA EMIGRANTS. As the season for emigrating to California overland approaches, we wish to call the attention of those intending to make the trip to the advantages of St. Joseph as a starting point on the western frontier. With those who came here last spring there was but one opinion, and that giving preference to this place over any other; they wrote back to their friends to that effect, and as such St. Joseph gained a name and reputation by which it is more generally known than it would otherwise have been, yet from the many slanderous reports and lieing [sic] hand bills, put in circulation last spring, in relation to St. Joseph by an *inland* rival town, intended to give the emigrant a false impression and wrong direction, it is fair to presume that such contemptible tricks will be resorted to the ensuing season."[35]

Not until 1851 did the rush of traffic on the wagon trails begin to subside and the outfitting of emigrant business return to levels prior to the gold rush. During that same period, another important western trail opened that connected some St. Joseph merchants to another distant hinterland. It did not originate near the town; however the same feeder trail led to it. The Mormon Trail originated at the site known as the Winter Quarters, on the Missouri River, north of Omaha, Nebraska. During the winter of 1846-1847, the first wave of four thousand Mormons, recently displaced from Nauvoo, Illinois, after the murder of their leader Joseph Smith, settled in to wait for the spring thaw. Their new leader, Brigham Young, planned to take them West across the plains into the isolated mountain valleys of Utah where they could practice their religion in peace. While they camped there in Iowa and Nebraska, they scoured the surrounding country to buy supplies for the long trip. Their wagons traveled south along both banks of the river, reaching into northwest Missouri. At Oregon and Savannah, Missouri, two small towns north of St. Joseph, the Mormons initiated a business relationship with grocers James McCord, his partner and brother-in-law Abram Nave, and Milton Tootle.

The young merchants, as well as several mercantile houses in St. Joseph, provided the Mormons with needed supplies that winter. As the years passed they established a continuous mercantile relationship. Milton Tootle moved his dry goods and grocery business to St. Joseph in 1849 to take advantage of the gold rush boom, and McCord and Nave moved their main operation to the town in 1857. Both firms grew substantially in the years to come and maintained connections with the Mormons in Utah. They not only provided wholesale dry goods, but also drove cattle on the hoof to their buyers in the Salt Lake valley.[36] The overland connections with Salt Lake City became part of the extensive network of trails, freight roads, and stage lines that either passed through St. Joseph or used it as a hub.

The rush to California subsided after 1852. Migration however continued through the rest of the decade. St. Joseph merchant houses shifted their economic focus from outfitting emigrants to establishing an extensive wholesale hinterland, dependent primarily on overland wagon connections to deliver their products. Connections had already been made with points throughout the transmountain West. When Kansas and Nebraska were organized as territories in 1854, the influx of settlers provided a new source of ready customers. Competition from Westport and Kansas City to the south, both of which had by then surpassed Independence as the major freight shipping hub into the Southwest, increased. Further upriver from Kansas City, the town of Leavenworth, built next to the military base, Fort Leavenworth, developed shipping connections of its own to the West. By 1860 it had grown into a boom town, even larger than Independence or Kansas City. A bit further north still, another river town, Atchison, began to develop. A number of freight companies based in St. Joseph competed for overland hauling dollars and, particularly, for government contracts to carry either the mail or supplies to western military outposts. Those contracts amounted to tens or even hundreds of thousands of dollars.[37]

The size of companies varied from just a couple of wagons and teams, operated by an individual and his family, to larger firms with a couple of hundred freight wagons and stage coaches, thousands of draft animals, oxen, mules, horses, and strings of stations from the Missouri River west to California. Typical of the larger companies were ones like Blodgett & Company. Owned by Colonel Blodgett, Major McCoy, and Mr. K. D. Raymond, and advertised to entice both overland traveler and mail service, the express company promised regular transportation to and from California. The *Adventure* reported the company had "at great expense" built a train of light wagons, secured the best horses, and hired "experienced and competent drivers" to operate their express train, carrying emigrants, letters, and small packages to both California and Oregon. The company advertised that they had relays of horses and mules at points 500 miles apart through to the West coast. It also guaranteed that all letters would be promptly deposited at the post office upon arrival of their express. Like many freight companies, it had agents in every town of any size throughout the region. The company agents in St. Joseph operated out of hotels. Some of the larger express and freight companies built their own terminals and warehouses in the town.[38]

With the opening of the Kansas and Nebraska territories, St. Joseph merchants found some compensation for the gradual decline in the number of emigrant trains to be outfitted for going to Oregon and California. Unlike the emigrants for the West coast, those in Kansas and Nebraska would tend to remain steady customers. St. Joseph continued to provide the primary ferrying service across the Missouri into those territories. The local papers made certain that the emigrant continued to be well informed about the advantages of outfitting in St. Joseph, and they heralded the arrival of a new steam ferry in 1854 as follows: "Messrs. Wright, Williamson & Co. have purchased a superior Steam Boat, the "GENERAL GAINES" and have her lying at our town *now*, for the purpose of ferrying Emigrants the coming season. She is a Boat of admirably adapted to the purpose; capable of crossing at one time at least 300 head of cattle and 12 wagons and teams. Arrangements have been made to accommodate at least 125 persons with board and lodging on the boat. Emigrants can have every comfort and convenience, and at the same time be certain of not being delayed. A good road through the bottom, on the opposite side of the river, is being cut out 100 feet wide to the Bluffs. Good pastures can be obtained for stock at this point, and St. Joseph is on the great Western Thoroughfare for emigrants going West either to California, Oregon or Nebraska."[39]

By the middle of the decade of the 1850s, St. Joseph could boast of her fine ferry services and of being an ever growing city that had become the premiere supply base for the Great Plains. By then the city had 5,000 inhabitants, telegraph communication with the East, two dozen large wholesale merchant houses, its first bank owned and operated by John Corby, and five mills processing locally grown grain into a flour "of superior quality and sold lower than it can be procured in St. Louis." The local press reported "an immense amount of Pork" slaughtered in St. Joseph during the winters. This resulted in what the papers declared the lowest price for bacon in the state. Most of the hog slaughtering took place in seasonal packing houses located along Blacksnake Creek. Because of the volume of the kill the little creek apparently became so fetid with blood and other unwanted animal parts that the city council passed an ordinance in 1856 forbidding area butchers from dumping their waste in any stream except the Missouri River.[40]

PIKES PEAK AND OVERLAND MAIL

Another major burst of overland trail business occurred just before the Civil War in association with the gold rush located in the Pikes Peak region of Colorado in 1858. That event launched nearly 100,000 emigrants across the Great Plains. St. Joseph again captured its share of the outfitting and supply business, along with Leavenworth and Kansas City.[41] Although it must have seemed like a revival of the prosperous heyday of the 49ers, the 59ers were in fact of much shorter duration and contributed to a false sense among merchants that the prosperity created by the wagon trails would continue indefinitely. The St. Joseph paper *The Weekly West*, which in 1859 replaced the *Adventure* as the "loyal opposition" to the Democratic *Gazette*, even warned in the middle of the emigrant season that the rush to Pikes Peak was a "humbug." The St. Joseph paper took the opportunity to condemn the Kansas City and Leavenworth papers for leading the emigrants on with "flaming editorials" in full "complicity with the humbuggers," while defending its own journalistic integrity. The article stated: "Kansas City, Leavenworth City, and St. Joseph are the points whence started on their wild goose chase, a majority of the emigration, and to these places is attached the infamy of having originated the humbug. No thinking man, however, knowing anything of the circumstances but will at once acquit St. Joseph, whose papers have from the beginning published, with like alacrity, both

42

favorable and unfavorable accounts."[42] Nonetheless, St. Joseph outfitters, wholesalers, and freighters made small fortunes from the Colorado "humbug."

Four Pony Express Riders. *Courtesy of the Boder Collection*

The final offshoot of the drive to establish a comprehensive system of wagon roads across the West directly linking St. Joseph and other towns on the Missouri River to California did not on the surface appear to have anything to do with moving emigrants or hauling freight in wagons. That brief, eventful period involved the short-lived Pony Express, which the modern city of St. Joseph takes so much pride in promoting as a symbol of its history. The connection began with the operations of one of the biggest freight firms at that time in the West that of Russell, Majors, & Waddell. The idea behind the Pony Express, which would carry mail from St. Joseph to Sacramento and back, over a 1,900 mile trail in ten days, was the brain child of William H. Russell. The idea for a rapid mail service to California came to him, probably in 1858, while he thought through the advantages of monopolizing the central overland route, a freight and stage road, to the Pacific.

He presented the idea to his partners in October 1859. Russell and his partners primarily used Leavenworth as their main base of operation. They competed directly for most of the big government contracts for mail and freight with firms like John Butterfield's Overland Mail Company. Butterfield's firm held a six year government contract, valued at $600,000, to deliver mail to California via the southern route, which originated in St. Louis and Memphis, then swung through Arkansas, Texas, New Mexico, and Arizona. The normal delivery time took 25 days. Russell believed that a more direct central route, which basically followed the old California Trail saving 800 miles, to be not only faster but also more economically viable, once it could be demonstrated that it could be traversed year round. To show its year round viability, Russell planned to use the Pony Express. In doing so he hoped to win the government's next big California mail contract away from Butterfield.

After Russell had discussions with California Senator William M. Gwin, and received only questionable assurance that the government would provide some subsidy for the operation, Russell traveled west to meet with his two junior partners, Alexander Majors and William Waddell. Their firm, and Russell's other various subsidiary companies—Jones, Russell & Company, the Central Overland California & Pike's Peak Express Company, and the Leavenworth & Pike's Peak Express Company--were already deeply in debt when Russell tried to convince his partners to back the Pony Express. Initially both thought the whole concept a bad idea. Majors and Waddell were certain the expense of setting up and maintaining the operation would never be covered by the potential income. Plus they already had a huge deficit from previous operations and mergers in trying to gain dominance of the central route. Besides, the transcontinental telegraph was likely to be completed in the near future. Russell, well known for his flamboyant business dealings, believed in the old axiom, to make money one had to spend money. Therefore the promotion of the central route, which by then they controlled, would be worth it. And because he had already made a lot of noise in Washington and some eastern papers were picking up the story, his personal reputation was at stake. Plainly stated, the Pony Express originated as an expensive promotional gimmick, a "fantastic scheme." When questioned about his motives for the services Russell answered: "I was compelled to build a world-wide reputation even at considerable expense." Majors made the scheme even plainer when he said, "It was undertaken solely to prove that the route could be made a permanent thoroughfare at all seasons of the year. . . .as far as the paramount objective was concerned, it was a complete success."[43]

The leaders of St. Joseph wholeheartedly signed on with Russell's promotion. St. Joseph had been chosen over Leavenworth as the eastern terminal due to the recent completion of the Hannibal & St. Joseph Railroad line into the city, which made the transfer of eastern mail more direct. Twenty city fathers signed a contract, granting Russell's firm, the Central Overland California & Pike's Peak Express Company, a number of economic concessions.[44] The company advertised in St. Joseph for two hundred horses, riders, livestock and station attendants, and purchased everything from harness and saddles to hay and lumber from local suppliers. Stations were about ten miles apart with riders getting fresh mounts. They relayed the mail pouches to other riders every four or five stations. Riders carried mail both directions on the route at the same time. From St. Joseph they left the company's stables and crossed on the ferry into Kansas to start the westward run. From San Francisco, California, they left for the first eastward leg from the office of the *Alta Telegraph,* a local newspaper where the San Francisco agent of the Pony Express had rented space.

Russell put the whole Pony Express operation together in quick order. It was barely three months from the time he made the final decision to go ahead with the project in January 1860, until it sent off its first rider at 7:15 p.m. on April 3, 1860, from St. Joseph. The scene, described by one local paper as "the greatest enterprise of modern times!" began with speeches by the mayor of St. Joseph, M. Jeff Thompson, and Mr. Majors, representing the express company. After the talks finished, Thompson reportedly personally put the mail bags on the back of the animal, "a fine bay mare," and amid the "loud and continuous cheers of the assembled multitude, all anxious to witness every particular of the inauguration of this greatest enterprise," sent the first rider on his way. Who the first rider was is often disputed, at least from the St. Joseph end of the route. The popular consensus is that a wry young lad named Johnny Frye rode the first leg. However, the account of the initial sendoff, reported in *The Weekly West,* identified the first rider as a "Mr. Richardson, formerly a sailor, and a man accustomed to every description of hardship."[45]

The Pony Express ran on a published timetable that outlined the route and the number of hours it took to reach each major point along the 1,966-mile journey. The advertisement called it "the fastest route on record to be run by horse flesh."[46]

Marysville, Kansas	12 hours
Fort Kearney	34 "
Fort Laramie	80 "
Fort Bridger	108 "
Salt Lake City	124 "
Camp Floyd	128 "
Carson City	188 "
Placerville	226 "
Sacramento	232 "
San Francisco	240 "

At first the cost of sending a message over the Pony Express route was quite high. The company expected most of its business to be generated from telegraph traffic originating on the east coast. According to an article in the *Weekly West*: "the tariff on this route has been fixed at $6.90 for a message of ten words from any point in the United States, on telegraph lines, to San Francisco; add ten cents for each additional word."[47] Rates for letters fluctuated, downward over time, but one had to pay for speed. The efficiency of the route's operation has never been questioned, nor has the bravery of the riders or station keepers along the way. However, there has to be a question regarding Russell's "stock in sensibility" at the time. The Pony Express operated only 18 months, until October 24, 1861, when the completion of the transcontinental telegraph made it obsolete. It completed 308 runs both ways, carried 34,753 pieces of mail, and produced receipts of $90,141 for the company. The bottom line indicates that it hardly made enough to cover the cost of the horses, and did not even make close to the estimated $700,000 it actually cost to operate during that short period.[48]

Although freight wagons provided the primary method of moving goods into St. Joseph's hinterland during the 1850s, steamboats proved the most effective way for St. Joseph merchants to resupply since much of their own wholesale buying took place in St. Louis. The link between St. Louis and St. Joseph by boat proved just as important for the large city on the Mississippi as its upriver partner. The link with St. Joseph meant that St. Louis could maintain northern and western Missouri as part of its hinterland. At first St. Louis took for granted that there would be no defection of St. Joseph merchants because the steamboat was the dominant form of western transportation. Dependence on the steamboat eventually proved costly for St. Louis in its own battle with Chicago for economic hegemony in the nation's heartland.[49]

THE POLAR STAR Captain Brierly's record setting steamer. *Courtesy of the Boder Collection*

Many people embarking from St. Joseph for the Oregon and California trails got to the town by steamboat. Articles in the *Gazette* encouraged emigrants to use the steamboats to come to St. Joseph to outfit: "Emigrants wishing to travel by water can find plenty of steamboats at St. Louis, for the Missouri river, on which they can procure a passage to St. Joseph, at as cheap a rate, as to Independence, or any intermediate point."[50] Independence did not sit directly on the river and used a landing a few miles distant. This was not overlooked in promoting St. Joseph. Regular packet service from St. Louis began nearly as soon as St. Joseph formed and reached its peak during the period 1848-1852. Although boats plied on to Council Bluffs and even as far up the Missouri as the confluence of the Yellowstone during that time St. Joseph represented the head of regular scheduled navigation on the river. The one-way ride upriver from St. Louis to St. Joseph normally took a week with a number of intermediate stops. Later record breaking runs would be accomplished in as little as three days.

Despite what it may have looked like from the embankment, the Missouri River was a wild, uncontrollable, and dangerous body of water. In those days no modern Army Corps of Engineers existed to build dams, control run-off, dredge the channel, or remove other obstacles to navigation. The state of Missouri eventually funded "snag boats" at the insistence of the St. Louis operators; however, they were not very effective in keeping the channel clear. In the spring, the river ran high with water from mountain runoff and spring rains. Sunken logs or snags lurked just below the surface of the swirling brown water. Late in the summer and into the autumn, it ran low. In winter, it could be clogged with ice flows. There were no levees so when it flooded it went wherever it wanted, gouging out a new channel or leaving sinkholes or lakes where none had been before. It shifted and deposited sandbars so routinely that even experienced navigators could get caught unaware. Because of that, freight and passenger rates ran seasonally high. There was no such thing as guaranteed arrival or departure times, though some packet lines attempted to meet their schedules. Some years the navigation season might be as short as five months, but even during a good year, it rarely lasted more than seven.

The first packet service to advertise in the *Gazette,* in 1845, was the *John Golong,* a boat mastered by William W. Baker. "The *John Golong* has been fitted up expressly to run as a regular packet between St. Joseph and St. Louis, and all intermediate ports. Shippers and passengers may rely upon her regularity and prompt attention. The lightness of the draught of the *John Golong,* and the greater security to persons and property, should recommend her to the traveling public as well as shippers. Her speed and accommodations are equal to any boat in the trade."[51]

Ads for various packet services appeared weekly in the paper, but many boats did not have the need to advertise. Plenty of business developed as the traffic on the overland wagon trails increased. As a result of that increased traffic, the boat operators, particularly the regular packet services, often stood accused of price gouging. In a June 1845 editorial, Ridenbaugh of the *Gazette* took some of them to task thus: "Within the last few days we have had at our landing three Steamboats, the White Cloud, the John Aull and Lexington, all of which are "independent" boats. Our merchants seem disposed to patronize them and give the 'combination' [packet] boats the go-by. We are glad to see this, for with much abhorrence do we regard all such encroachments upon the principles of 'free trade and sailor's rights,' as are made by (we would almost say) this infamous conspiracy of the steamboats against the merchants, the farmers, and those other boats who would not join them. The effect of such a combination is to make the consumer pay more for his goods, and as the up-country merchant could not rise so much in his prices at once, to make him lose some of his profit, and all are consequently interested directly in putting down such an association. As for ourselves we are and hope ever to be at war with monopolies and exclusive privileges in all kinds of business, considering such unfair, anti-democratic, and highly injurious."[52]

Early on the town fathers--as they had done with the ferry operations--ensured the town's steamboat service would not be hindered by poor landing facilities. They considered constant attention to the riverfront imperative to the town's growth. The landing of steamboats took precedence even over ferry operations. The granting and renewal of ferry licenses stipulated that they not interfere with the steamboat landing and that any money made from ferry operations by the town were to be used "to improve the wharves and landings of the town."[53]

In an ordinance passed in July 1846, the board of trustees preempted land along the riverbank to insure some order to the landing operations of the steamboats. It stated that all the embankment, starting on the north side of Jules Street and running south for 150 feet, be declared a steamboat landing. Thereafter, flatboats, wooden boats or rafts of any description could not land or discharge cargo there. The ordinance called for a fine of not less than five dollars for anyone violating it.[54] The board of trustees, in July 1847, acquired land for the construction of a city-owned wharf at the same location, the foot of Jules Street.[55] Subsequent actions by town fathers included appropriations of funds for pilings and stone and a proposal, presented in November 1849, to allow the city to borrow $5,000 to $10,000 for wharf improvements. It was one of the first fiscal propositions to be recommended for submission to the town's voters.[56] On October 30, 1850, the voters approved borrowing of $10,000 for grading and paving the riverbank and the construction of a more substantial stone wharf.

The influence the steamboat captains exercised with the town's board of trustees demonstrates the power to control the import of merchandise, and thus the economic health of the town. The captains needed and wanted certain conditions on the riverfront, to satisfy not only themselves, but their merchant clientele as well. For instance, in September 1849, Captain John Whitehead, a prominent local boatman, convinced the board to revoke the ferry licenses of two of the town's better known steam ferry operators, John Corby and Thomas James. The stated reason for the revocation involved the continued violation of steamboat landing access by the ferrymen. Considering the three and four day backlog of emigrants waiting, during the spring rush, to hit the trail to California, the ferrymen no doubt felt they had just as much right to keep their boats moving back and forth across the main channel as did the bigger steamers to make a landing.[57] That Corby also promoted railroads did not endear him to the steamboat operators either.

The town hoped to regulate the flow of freight to and from the wharves by licensing draymen. Draymen hauled freight in wagons from the riverfront to elsewhere in the town. Although originally limited to a charge of 15 cents per load inside the town, by 1849, the board had increased the charge to 20 cents.[58] An ordinance set the limit of a daryman's load at 1,200 pounds, or the equivalent of: twelve 100 pound sacks of flour, six sacks of salt, four bales of hemp, four barrels of whiskey, or three barrels of molasses. They also created the office of wharf master, to supervise the riverfront and collect wharfage fees, which amounted to $3 per boat from all steamboat captains.[59] During the summer of 1850, amid the rush of departures for California, the town began constructing the municipal wharf, which extended from Jules Street south to Charles Street, nearly four blocks long.[60] Afterward the city continued to pass ordinances appropriating funds for the repair and upkeep of the wharves.

In response to the huge influx of emigrants, many of them arriving in poor physical condition, the board of trustees, in July 1849, also passed an ordinance that required all steamboats, flatboats, or trading craft landing or discharging freight or passengers at St. Joseph's wharf to be examined by the town's newly created board of health. A subsequent ordinance, passed in May 1850, required a physician appointed to the board of health to personally visit every steamboat landing. He could search every boat, and if any person on the boat had a contagious disease, he reported it to the town constable and the boat's captain. The constable could then forcibly prevent any sick person from landing.[61] The ordinance apparently proved too much of a demand on the city's physicians and the city repealed it, although inspection of boats continued on a random basis.

At the peak of the spring emigrant rush, boats landed nearly every day, sometimes more than one at a time. For example, on April 27, 1849, four boats— the *Meteor No. 3*, the *St. Joseph*, the *Boreas No. 3*, and the *Mandan*—all called at St. Joseph with loads of emigrants and supplies.[62] The combination of transportation links between the river and the overland trails made St. Joseph the transportation hub for crossing the Great Plains. For the decade of the 1850s, the town's growth and prosperity rode on wagon wheels and paddle wheels. The town became the building site and home port of a number of noted steamboat captains and their boats, like the *Silver Heels*, owned by Captain Silvers; the *Hesperian*, by Captain Frank Kercheval, the *St. Joseph*, by Captain Tom Scott; and the *A. Saltzman*, built and operated by Augustus Saltzman. Advertisements for regular packet service to St. Louis steadily increased. During the summer months of 1851, at least six boats—the *Timour, Banner State, Clara, Alton, El Paso*, and *Isabel*—all offered regular weekly arrival or departures. The big boats and their dashing captains became household names in St. Joseph.

Typical of the boats that served the emigrants was the *Timon*, owned by Captain William Miller, a master well known in St. Joseph. The *Adventure* published a technical description of the *Timon*, being outfitted for the St. Joseph packet business, in St. Louis: "The hull measures 160 feet straight keel, 172 feet on deck, 29 feet beam, 28 feet floor, and 5 1/2 feet hold. The engines and machinery which are being built at Gaty, McCune & Glasby's are to be of the best description, with the latest improvements and all finished *bright*. The cylinders are 19 inches in diameter, and 6 feet stroke, and the pittmans are 21 feet in length; she will carry three 40 inch boilers, 26 feet in length, and will have a neat compact *doctor* to work the pumps & all entirely new. The wheels will be 23 feet in diameter with 10 feet buckets. The cabin is to be 134 feet straight and will contain 30 state rooms."[63]

Probably the most celebrated boatman from the city was Captain Tom Brierly, who lived on a fine large farm just east of the town. A more experienced

51

navigator, on the Mississippi or the treacherous Missouri River channel, could not be found. Adept at dodging snags and sandbars on regular runs between St. Louis and St. Joseph, he continually broke the speed records he had set himself on previous trips. He commanded a number of fast boats during his career and even operated the successful Union Packet Line which had at one point eleven boats. His most famous boat, the *Polar Star*, made a record run from St. Louis to St. Joseph in August 1853 in the time of two days and 20 hours. His arrival at the town's wharf prompted the cream of St. Joseph society to visit the famous captain aboard his boat and present him with a set of silver mounted elk horns. The local paper reported: "The "Robidoux Greys," a uniformed Military Company of our city, were selected as the medium through whom this presentation was to be made." Captain James Craig of the "Greys" made the presentation and afterward the citizens were invited aboard to "partake of an abundant repast prepared by the hospitable officers of the boat. The edibles were discussed and dispatched: champagne was introduced and flowed freely, and numerous witty, patriotic and enlivening sentiments were proposed and drank to with hearty good will." The only complaint on the evening arose when "the heavy rain descending before all were safely *moored* on board, prevented the ladies gracing the occasion by their attendance, to the great mortification and regret of the bachelors." Brierly reportedly mounted the horns on the steamer's forecastle along with a banner inscribed: "Beat our time, take our horns. St. Louis to St. Joseph, 2 days, and 20 hours."[64]

The *Polar Star* stood as a prime example of the ever increasing size and speed of the river steamers that served St. Joseph with cargo and passenger service after 1852. A side-wheeler, 227 feet long, with a beam of 34 feet, she could float in only two feet of water. She carried up to 300 passengers who could be fed and entertained in her grand saloon. The saloon seated 100 for dining or dancing to the ship's band. The interior, decorated with the finest hardwoods, gilt carvings, crystal chandeliers, and velvet curtains caused many exclamations of awe. Cabin doors led out to the promenade deck where first class passengers could watch the river flow serenely by. Many emigrants who could not afford a first class cabin rode on the lower decks, sleeping with their baggage and eating where they could find a place to sit down. Beneath the luxury of her upper deck appointments were boilers that fed her two large engines with steam, and storage for 100 tons of cargo, that covered the spectrum from finished manufactured products to farm produce. The engine stokers were often black slaves. Like so many river steamers, the *Polar Star's* life proved too short. Snags and sandbars took their share of boats, but fires and boiler explosions were just as fatal. The *Polar Star* burned to the waterline in 1859 near St. Louis. Brierly's record run to St. Joseph stood for three years, until the boat *James A. Lucas*, captained by Andy Wineland, broke it on July 22, 1856, with a time of 2 days, 12 hours, 57 minutes.[65]

The era of the river steamer brings to mind a period of excitement and romance for many. The elegance of the boats, their luxurious appointments, the legend of big poker games, and of shifty scoundrels being tossed overboard for cheating, and the chivalry of the captains, who would risk all to win a race or set a record, belies the reality of steamboating. The steamers were in the transportation business. They transported passengers, freight, and the mail. They operated not for some backdrop to a Hollywood period piece, but to make profits for their owners. As a mode of transportation, steamboats were the unchallenged waterborne counterpart of the overland wagons. In a greater sense, the belief in the dominance of the steamboat as "the" means of heavy transportation for the Mississippi and Missouri river valleys spelled trouble down the road for many towns and cities. Even though the "natural" advantage of river trade strongly supported the decisions of city fathers in St. Louis, Memphis, New Orleans, and Louisville, the entire commercial network of the West faced an impending and irreversible change.

During the 1840s, there began to emerge a third form of transportation company that combined the better elements of both boats and wagons with fewer restrictions. When it arrived, it transformed the transportation hub of St. Joseph, and for that matter the entire nation's economic future. Those towns which embraced the new transportation system saw new potential to prosper and grow to greatness.

CHAPTER 3

The Coming of the Iron Horse
1645-1860

Wagon roads and the bountiful waterways provided by nature were used as transportation links to extend a town's hinterland in mid-nineteenth century America. To have any chance at real urban success, it became almost imperative to have railroad connections. St. Joseph was no exception to that rule and, showed an enormous potential to develop into the region's preeminent rail center. Decisions made by town fathers and promoters, along with their hard work, initially put St. Joseph at the forefront of any discussions about railroads in the state of Missouri and, for that matter, the entire American West. But most western towns, even those with prodigious futures tied to rails, like Chicago, could not build them on their own. It also took critical decisions by the government and capitalists from the East to pull it off. St. Joseph certainly gave itself a head start, but like the story of the hare and the tortoise, the first away from the starting line does not always finish first.

As early as 1846, only three years after St. Joseph had been born, agitation began within the community and the state to build a trans-Missouri railroad. Initial proposals included a line from St. Louis to Independence and Westport, through the state's capital, Jefferson City; and a line directly connecting St. Joseph on the west side of the state with Hannibal, on the Mississippi River, on the east side. In St. Joseph, several business and civic leaders saw the enormous economic potential a rail line could add to the town's growing commercial prospects. In November 1846, an article in the St. Joseph *Gazette* pointed out the problems with river transportation as the main arguments in favor of building rail connections with the east: "Our country is destined to suffer much and is now suffering from the difficulty of navigation and the extremely high rates the boats now charge. Our farmers may calculate that they will get much less for produce and will be compelled to pay much more for their goods than heretofore, and this will certainly always be the case when the Missouri River shall be as low as it now is. The chances are fearfully against having any considerable work bestowed in improving the river, and until it is improved by artificial means, the navigation of it to this point must always be dangerous and very uncertain."

The article continued the argument in favor of rail transportation: "We suggest the propriety of a railroad from St. Joseph to some point on the Mississippi, either St. Louis, Hannibal or Quincy. For ourselves, we like the idea of a railroad to one of the latter places suggested, for this course would place us nearer to the Eastern cities, and make our road thither a direct one; we like this road, too, because it would so much relieve the intermediate country which is now suffering and must always suffer so much for transporting facilities in absence of such an enterprise."[1]

The article represented progressive thinking, by anyone's yardstick, in the 1840s. There were practically no railroads west of the state of Ohio at all. The river steamer and canals still dominated as the most popular means for heavy freight transportation. So anyone with a vision of expansive rail links, connecting the distant West with the cities of the East, was still considered to some extent a dreamer. But even as early as 1846, the notion of a true transcontinental railroad circulated among visionaries and a few people in government. In 1846, Chicago, destined to become the great rail hub of the entire nation, had begun to build its first line west to Galena. For St. Joseph, the vision of the town as the eastern terminus for the railroad to Oregon had been bantered around in the East and by certain members of Congress.

Robert M. Stewart.
Courtesy of the Boder Collection

Among St. Joseph's dreamers, Robert M. Stewart stood above all. Born in Truxton, New York in March 1815 to a family of limited means, his took up school teaching as his first profession. While teaching he studied law and at age 21 switched to that practice, moving to Louisville, Kentucky for a short time. He became a partner in a newspaper and continued the practice of law in St. Charles, Missouri for a year before moving to Buchanan County in 1839. Stewart came to St. Joseph in 1845 shortly after the town organized. As an active Democrat, he drew support from Ridenbaugh's *Gazette* and won election to the Missouri senate in 1846.[2]

Stewart believed in building internal improvements. He viewed the proposed 200-mile railroad between his new hometown and Hannibal as an important investment in the future of the town and the state. Late in 1846, Stewart traveled to Hannibal and met with other railroad promoters at the office of John M. Clemens, also a lawyer, and the father of a son named Samuel, later known as Mark Twain. The meeting resulted in a petition to the state legislature to charter a railroad company. As the state senator from the district including St. Joseph, Stewart took the lead in introducing the chartering bill during the 1847 session. The Hannibal and St. Joseph Rail Road received its charter on February 16, 1847.[3]

Among those named to the company's board from St. Joseph were Joseph Robidoux, the town founder; John Corby, a businessman, banker, land developer, and ferryboat operator, who had invested in railroad building back East before coming to St. Joseph in 1843; and Robert J. Boyd, a prominent dry goods merchant. The positions of Robidoux and Boyd on the board reflected their community standing and financial investment capabilities, respectively. Corby had been one of the real drum beaters for the proposed railroad. Born in Limerick, Ireland, he spent his youth in Pennsylvania. As a young man, he became a contractor in both canal and railroad construction. He traveled and worked throughout the Midwest and South. He came to St. Joseph in 1843 and immediately invested in property, much of it bought directly from Robidoux. He wrote several letters to the editor in support of the railroad, which he signed only with the initial "C." He received front page space, and used it to blast the costs and problems of river shipping and promoted the railroad as a practical and desirable alternative. He wrote: "The residue of the year being fully nine months the Missouri River is obstructed by the numerous shoals and bars, in consequence of the low water, and during the winter months by ice. These impediments being the result of natural causes, are in my opinion irremediable, unless by the plan you have suggested, a rail road from St. Joseph to the Mississippi River."[4]

JOHN CORBY
Courtesy of the Boder Collection

56

The initial proposal called for raising two million dollars to begin construction through public subscription of 20,000 shares at $100 per share. The General Assembly's action touched off a flurry of railroad meetings and activities surrounding the initial survey in every county in the northern part of the state. Not unnoticed, especially by the riverboat interests in St. Louis, lay the fact that at the same time charters had been granted to six other railroad companies. By the start of the Civil War the trend saw over 100 railroads chartered by the state.[5] The people of St. Joseph got exciting weekly updates and editorials about the railroad. They also read about the "river convention" to be held at Glasgow, an important river port in the center of the state. There boat operators discussed ways of combating the newly emerging competition.[6]

On June 2, 1847, a railroad convention for all the counties between Hannibal and St. Joseph convened at Chillicothe. Representing St. Joseph were Benjamin Loan, the town's first clerk, a lawyer, and later a member of Congress, and Lawrence Archer, also a lawyer and sometime editor of the *Gazette*. The convocation of civic and economic leaders passed numerous resolutions, the most important being the following:

> "1st. A liberal subscription by the citizens of the State to the capital stock of said company.
>
> 2d. That Congress be petitioned for a grant of alternate sections and parts of sections of all vacant lands ten miles on each side of said road when located.
>
> 3d. That the company procure a subscription to the stock by Eastern Capitalists. And should the foregoing means prove inadequate, we then recommend that the Legislature pass an act authorizing the company to issue bonds to be endorsed by the Governor or Secretary of State for the residue: the company to give a mortgage on the whole work to the State for the liquidation of said bonds."[7]

Despite the newness of the railroad industry in general, the Chilicothe convention demonstrated a complete grasp of the economic structure of railroad building that lasted through the rest of the century. Local private investors needed soliciting as with any company that required a large capitalization. But, the concept of receiving land grants from the United States Congress for such ventures and the belief in the importance of attracting Eastern capital demonstrated their grasp of where the real financial power lay in the United States. In simple terms, the men attending the Chillicothe convention knew what they wanted and had a realistic idea of how to get it done.

A SLOW START

Unfortunately, some of the ideas presented at Chillicothe were a bit ahead of their time. To pay for the initial "viewing" or survey of the proposed line, the directors opened subscription books for 1,000 shares at $100 per share in July 1847. In September 1847 the *Gazette* reported shares were selling rapidly, not in St. Joseph, but in Livingston County, site of Chillicothe, 70 miles east of the city. The paper reported that in two days 129 shares already sold there and within the week they expected 250 to 300 shares to be sold.[8] But, the enthusiasm in Livingston County and the number of investors there soon petered out. In January 1848, the *Gazette* lamented that only 711 shares had been subscribed to leaving 189 shares left of the initial $100,000 to be raised locally. Since that was barely enough to pay for surveys or operating expenses, the money for any type of construction would have to come from elsewhere.

To that end, elected officials representing St. Joseph and others along the proposed line to Hannibal, in the General Assembly or the United States Congress, began soliciting government support for the railroad. The *Gazette* and other papers in the area editorialized the importance of the proposed railroad: "Strong reasons are shown why Government ought to make an appropriation of land to aid in the construction of such road, among the most important of which is the fact that it will form a material link in the great Oregon Rail Road."[9]

In May 1848, area Congressmen Willard P. Hall, and James Green published a letter to their Senate colleague, Senator Sidney Breese, Chairman of the Committee on Public Lands. They requested his attention to a bill granting lands to the state for the "purpose of aiding in the construction of the Hannibal and St. Joseph Rail Road." In the letter they cited the rapidly growing size and importance of St. Joseph, the high cost of river transportation, and the lack of access to the river landings for most northern Missouri farmers as reasons to support the bill.[10] Unfortunately for railroad promoters, the committee tabled the bill, along with dozens from other states, all wanting assistance to build their new transportation networks. There was no precedent for the granting of government land to railroad companies yet, though it had been practiced in regards to overland roads and some canals. Some members of Congress still believed in the viability of canal building, the transportation revolution that swept the East in the decades since 1820. Railroad building remained too "new" a risk into which to sink the nation's money.

However, by 1850 a breakthrough regarding federal land grants to railroad companies appeared on the horizon. The breakthrough did not come as a direct benefit to the Hannibal and St. Joseph or any other Missouri railroad. The first line to receive the federal land subsidy was the Illinois Central Railroad. The political astuteness of Illinois Senator Stephen Douglas and the support of powerful eastern investors, proved to be decisive for making that line the first.[11]

With minimal funding from the public stock subscription, a small appropriation from the Missouri General Assembly, and the private backing of men like Stewart, the dreamers went ahead the best they could. Stewart worked tirelessly to promote the Hannibal and St. Joseph. Even the political opposition praised him for his endeavors. The Whig paper, the *Adventure*, described the Democrat Stewart in glowing terms: "To the energy, enterprise and untiring perseverance of our fellow citizen, Robt. M. Stewart, Esq., the friends of this contemplated rail road are indebted, for the active part he has taken in this enterprise."[12] However, in the same article the editor took the Democratic-controlled state legislature to task for only appropriating $5,000 to help the fledgling railroad company with its cross-state survey. "The State Legislature at its last session: reluctantly appropriated, for this survey, five thousand dollars, *provided* Congress would make a grant of land, and further conditioned that the State should hold stock in the corporation, to that amount. This *liberal donation*, by the State, amounts to just nothing:" Furthermore, Stewart himself reported that the stock subscription to the railroad, from Buchanan County and St. Joseph, was the lowest of any of the counties along the proposed line. With so much to gain from being the western terminus of the first trans-state line, Stewart could not explain why Buchanan County was "in proportion to the number of inhabitants and wealth, below every other county in the amount subscribed."[13]

A survey of the line finally began in late summer 1849. Two local surveyors, Simeon Kemper and James O'Donoghue, their crews, and military surveyor Major M. F. Tiernan formed the team. Stewart accompanied the survey party for part of their expedition, arriving with them when they entered Hannibal in December 1849. He spent much of his time soliciting more stock subscriptions along the way. He left the State Senate in 1850 and became the Hannibal and St. Joseph Rail Road's first president. Stewart, local promoters like Corby, and the newspapers continued to prod the government and the public about the importance and the need for the railroad connection. Papers published a steady stream of railroad news to keep the issue in the public eye, but the gold rush story seemed to dominate everything and every mind in St. Joseph. Rail promoters tried to tie the need for better transportation to the west coast to their cause. They said if a rail link to the Pacific Coast to transport the thousands of emigrants were built, "the Hannibal and St. Joseph road must form an important connection with it."[14]

When the surveyors completed their work, they published and filed reports in Washington for Congressional consideration. St. Joseph received a glowing report card about its potential. In a letter to Missouri congressman Willard P. Hall, Tiernan reported his conclusions: "St. Joseph occupies so important a geographical position with reference to all parts of this Continent, and is surrounded by such extraordinary natural advantages, that it requires no uncommon degree of sagacity to foresee the influence she is one day destined to wield, and the consequences she will assuredly attain in the future chronicles of the West."[15] So gushing was his account, it would have even made Independence promoter William Gilpin blush.

Finally, in 1851, the state realized the need to financially back the railroads, and authorized $3.5 millions in bonds. There had been some bitter infighting within the legislature among groups representing various parts of the state and their railroad factions in regards to the state bonds and pending federal land grants. Papers in the northern part of the state referred to the St. Louis press as taking the position of "usual jealous selfishness, claims the whole benefit of the grant for their road, upon the south side of the river."[16] The powerful St. Louis delegation managed to garner the lion's share of the state bond money for the Missouri Pacific line. The Hannibal and St. Joseph Rail Road received $1.5 million. The state would hold a mortgage against the railroad's land and stock, just as the Chillicothe convention had proposed. The state further stipulated it would not release the bonds until sufficient matching capital had been raised by the company from other sources.[17] Thanks to the precedent set with the Illinois Central regarding federal land grants, along with the consistent lobbying of Stewart and the Missouri congressional delegation, President Millard Fillmore, in June 1852, signed legislation approving land grants to Missouri for the Hannibal and St. Joseph line. Despite the tremendous effort of the Missouri leadership in Washington, the legislation would not have been passed without the support of Illinois congressmen, particularly Quincy representative, W. A. Richardson. Richardson wanted to ensure the proposed Hannibal and St. Joseph line connect with his town on the eastern bank of the Mississippi via a short branch line to Palmyra, Missouri which is fifteen miles north of Hannibal and opposite Quincy.[18] The consequences of that action were to have far reaching effects on the development of the railroad to St. Joseph, but in a much larger scope, on the transportation hinterlands of Chicago and St. Louis as well.

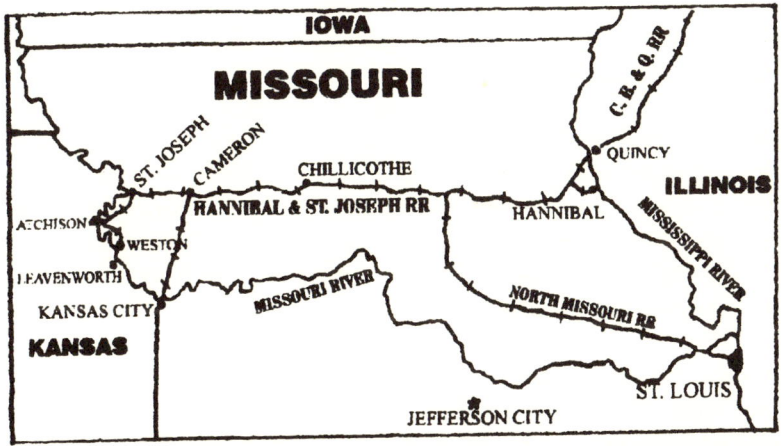

Map of the Hannibal & St. Joseph RR.   *Map by the Author*

Stewart's perseverance and final success in getting the federal land grant from Washington earned him much public acclaim at home. The local papers lionized him as the "champion of the Hannibal and St. Joseph railroad." After his extended stay in Washington, his friends in St. Joseph wanted to throw him a welcome home party. The editor of the *Adventure* wrote: "In consequences of

61

his great services in behalf of this important enterprise, with the people, at Jefferson City and at Washington City, our citizens have tendered to Col. Stewart a public dinner, a tribute justly due him; this compliment he has declined to accept. He has the confidence and heartfelt congratulations of the people of northern Missouri, which without doubt, are more acceptable to him than any public demonstration."[19]

The federal grants gave access to a 30-mile-wide path across the state. The company received a section [640 acres] for each mile laid. This provided the Hannibal and St. Joseph with revenue potential from 600,000 acres of right-of-way land, some of northern Missouri's prime farmland. Once the railroad company surveyors, Colonel M. F. Tiernan and M. Jeff Thompson, completed a second and more detailed survey in 1852 selecting tracts best suited to railroad construction, the government returned to public domain the remaining land from the 30-mile swath. It was then put up for sale, but with a price per acre double what it had been. The final transfer of land title to the railroad would officially take place on completion of the line. In exchange for the land grants the railroad would carry federal troops and supplies at no charge, and also the mail at a minimal rate set by the government.[20] With some private stock subscription money, the promise of state loans, and federal land subsidies granted, Stewart and the board of directors were ready to see some rails and ties laid down. But, they still needed hard cash to get things moving. John Corby traveled east to "close a contract with some one of the companies, which have made proposals for the construction of the road."[21]

One of the companies Corby met with in 1852 belonged to John Duff. A wealthy New England railroad contractor, Duff bought in excess of one million dollars of Hannibal and St. Joseph stock to secure the construction contract for his firm--on favorable terms, from a cash poor board of directors. His stock purchase made him for all intents and purposes the controlling interest in the railroad company. The construction contract paid him $23,000 per mile and he retained the right to operate trains, hauling both passengers and freight, and collecting fares and freight charges until the completion of the entire line. The actual laying of track on the Hannibal and St. Joseph line did not begin until 1853. Duff came to St. Joseph in March that year and "gave assurances that the contractors will commence the work both at St. Joseph and Hannibal as soon as the laborers and the necessary means can be obtained, which will probably be as early as the first of May next."[22]

As soon as Duff left, the engineers were to stake out the first twenty-five miles of the construction route. In April 1853, bidding opened at the city hall for local contractors to do grading, bridging, and masonry work for the first section. The papers reported the arrival of numerous railroad hands ready to get started. But, the initial excitement caused by the start of construction soon paled as the work crept along at a snail's pace. Topographically, northern Missouri did not present anything as challenging to the engineers as say, crossing the Rocky Mountains. But dozens of streams with soggy embankments had to be bridged and the necessary building supplies or the money to buy them failed to materialize. After four years, the amount of time Duff had originally promised for completion, the number of miles of actual track laid had only reached thirty-four, with only seven of those built on the St. Joseph end.[23]

By that time, the elements that the Chillicothe convention had identified as necessary to build their line had all been brought to bear on the financing of the Hannibal and St. Joseph line. The last major step in the project, which initial railroad boosters no doubt felt had grown beyond their anticipation, involved the transfer of controlling interest from the local promoters and the builder to the eastern capitalists. It was their vision that controlling interest in the Hannibal and St. Joseph remain in the hands of local stockholders from the two towns which gave their names to the road, and of investors at all the points in between. But financial support in the form of local stock subscriptions was not forthcoming in any amount near what was needed, least of all from St. Joseph investors.[24] The capital of the merchant class of the town was either insufficient or focused elsewhere. Apparently many still believed the wagon roads and steamboats would fill their commercial needs. A monumental decision loomed before those men; a decision that would have far-reaching effects on who would control the destiny of St. Joseph's transportation network. But, hard cash had to be found to build the road. When the government made the land grants, promising some tangible prospect of return, the project became more attractive to those with cash. Subsequently, the eastern capital so desirous to help build the road turned out to be the same eastern capital that would financially dominate the line and its ultimate management. Enter John Murray Forbes.

THE BOSTON CONNECTION

In the autumn of 1854, Forbes, a native of Boston who had made a fortune in the China trade, bought one million dollars worth of stock in the Hannibal and St. Joseph from contractor John Duff. As a result Forbes bought control of the railroad and the future of modern transportation in and out of St. Joseph.[25] Forbes was not new to the railroad business. In 1846, he led a group of fellow Boston investors in the purchase, extension, and operation of the Michigan Central Railroad. Through his efficient management that railroad completed construction across Michigan by 1848, and by 1852, linked Chicago with the cities of the east coast. From there Forbes and his group began building the Chicago, Burlington and Quincy line, which would reach the bank of the Mississippi, at Quincy, Illinois in 1856. Forbes' next logical link meant crossing that river and striking west toward the Missouri River at St. Joseph. It is doubtful at that moment, that Forbes had aspirations to span the continent. He invested cautiously in the still thinly settled areas west of the Mississippi River.[26] It is even less likely that he had any interest in the city of St. Joseph, other than as a spot on the map where his next railroad venture ended. Certainly, he was driven to accomplish his goals. His desire to see the line to St. Joseph completed and to become a viable source of income and return on his investment had an enormous influence on St. Joseph's hinterland from that time on.

Forbes increased the amount of working capital, secured more state bonds, hurried the pace of construction, and found ingenious ways to raise speculative capital from overseas investors. He also raised capital from offering land at potential town sites along the route even though legally the federal lands would not be transferred until work on the line finished. After purchasing the majority share of the company's stock, he made the decision to retain Stewart as the company's president. That move, designed to overcome criticism within the state that easterners bled Missouri of revenues, by sending the money back to Boston and New York banking houses, proved a cosmetic move at best. The real power behind nearly all the railroads west of the Appalachians lay with investors in New York, Boston, Philadelphia, and even Great Britain. Even large, more economically powerful cities like Chicago and St. Louis, had little control over the venture capital that built their proposed railroads.[27]

Stewart resigned as president of the Hannibal and St. Joseph in 1857 to run for governor of the state. He had served pretty much as a figurehead after the Forbes group took charge, and no doubt that influenced the decision of the skilled and ambitious leader from St. Joseph. In a close election he defeated his Whig opponent by only 329 votes statewide. Meanwhile, beginning in mid-1857 and extending for the next eighteen months, into early 1859, construction of the line accelerated to almost breakneck speed with crews laying down over 160 miles of track. During the spring of 1857, the first iron horse, a small construction engine, arrived in St. Joseph aboard the river steamer *Saranak #3* to carry construction materials and men to the east. In preparation for the completion of

New Short Route to the East, North and South,

BY THE

HANNIBAL & ST. JOSEPH

RAIL ROAD.

TO CHICAGO, ST. LOUIS, & POINTS EAST, NORTH & SOUTH

SAVING FROM

5 TO 7 DAYS TEDIOUS NAVIGATION

Of the Missouri River, and Tiresome Staging.

J. T. K. HAYWARD, Superintendent.

D. C. SAWIN, General Agent, St. Joseph. **City Directory 1860**

the line, John Patee donated a 40 acre tract near the center of the city for a railroad station. The first depot had an engine shop for repairs and maintenance nearby. Due to the speed of construction, the quality of much of the line proved substandard.

On February 13, 1859, construction crews pushing west from Hannibal and east from St. Joseph met. Railroad officials drove the last spike near Chillicothe, the town where a convention twelve years earlier had first undertaken the idea of building the road. The next day, the first passenger train arrived in St. Joseph. At the controls of the engine was Edgar Sleepy, with Benjamin

65

Colt the first conductor. The "grand opening" of the railroad took place on February 22, 1859, when a train carrying company officials and dignitaries from St. Louis and Chicago arrived in St. Joseph. Met by the mayor, M. Jeff Thompson, the dignitaries proceeded to Blacksnake Creek. There, in the presence of old Joe Robidoux, they conducted the traditional "marriage of the waters" by pouring jugs from the Atlantic, Lake Michigan, and the Mississippi into the Missouri at the mouth of the creek. A banquet for about 600 guests followed on the upper floor of the Odd Fellows' Hall at the corner of Fifth and Felix Streets.[28]

In April 1859, the noted journalist Horace Greeley, traveling from New York City across the United States, rode on the Hannibal and St. Joseph. He left a remarkable description of what the road was like shortly after it began operation: "We took our course westward, almost as the crow flies, to St. Joseph on the Missouri, two hundred and six miles distant, which we reached in a little over twelve hours, or at half past ten last evening. The road was completed in hot haste last winter, in order to profit by the 'Pike's Peak' migration this spring; no gravel is found on its line, unless in the immediate vicinity of the Mississippi; and it was raining pitilessly for the second day nearly throughout, so that the roadbed was a causeway of mortar or ooze, into which the passing trains pressed the ties, first on one side, then on the other, making the track as bad as track could well be."[29]

On arriving in the city, after a somewhat long and jostled ride, Greeley wrote an insightful and complimentary sketch of what he saw: "St. Joseph is a busy, growing town of some ten thousand inhabitants. It is beautifully situated on a bend in the Missouri, partly on its interval (which the river is gouging out and carrying away), and partly the southward slope of the bluff, which rises directly from the river bank, at the north end of the town. Other towns on the Missouri may have a grander future; I doubt that any has a finer location."[30]

In June 1859, Governor Stewart certified most of the track leading into St. Joseph as acceptable, despite some of the shoddy sections built by Duff, and the railroad company began to advertise its 600,000 acres for sale. The Hannibal and St. Joseph had become the city's most important transportation link with the great cities of the East. With daily connecting service to the Chicago, Burlington & Quincy line, which then tied into the Pennsylvania Central line, through rail service from New York or Boston to St. Joseph became a reality. Other railroads, designed to open and expand the city's more immediate hinterland, suddenly seemed more than possible to local promoters. Unfortunately, most of those railroads existed only on paper because the investment capital to actually build them proved more difficult to raise among local businessmen than it had for the Hannibal and St. Joseph. Still, most of the paper railroads received state charters, and that first step helped them to raise money legally through stock subscriptions. Among the roads proposed by 1859 were spur lines to towns in the immediate vicinity—Weston, Savannah, Maryville, and Atchison—as well as more substantial lines, including the St. Joseph and Little Rock Rail Road, the St. Joseph and Topeka Rail Road, the Marysville and Roseport Railroad, and the Kansas City, St. Joseph, and Council Bluffs Railroad.

The concept of the Marysville and Roseport line represented an important key to St. Joseph's future. The proposed line lay in Kansas Territory, directly across from St. Joseph. Because it ran west, it promised to open the great untapped hinterland of the Great Plains. Marysville, Kansas, had grown up near the point where the St. Joseph feeder trail joined the California and Oregon wagon trails. Roseport was an early name for the little town just opposite St. Joseph on the Kansas side of the Missouri River, later to be called Elwood. The charter for the line had been granted by the Territorial Legislature of Kansas on February 17, 1857. The first public meeting about organizing the company took place in St. Joseph nine days later on February 26.[31] A board of local business leaders formed and stock subscription books opened. After a month, according to some reports, $100,000 in subscriptions had been received, but how much of that was actual cash remains questionable. Due to its small scale, the company did not attract the attention of eastern capitalists, but its inception contained a seed of what might grow into enormous potential for St. Joseph.

Not until the summer of 1859, after the Hannibal and St. Joseph had been completed and begun operation, did serious work on the Marysville line begin to take place. A new board of directors, appointed by actual stockholders, took control. It included some of St. Joseph's most notable citizens among them Governor Robert M. Stewart, Frederick W. Smith, and Mayor M. Jeff Thompson. Thompson, elected by the board of directors as president of the line, pursued its development with vigor. He appointed an engineer to lay out the line, supervise grading and bridging, and hire a construction superintendent. Thompson had a small work engine ferried across the Missouri, the first steam powered locomotive west of that great river. In 1860 three miles of track, laid to the little town of Wathena, nestled against the bluffs opposite St. Joseph, opened. Within two years, the name of the line changed to the St. Joseph and Denver City Railroad reflecting the real vision of its owners. Some murmured of a bridge over the Missouri to connect it with the Hannibal and St. Joseph.[32]

COMPETITION FOR THE TRANSCONTINENTAL

The advent of the little Marysville and Roseport line carried some potential for the future expansion of St. Joseph's hinterland, but that became lost in a much larger debate taking place in the last two critical years before the outbreak of the Civil War. The debate simmered over the proposed Pacific railroad. From the inception of the Hannibal and St. Joseph line in 1847, its supporters had dreamed that it would one day form a vital link in the first transcontinental railroad, to either Oregon or California. During the early 1850s, the United States government conducted surveys by the army, to explore the feasibility of a number of routes, ranging from a southern route connecting at New Orleans to a northern route connecting Puget Sound with Lake Superior. A more central route, not far off the line of the great wagon trails, was popular from the beginning, and particularly after sectional differences between the North and South grew more intense. Just where the central route would begin in the east remained a question of immense importance to the commercial interest of a number of cities. The two most prominent competitors being Chicago and St. Louis, which had already locked horns in a battle for hinterland. Chicago had clearly become the western rail hub of the nation by 1859. A route directly west across Iowa was possible, but the connections already existing to St. Joseph, via the Hannibal and St. Joseph, and the Burlington and Quincy line certainly looked attractive. St. Louis had connections to the Hannibal and St. Joseph line too, via the North Missouri Railroad coming up from the south, but the Pacific Railroad Company line, striking west directly from St. Louis on the south side of the Missouri River provided that city's most direct route.[33]

The battle to see which of the two western giants became the main eastern terminus of the transcontinental railroad embroiled not only St. Joseph, but revived old resentments and touched off new ones along with a propaganda battle with other towns on the Missouri, also anxious to be the jumping-off point for the dash across the Great Plains. Primary in site competition lay Kansas City to the south. St. Joseph, clearly the larger of the two with the 1860 federal census showing a population of 8,932 persons against Kansas City's 4,418 had the advantage.[34] The same kind of battle fought between the newspapers of St. Joseph and Independence that prevailed during the gold rush days, reappeared over the issue of the Pacific railroad. Featured were Kansas City editors arguing with St. Joseph editors over the merits of starting from one point or another.

The fact that St. Joseph, and not Kansas City, had completed its railroad first became a nasty point of contention. The Kansas City *Western Metropolitan*, published on June 2, 1859, fired one of the opening shots with an editorial that read: "The notion, however, that St. Joseph may be possessed with namely: that trade will be diverted from the river, and she, by reason of her railroad facilities, be vastly benefited over other points, is as ridiculous as her efforts will prove futile. So long as there is a channel in the Missouri which boats can navigate, so long will there be business for them to do and the superior advantages which other points possess over St. Joseph, in a commercial sense, will be an insuperable barrier to all her efforts, backed no matter how strong by railroad facilities."[35]

One might attribute that way of speaking to blatant jealousy, and maybe to the dying belief that the riverboat would never be surmounted by the railroad. But either way, the thinking in that Kansas City editorial seemed to belie conventional wisdom regarding the future of the railroads. *The Weekly West* responded with a question that put their neighbors to the south on the spot: "Why, then, have our Kansas City friends been making such unwearying, almost superhuman exertions, for the past five years, to have the Pacific Railroad completed to their town? . . . Do not her editors fondly hope that the next Legislature will kindly step forward and build their miserably misnamed road for them, and so help them out of this, "slough of despond"?" And for extra measure, the St. Joseph paper threw in a barb or two of its own: "In spite of her excellent location at the mouth of the Kansas river, and her monopoly of the New Mexico trade, for low these many years, Kansas City has lingered along, but little more than a peer of the enterprising inland village of Westport." And adding insult to injury: "We expect better things of the *Metropolitan* at least, for it is in the habit, if we remember rightly, of rising above the petty jealousies of *some* of our down-river contemporaries."[36]

A primary and easy target for the St. Joseph papers lay in the apparent incompetence and overspending that plagued the Pacific Railroad coming out of St. Louis. It had still not reached Kansas City by the time the debate between the two cities really began to intensify. In September 1859, *The Weekly West* published a chart comparing the construction costs of the Hannibal and St. Joseph to those of the Pacific Railroad. To that date, the H. & St. J. had cost the company $6,500,000 and the state $3,000,000 for a completed 206 miles of track, averaging $46,116 per mile. The same chart showed the Pacific had cost the company $4,500,000, and the state $7,000,000, for 168 miles of track on an incomplete line, for an average of $68,451 per mile. The broadside continued by blasting the St. Louis supporters and the state legislature for pandering to the incompetent management of the line.[37]

The directors of the Pacific Railroad, primarily St. Louis capitalists, apparently did not view Kansas City as an important link to the western trade played to the benefit of St. Joseph. Initially the Pacific line proposed to bypass Kansas City altogether, passing through southern Jackson County, with only a spur to the city on the river bend. Promoters, businessmen, and editors of Kansas City pleaded for the railroad to connect directly to the town, passing through Independence first, then pushing directly on into the Kansas River valley. The leaders, pressured by the railroad to increase their stock subscription to get guarantees, were so worried that they petitioned the legislature for a charter to allow them to build a spur northward to connect them with the Hannibal and St. Joseph line.[38]

Meanwhile, St. Joseph's hinterland relation with St. Louis had developed a sour note, urged on by the competitors down south, creating a triangle of squabbling. The Independence *Democratic Gazette*, representing a town that as yet had no railroad, printed an article that slapped and chastised both St. Joseph and St. Louis for their railroad practices saying: "The Hannibal and St. Joe. road, owned by eastern capitalists, and now discriminating against St. Louis in favor of Chicago, in anticipation of and to meet this Kansas Valley trade, has already *projected a branch to intersect it*; even yet the Directors of the Pacific Road, principally citizens of St. Louis, have terminated the road and located their depots three miles from the terminus of the Kansas Valley Road."[39]

The St. Louis papers, responding to the growing importance of Chicago, criticized St. Joseph's rail connections with that city as an economic stab in the back and unpatriotic toward the state of Missouri and its largest city. The contention that the rates offered helped to deflect trade and passengers away from St. Louis galled that city. Continued criticism prompted the St. Joseph paper *The Weekly West* to publish an open letter from J. T. K. Howard, the Hannibal and St. Joseph's superintendent, defending the city and the line's practices. "Since the opening of the road, the passenger fare between St. Joseph and the east has always been the same by Chicago and by St. Louis, and strict orders are given to the ticket agents to require persons to *select their route*. At all times we receive less on our Eastern passengers by St. Louis than by Chicago."[40]

From all the intrastate bickering, St. Joseph could take some solace that as a decision by the United States Congress approached, they were almost certain to be the terminus for launching the transcontinental railroad across the Great Plains. The city received powerful endorsement from Chicago and other eastern newspapers. Chicago rail promoters pressed Congress to adopt the central route. In effect this would make St. Joseph the starting point by default, since it was the only city on the edge of the Great Plains that had a railroad. A correspondent of the Chicago *Press &Tribune* reported from Washington the proposed route of the transcontinental railroad: "The road commenced at St. Joseph, thence West to the Platte, up that river to the Rocky mountains, crossing them at or near South Pass; thence via Salt Lake and Carson Valley to San Francisco." According to him a congressional committee seemed likely to endorse the central route over a southern route.[41]

In April 1860, the report issued by the Special Committee on the Pacific Railroad filled the local papers. The report's conclusion clearly favored the central route, with branches feeding in from both north and south. All traffic would funnel into an eastern terminus. There was no doubt that Chicago would grab that honor. That St. Joseph would ride those coattails to commercial success and dominance of the Great Plains hinterland looked clear to most in the city. The editor of the *Weekly West* felt so confident that he wrote: "The conclusion, as will be seen, is that the road should start from St. Joseph and pursue what is known as the Central route. Every argument in favor of other routes was presented in a forcible manner, and was carefully weighed by the Committee in making up their decision; but the superiority of the Central route was too evident to admit of a doubt as to the proper location. We think that there can be no longer a question in regard to the route or the starting point. The only trouble is to determine when the work shall be commenced."[42]

If the decision had been made by the Congress, that spring, to adopt the committee's recommendations, then St. Joseph would have already made a head start on the transcontinental road with the initial construction of the Marysville and Roseport line. All that was needed was a bridge over the Missouri River at St. Joseph. The ultimate success of St. Joseph to become the "queen" of western cities lay with the vote of the Congress. But as the local editor questioned, how soon would that be forthcoming? There were dark clouds on the immediate political horizon that no one could deny. The possibility of distraction by more intense sectional issues loomed: "Will Congress act upon it at once, or are we to wait until parties shall have an opportunity to use it as a hobby in another Presidential contest? We hope the members from this section will at all events, use their best endeavors to urge the matter to a speedy vote."[43] And in the anxious little city on the Missouri, they waited.

View of St. Joseph from the Kansas bank of the Missouri River, circa 1860.
Courtesy of the Boder Collection

CHAPTER 4

Weaving a Social Fabric
1845-1860

The formation of towns and cities in nineteenth-century America represented one of the most important aspects of the eventual conquest and extension of white civilization into the American West. Towns and cities were the points from which not only trade and transportation emanated, but American culture as well. The social fabric of small towns became the model of American life by the middle of the nineteenth century. They replaced the eighteenth-century Jeffersonian model of the yeoman farmer, tilling his expanse of free land as the idealistic American lifestyle. But large cities, grown beyond the small-town setting, represented another image. In nineteenth-century America, the majority who lived on the land or in the small towns viewed the growing major cities with suspicion. They were places full of foreigners, and the site of unspeakable materialistic evil, depravity, and depression. Cities were places good people kept their children away from lest they be mesmerized and corrupted. Urban promoters on the other hand saw them as the glowing symbols of what America could become. There stood no doubt, in the minds of urban supporters, that America's cities represented true pillars of economic prosperity, inventiveness, modernity, and culture, after which everything else should be modeled. The social institutions and the life style that evolved with them stood second only to economic prowess as the major attraction for people moving from rural environments into the urban world.[1]

From the beginning, St. Joseph people favored the urban way of thinking. St. Joseph had the best of everything to offer the people occupying its hinterland, and showed no reluctance to export it to them. The wealth that came from the product of its hinterland and its geographic position provided the economic basis for building the city and for weaving the social fabric of the people who lived and worked there. St. Joseph developed with more than one distinct fiber. First, it clearly had a western thread. In many ways it epitomized a frontier town serving as a jumping-off point into the great expanse of the American West. Classic models of frontier characters, ranging from fur trappers, cattle drovers, army troopers to missionaries and Indians frequented its streets. Wagon trains

73

organized there and seasonal waves of emigrants passed through.

But because the majority of people who made up the town had come from where they did, it was also a southern town.[2] The social structure reflected strongly southern attitudes, not only about the obvious question of race relations, but in the style of living of many. In that context it is safe to say that someone from Louisville or Atlanta or Memphis would have been more comfortable in the St. Joseph environment than someone from Boston or Philadelphia. By 1860 the town also had a definite Germanic filament running through it. More numerous than any other single minority, they had their own newspaper, parish, social clubs, a school, and various businesses, reflecting their prosperity and influence.

When one thinks about how people lived in nineteenth-century American cities, particularly in the West one is often drawn to the Hollywood image of a single main street, with shops and saloons packed together, a church and a school house, and neat little houses with porches and white picket fences. Horses, pulling wagons and buggies, pass in neat order and women in long dresses raise hardly a cloud of dust as they walk in lady-like fashion across the wide thoroughfare or along the neatly swept boardwalks in front of linen shops and general stores. The picture is all so tidy, but fails to capture the true dynamics of most burgeoning cities of the West. St. Joseph, like many other cities of its size and geographic position in the pre-Civil War period, had its share of colorful people from a wide mix of backgrounds. They, along with the social institutions dealing with urban problems, constructed a social fabric probably nothing like those represented on the Hollywood sound stage.

Throughout history, the congregation of large numbers of people in the confined space of an urban setting has created special problems that have influenced how society developed. In the nineteenth century, and still true today, the major concerns of citizens are most often verbalized in some type of public forum. First, people complain to their neighbors, and then to city hall, the mayor, or aldermen, either directly or through the news media. If the snow is not removed, or the trash is not picked up, people call city hall. If the neighbor's dog is a nuisance, or there's a pothole in the street, they call city hall. So by examining what the town fathers in St. Joseph dealt with in the nineteenth century, one can better understand what happened there and how people lived their day-to-day lives.

74

PUBLIC HEALTH AND SANITATION

To begin with, towns like St. Joseph were not very clean. Like the streets in those Hollywood western sets, St. Joseph's thoroughfares were unpaved, but there the resemblance ends. During dry periods the amount of wagon traffic on them kept the air swirling with dust. When it turned wet, they became deeply rutted, and after heavy rains the low spots became quagmires or small ponds. Anyone attempting to cross or navigate up or down one of those streets in that condition likely lost a shoe or boot in the sticky goo, or faced getting stuck in the mud and run down by a wagon or carriage plowing through. By 1846, the town had passed an ordinance calling on all property owners to install sidewalks, preferably of brick "nine feet wide and level with grade."[3]

From the beginning the town fathers attempted to deal with the continuous problem of having passable streets by approving an ordinance requiring "that all the male inhabitants of said town, over the age of 16 and under the age of 45, shall work on the streets and alleys of said town not more than six days in each year, which may be discharged by the payment of 50 cents [per day] to the street commissioner." If a man did not show up to do his civic duty with shovel and rake then he could be fined one dollar for each day he missed. According to the same ordinance the street commissioner had to give the men two days advance notice of their public service. Besides calling out the citizenry to periodically grade the streets, which meant filling in the deep wagon ruts, the street commissioner was to "see that all streets and alleys are kept free of all obstructions or filth." That meant he could write a citation for "any citizen who shall permit to remain on his premises any dead animals or filth or other nuisance longer than one day," with a potential fine "not exceeding $10."[4] Not until 1859 did mayor, M. Jeff Thompson, begin to push the idea of "macadamizing" the town's streets, paving them with crushed stone and river rock.

Adding to the problem of dirt, in the form of dust or mud was the nasty situation of animal waste. Unlike the streets of the Hollywood western, in real towns the hundreds of horses, mules, and oxen that passed through the streets or were tied to hitching posts everyday left tons of manure and urine to be mixed with the surface dirt. Stepping in something unpleasant during a walk through town had to be a foregone conclusion for all but the most ginger of foot.

American cities of the nineteenth century simply smelled bad. On top of the nuisance of waste from draft animals, St. Joseph, like a number of other towns and cities, both large and small, had a problem with hogs. Hogs roamed everywhere, in yards and in the streets and alleys, scavenging for food. And a hog will literally eat anything, no matter how detestable. In reality, because of a lack of, shall we say, discriminating palate, hogs provided a natural garbage disposal on the hoof. By eating the garbage and other human refuse that people routinely tossed out into the town's streets and alleys, the animals offered a public sanitation service. Herds of hogs roamed many of America's major cities during the ante-bellum period, providing a distasteful, but necessary public service. When the number of hogs roaming unattended about the town grew too large, they disrupted   traffic, attacked gardens, tipped over outhouses, and chased dogs and small children, becoming not only a nuisance but dangerous as well.[5]

By 1850 the town fathers had received enough complaints to pass an ordinance establishing a "hog" pound. The ordinance prohibited any hog from "running at large in the streets" and instructed the town constable to round up the stray swine and take them to the pound. The owners of errant hogs could be fined and charged for the cost of feeding the animals until they came and collected them. The constable charged a finder's fee of ten cents for each "hog apprehended." Room and board at the hog pound amounted to five cents a day.[6] The "final solution" to the hog problem in many places, ranging from big cities like New York or New Orleans to smaller ones like St. Joseph, involved replacing the four-legged variety of street cleaner with the two-legged kind that pushed a broom. Unfortunately for the hogs, they were not retired with a gold watch at the end of their service, but sent off to the packing house to be made into breakfast bacon.

Along with hogs roaming wild, dogs presented another problem in nineteenth-century towns and cities. Packs of dogs, not unlike packs of wolves, unkempt, and unattended by an owner, scavenged the town for food. They were often sick, full of fleas and ticks, and occasionally rabid. Like the hogs, they quickly became a nuisance as they competed with humans for space in the town. By the middle of the 1850s, dogs had become enough of a nuisance that the town council reacted vigorously, stating in an ordinance, "Whereas the council has received reliable information that there has been among dogs in this city several cases of hydrophobia and numerous dogs and other animals have been bitten and

76

the lives of persons endangered therefore." Thereafter, no dog was to be permitted by its owner to "run at large"; any dog doing so would be declared a nuisance, and the city marshal authorized immediately to kill the animal and "throw it into the river"[there was obviously no thought then either about water sanitation]. The ordinance further stated that no person should be punished for shooting any dog found at large, and the street commissioner received a bounty of fifty cents for every dog killed and disposed of accordingly.[7] It must be noted that the dog policy mentioned above, which would make any dog lover cringe in disbelief, created enough dissent that the council amended it in 1857, after only a year. It allowed the marshal to impound dogs for three days before destroying the animals and charge the owner a fee if they claimed their pet in time.

Of course, humans create a great deal of waste, and foul the air as well. In towns and cities where people concentrated, the waste situation went from bad to worse as the population increased. One problem connected to public sanitation in the early nineteenth century involved the lack of a sewer system in towns, St. Joseph not being an exception. As such, every household had to deal with its own sewage. That could mean simply dumping the chamber pots and garbage pails periodically in the street or alley and waiting for mother nature, in the form of a rain shower, to dilute it. In many towns, homeowners assumed the roaming hogs would take care of it. Most households built a privy. Early on, the town's board of trustees dealt with the problem of the proper maintenance of privies, or outhouses. One of the board's first acts in early 1845 mandated that "all privies in the city shall be over a vault no less than five feet deep and the mouth of which shall be tightly enclosed so as to prevent the caving in thereof." Old privies had to be brought up to that code by August 1, 1845, or owners faced a fine of $2.50.[8]

Besides using the Missouri River as a disposal for the town's dead animals, townspeople turned Blacksnake Creek into an open sewer as well. In the early days, settlers drank water from the creek, but by the time of the wagon trail boom, the banks along the creek had become a popular site for butcher shops. In May 1849, the smell became so bad from the slaughter refuse dumped in the creek that the board of trustees ordered "the pork houses of Messrs. Holliday and Baker [the two largest packers in the town] be required to cleanse the same as to preserve the health of the neighborhood there abouts." The trustees backed the order with a threat to abate the property if they did not comply.[9] Subsequent ordinances provided for fines for any person who would leave or deposit in any city stream, except the Missouri River, any offal from slaughtering or pork packing houses.

A common belief throughout the nineteenth century held that "miasma," or bad air, carried or caused most diseases. That belief instigated some action on the part of urban leaders. Air that smelled bad was dirty or full of miasma and therefore unhealthy. People did not know about germs or viruses. Whether the belief in the miasma theory proved clinically correct or not, it did have a positive effect in that it stimulated most large American cities in the later nineteenth century to adopt the practices of cleaning streets, building sewers, providing parks, and planting trees to give people cleaner air.[10]

Having clean drinking water offered another problem. People viewed the quality of their water based on how it looked or tasted. Without knowledge of bacteria counts, city people depended on their tastebuds to tell them if the water was good or not. Of course, a person can not taste cholera or typhus bacteria, and outbreaks of waterborne diseases were routine in St. Joseph as in other American cities.[11] As in most towns and cities of the mid-nineteenth century, people in St. Joseph depended on wells for their fresh water. Geography provided the area with a fairly high water table, so digging a private well, particularly in the river bottom, presented no indomitable task. In the hills that formed the amphitheater of the town there were numerous springs that families could tap for fresh drinking water. They often had a stone basin and even a shed built over the place where the spring water emerged from the ground. Such springs attracted not only area families who liked the taste of the water, but some of the town's first breweries. Some households got water from the centrally located city wells or from a cistern that caught rain water from the roof. The Missouri River flowed by, nearly always murky and laden with silt, so no one of right mind drank from it, though it was used to water livestock, nor did anyone drink from the creeks that had become open sewers.

Personal health care existed in a primitive state. The town's newspapers carried dozens of advertisements from local druggists and merchants for all kinds of wonder drugs, patent medicines, toothache remedies, and mustard plasters, for those wishing to treat themselves for everything from gout to whooping cough. As far as attending physicians, St. Joseph seemed to have been blessed with its share. In 1845, a public notice, printed by the "practicing physicians of the town of St. Joseph and vicinity," advertised set rates for their services. Typical rates charged for common ailments included: for a house call within one mile, $1.00; for each succeeding mile, $.50; attending the whole night, $5.00; a "simple cast of Midwifery," $5.00; twins, $10.00; bleeding, $.50; administering enema, $1.00; amputation of finger or toe, $5.00 each; amputations from forearm to thigh, $10.00 to $25.00; treatment of syphilis, $10.00 to $20.00. The doctors stated they required payment in advance for the treatment of syphilis, maybe indicating they did not have much faith in their cures. The notice, signed by eleven doctors, represented a good number of physicians for a town of St. Joseph's size.[12]

The board of trustees had created a board of health in 1849, ostensibly to handle the health problems caused by the influx of emigrants. Subsequently, the trustees also decided to lay off the town into three districts and appoint a physician to oversee each one. Besides inspecting the flow of emigrants through the town for signs of cholera, typhus, or other infectious diseases, they were to inspect steamboats, the city market, and living conditions in general in their respective wards. City fathers also proposed the building of a public hospital, but that would not be accomplished until after the Civil War.

Fire provided a constant and serious threat to public health and safety in every American town during the nineteenth century. The root of the problem was that most heating and cooking took place over an open flame with a fireplace or flue to carry away the smoke, sparks, and hot cinders through the air. Neighboring roofs, generally made of dried wood shingles, made a highly combustible target. Because of these conditions, coupled with the primitive state of fire fighting machinery, the fear of the firebell in the night proved very real. The St. Joseph board of trustees attempted to deal with the problem of fire in a number of ordinances that reflected the level of municipal involvement in many towns and cities during the ante-bellum period.[13]

The first priority, in 1845, dealt with having proper chimneys: "For the better protection of property in said town, no person shall hereafter build or cause to be built in said town any chimney or part of chimney of wood or any combustible matter." Chimneys had to be "at least three feet above the comb of the roof," and also "three feet above any adjoining roof." The same applied to stovepipes. Two years later, the next step prohibited the building of open fires in the town within twenty feet of any building. Another ordinance followed, in 1850, to "prohibit the depositing or keeping in any building in the town, powder,

79

hay, or other combustible materials for any longer than necessary." The ordinance discouraged blacksmiths from keeping an open forge within 40 feet of any building "without the plastering of said building to prohibit the spread of sparks." A final action prior to the Civil War involved the institution of a zoning ordinance that prohibited the building of wood or frame buildings on lots in the central business district, west of Third Street to the riverbank.[14]

No municipal fire department existed prior to the Civil War, but volunteer groups of fire fighters organized in St. Joseph, as they did in other American towns and cities. During the nineteenth century, fire fighting equipment consisted of the basics: buckets, ladders, hooks and axes, provided by the fire fighters themselves. A pumping apparatus of some type, either hand operated or powered by a steam engine, gave pride to any town. In December 1850, the city heard a proposal from Lewis Tracy, representing the town's fire companies, for funds to build a house on the south side of the town's market square "for the purpose of keeping the apparatus of the fire companies of the town." Volunteer fire companies were social organizations, often like clubs, that promoted camaraderie, and civic spirit among members.[15]

CRIME AND PUNISHMENT

There is an old religious axiom that states that *when the number of humans in any given area increases, the amount of sin multiplies proportionally.* [That belief became the basis for entire generations of nineteenth century rural American preachers to warn their young men and women to avoid the temptations of the big city.] Whether or not that axiom had any firm sociological principle behind it, it somewhat accurately reflected the character of towns and cities throughout the West. Not that city people were any worse, or less religious, or had any more vices than people who lived in rural isolation. The close proximity of so many people made the vices seem more evident. Very large cities like New York, Chicago, or even St. Louis were said to be the devil's playground where every type of unsavory character could be found, committing every sin or crime imaginable and even some that were not.[16]

A quick survey of the ordinances passed by St. Joseph's board of trustees, defined what the people could and could not do. *Thou shalt not gamble.*

Gambling, as defined by the town fathers, meant playing cards or any other game of chance. The fine, if caught, was five to ten dollars. *Thou shalt not sell liquor to Indians.* "Any person selling or giving within the corporate limits of the town of St. Joseph to any Indian or half breed any spirituous liquor or any liquid which spirituous liquor is a part shall be fined no less than two dollars or more than ten dollars."[17] The same type of fine could be levied for selling liquor to Negroes in general, but particularly to slaves without the "written consent" of the master or mistress.

Citizens of St. Joseph were not to disturb the peace, defined as being in a state of intoxication and or "harming the inhabitants by blasphemy, profane swearing, quarreling, using angry words, or other types of boisterous conversation."[10] The fine for doing that was to be not less than one dollar. Assault and battery could get you a one dollar fine, but if you did it three times the fine jumped up to $100. Complete bans extended to horse racing, cockfighting, and the "exhibiting of stallions or jackasses within the limits of the town."[19] Liquor could not be purchased until after nine o'clock on Sunday morning, except if used as medicine. One can only wonder how many needed a "medicinal shot" to get them off to church after a late Saturday night of revelry.

The influx of emigrants and other western travelers during the late 1840s included many young, adventurous men. Those practicing the "world's oldest profession" accompanied their arrival in St. Joseph. The town fathers quickly passed an ordinance prohibiting within the town limits *bawdy houses*, or *houses of ill fame*. Any person living or boarding in such a place could be fined not less than ten dollars or more than one hundred dollars.[20]

During the decades of the 1830s and 1840s, a reform movement against drinking and the effects of drunkenness and alcoholism developed in the United States. While best known for campaigns in large eastern cities, which produced the "Cold Water Army" and groups like the "Washingtonians," towns and cities of the South and on the American frontier felt the effects too.[21] During the 1840s and 1850s, St. Joseph's newspapers regularly ran series of articles promoting the temperance movement. A number of temperance meetings and public parades took place in the city. They were usually affiliated with one of the local churches and well attended by the women folk. A typical notice in the paper read, "The Good Will Division, No. 30, Sons of Temperance, will form in procession at 10 1-2 o'clock this morning and march to the Methodist Church, where the Ladies of St. Joseph will present to the Division a splendid banner. The Rev. Mr. Rush will deliver an Address. The public and especially the Ladies, are invited to attend."[22]

City fathers regulated the sale of liquor within the town by licensing "dram shops," taverns, and "tippling houses." Tippling houses were those establishments licensed to sell less than a quart of liquor at a time. Dram shops, taverns, which also provided room and board, and tippling houses were social places, where men and boys could discuss all matters of business and politics, or engage in a game of cards, billiards or even ten pins, even though most of those activities had been declared illegal. Some catered to an upper class clientele, while others served primarily ruffians. Any business selling liquor had to post a $1,000 bond and observe the prohibition against selling to "Indians, minors, apprentice servants, or slaves." The barkeepers had sole discretion for the checking of age.[23]

To enforce its ordinances, the town's board of trustees created the office of constable, with Howell Thomas being the first to hold that post, beginning in April 1845. Like town constables and marshals elsewhere, the job entailed an endless list of duties that included routine patrol of the streets and riverfront, keeping the public peace, the serving of city court papers, the "suppression of bawdy houses," the rounding up of stray animals and their disposal, and overseeing a number of night watchmen, appointed by the board of trustees. In St. Joseph he also received the authority to deputize any citizen at any time. The town shared a log jail building with the county, after the county seat moved to St. Joseph in 1846.[24]

In 1855, a change in the city charter created the office of city marshal, also called captain of police. The new charter created a regular police force. Six officers assisted the marshal at the pay rate of 20 cents per hour. The policemen, in effect, replaced the night watchmen. The trend toward an organized police force took place in many cities throughout the United States at that time.[173] As the populations of cities grew, the part-time job of protection became by necessity a 24 hour occupation. Two months later, an ordinance raised the pay of policemen to 40 cents per hour.[26]

Like all growing towns in the American West, St. Joseph had its share of notorious crimes and local criminals. The concept of frontier justice remained strong, despite the trappings of being a civilized town. There were courts and practicing attorneys and law officers, but vigilante justice proved just as common

82

a rule of law. A good example involved one of the most noted local criminals, one Tom Farris, active during the heyday of the California gold rush. Farris, was described as a "pestiferous" petty criminal, who was involved in countless local break-ins and specialized in various larcenies against emigrants waiting to cross on St. Joseph's ferries. He led a gang of thugs who during the night would steal wheels and harness chains from emigrants' wagons. When morning came, the emigrants, desperate to get on the trail, would buy back the wheels and chains from Farris. Sometimes they bought their very own, which had been painted by the gang to hide their origins, for an exorbitant price. Farris ran his operation for two years, always outwitting the town constable and the night watchmen. Finally, in May 1851, and in typical western justice fashion, a mob of citizens took matters into their own hands. Reportedly they took "Old Tom and his first lieutenant, a handsome and finely dressed man," to the top of Prospect Hill [a river bluff overlooking the town] and gave each of them 100 lashes with a raw-hide whip, along with an admonition to leave town immediately. Tom Farris and his gang disappeared after that.[27]

Another incident that had the town talking for many years involved the tragic death of Joseph Robidoux's youngest son, Charles, in September 1850. The young man, a bright and dashing figure, who had recently returned from attending an eastern college, had been drinking in the company of some friends. After leaving the tavern late that night, they began carousing through the town rapping and banging on doors. At the door of MacDonald's dry goods store, the play got out of hand. The young men decided to pull up a hitching post and attempt to bash in a door or window. MacDonald, who lived above, and who had awakened, saw the activity in the darkened street below, and got his gun. He fired one blast from his shotgun at the figures in the street below. The shot hit young Robidoux in the head, and he died almost immediately. Robidoux's father rushed to the scene and proposed that MacDonald be lynched from the nearest limb. While tempers flared in the street, MacDonald told the constable that he had not intended to hit anyone, just scare the intruders away. He subsequently posted bail and left town for a while until tempers cooled. MacDonald, eventually tried and acquitted, protested his innocence, but bad blood remained between the two families for a long time.[28]

Like other frontier towns, St. Joseph had its share of mayhem and even murder. The first legal execution for a murder took place in St. Joseph on

September 2, 1853. Auguste Otis Jennings, in the presence of two other drunken acquaintances, had kidnapped, tortured, and beaten to death a local carpenter named Willard. Jennings gave a remorseful confession, blaming it on his alcoholism, but when his two friends turned state's evidence, the court condemned him. The county sheriff erected a scaffold in a vacant field just southeast of the city limits near John Patee's hotel. There Jennings became the first, but far from the last, to be hanged. The field remained the site of executions in the city until after the Civil War.

AFRICAN AMERICAN SOCIETY

African Americans provided another thread in St. Joseph's early social fabric. The number of blacks in the community never proved as substantial as in cities of the deep South, but an unofficial census of the city taken in December 1846 showed 70 slaves and two free blacks out of a total population of 967.[29] At about seven percent, there were enough African Americans to have a visible presence in the town and remind visitors of the town's southern influence. That percentage remained fairly constant through the decade of the 1850s, then dropped to under five percent after the Civil War. The activities of the slave trade routinely appeared in St. Joseph newspapers, which ran advertisements for the buying or selling of slaves, usually by individuals or agents settling an estate, though on a rare occasion a merchant might acquire a lot of slaves from downriver and sell them at public auction. A number of the town's leading citizens owned slaves, and house servants were bought and sold between the upper class residents. One recorded transfer involved Willard P. Hall, promoter and congressman, and Mrs. Mary Richardson, wife of a leading city merchant. Mrs. Richardson bought Hall's "Negro boy Alfred, aged about fifteen years," for the sum of $600 in July 1852.[30]

Requests for help in the return of runaways, as well as offers to hire slaves out at harvest time or during hemp breaking season, also appeared frequently in the papers. Most slaves living within the town were domestic servants; some worked for merchants, or as warehousemen, and some acquired specific skills or training. An advertisement requesting help in the return of a runaway helps shed light on the life of a slave in the area of St. Joseph.

"RUNAWAY a Negro man, known by the name of George Millet; said Negro is about six feet high, trim made, and of good personal appearance, age thirty six. His dress not exactly remembered, but when he left had good clothes—as he is a keen, intelligent Negro he may change his appearance as much as possible. Said Negro is a good house carpenter and painter. For his apprehension in this county I will give ten dollars, and if taken out of the county twenty dollars."[31]

As was the case elsewhere throughout the American South, the individual treatment of slaves in the St. Joseph area varied with the will of their masters.

City ordinances did describe the social limits for African Americans and prescribed the treatment of slaves who committed a crime.

"[I]f any slave shall commit an assault or an assault and battery upon any white person or any free person of color, or upon any slave, or if he be involved in any riots or unlawful assembly within the corporate limits of the town, he shall upon conviction receive upon his or her bare back any number of lashes not to exceed 39 to be laid on by the town constable."

As in all other slave holding areas of the United States, there were codes of conduct and rules that slaves had to observe when in public. Any legal costs incurred by a slave were taxed against the master. Slaves could not hire themselves out without the master's permission. Any pay from being hired out became the property of the master, and a master who allowed his slave to freelance could be fined. One city ordinance said that a slave riding though the town could not gallop the animal.[32] It was against the law for any "free Negro or mulatto residing in the city" to entertain or have on his property any slave without the permission of the master or mistress.

During the 1850s, tensions increased over the issue of slavery. In Kansas, just across the river from St. Joseph, the situation had deteriorated into a bloody brawl between pro-slavery and free state forces. Slaveholders influenced the city government to react to events taking place there. They feared that slaves in St. Joseph or the surrounding area might use the ferry boats to cross the Missouri River and escape into Kansas, which through the turmoil leaned toward becoming a free state. To that end, the city council passed an ordinance prohibiting free blacks or mulattos from not only working on river ferries, but even traveling on them unless they were "duly licensed" to live in the city. It forbade ferry operators from hauling any slave without written permission from a master or mistress. The fines for violating the ordinance were hefty for those days, ranging from $100 to $200.[33]

St. Joseph never became a hotbed of abolitionist activity, though a small percentage of the population did support an end to the abominable practice or at least a limit on its spread. St. Joseph's two main papers, the *Gazette* and the *Adventure*, rarely ran a story mentioning abolition. Help for a runaway in reaching the underground railroad or escaping to free territory reportedly could be found in the area of St. Joseph from a few individuals. In the little towns on the Kansas side of the river, and particularly on the Indian reservations along the Kansas-Nebraska border, runaways found more sympathetic supporters. St. Joseph stood too far to the west for much activity on the main routes of the underground railroad which channeled its passengers to freedom in Canada. However, Iowa, a free territory just 70 miles north of St. Joseph, provided an attractive haven for slaves escaping from Northwest Missouri. One or two safe houses reportedly existed in St. Joseph owned by German immigrants and a Quaker family.[34]

CHURCHES AND SCHOOLS

Primary among any town's earliest social institutions were its churches. In St. Joseph churches reflected the diversity of peoples, attitudes, and traditions from all the regions of influence: the West, the South, and Europe (immigrant). Jesuit priests, serving nearby Indian missions, regularly passed through, stopping at the riverboat landing or taking a rest from overland travels. One of them, the most noted of western missionaries, Father Pierre Jean DeSmet, stopped briefly at the Blacksnake Hills in May 1838. Robidoux was Roman Catholic, and people of that denomination, despite common religious bigotry in Missouri and throughout the country, found a welcome reception in his town. Catholics eventually became the largest single denomination, but the majority of St. Joseph's early settlers represented a variety of Protestant faiths.[35]

Father Christian Hoecken, a Jesuit missionary, celebrated the first Roman Catholic mass in St. Joseph [then still the Blacksnake Hills] in the same year that

DeSmet visited. Another missionary priest, Father Anthony Eysvogels, frequented the area around Blacksnake Hills during the early 1840s, traveling about in a long black coat with a large white cross sown to the back, like some errant crusader knight. He said mass for both whites and Indians and performed baptisms and burials. But the first official pastor of a Catholic parish in the town was Father Thomas Scanlan, who had been appointed to his position by Archbishop Peter Richard Kenrick, of the archdiocese of St. Louis. Father Scanlan arrived in October 1845.[36]

For two years, the parish, which took the name of St. Joseph, the town's patron saint, met in a room of a wood frame building owned by Robidoux. Originally, the parish had about twenty families, of Irish or French Canadian background. As the town's population grew rapidly, so did the size of the parish. By 1847 it reportedly had 300 members, or about 30 percent of the town's population. Having outgrown the room, in June 1847, parishioners laid the cornerstone for a new brick church, 28 x 55 feet in dimension, at the corner of Fifth and Felix Streets, a bit east of the main business district at that time. The lot had been donated by Robidoux. A two-story brick rectory was added the next year. Masses, weddings and baptisms became regular events and the parish grew proportionally with the city's population, strengthened by the increased number of German Catholic immigrants during the 1850s. A number of influential citizens of the town, like John Corby, and Robidoux's offspring, were members of the parish. Father Scanlan received assistance from other priests, and by the time he left the parish in 1859, it had grown to nearly 2,000 members. Father John Hennessey replaced Father Scanlan. Because of the number of German immigrants, the archbishop in St. Louis agreed to allow them to have their own parish. So, in 1860, Immaculate Conception parish formed, becoming the town's second Catholic church, with Father Francis Ruesse as the pastor.[37]

New School Presbyterians built the first Protestant church in St. Joseph. Like the Catholic church, all the Protestant sanctuaries had sites donated on the sloping streets within the close confines of Robidoux's original town plat. In 1843 the Reverend Thomas Reeve arrived in the newly organized town and preached his first sermon in the tavern owned by a Mr. Beattie at the corner of Main and Jule Streets, barely a block from the river. His first congregation consisted of "six devout Christian women." When the tavern could not be used on Sunday mornings, he preached at a grocery store or in private homes. By the spring of 1844, his congregation had grown to the point where a proper church building needed to be erected. A local landowner agreed to donate timber, so long as the pastor and his followers cut it down. Pastor Reeve took up the ax and felled the first tree, and by September of that year a log church had been built on a donated lot. It took the official name, Presbyterian Church of St. Joseph.[38] It remained in the log building only five years, until replaced by a modest brick structure. The congregation remained relatively small, but grew steadily under Pastor Reeve, and his replacement, the Reverend Frederick Gallager. By 1851 it had 102 members, up from the original ten in 1844, and by 1860, 195 members. Because of the theological conflicts arising from the issue of slavery and the Civil War, the congregation dissolved itself in 1861. A separate group of that general denomination formed the First Presbyterian Church, in 1854, affiliated to the Old School Presbytery of Missouri.[39]

The Methodist denomination began to organize in St. Joseph, also in 1843. There were several separate congregations, which when combined made them second only to the numbers of Catholics in the town for a number of years. The Reverend Edward Robinson served as the first minister, and the congregation, or class [a term used for the congregation] met in a frame structure owned by David Heaton, a maker of cabinets, furniture, and coffins. The early Methodist congregation affiliated with the Methodist Episcopal Church South circuit, reflected the southern fiber of the town's religious fabric. By 1847 the congregation had grown large enough to need a sizable new sanctuary. Joseph Robidoux, though a Catholic, donated a lot, and a new church, constructed of brick, became the place of worship. The Methodists outgrew that structure after only eleven years, sold that property and built a new larger sanctuary. It took the name Francis Street Methodist Church South. In 1849 a second Methodist congregation, under the banner of the Methodist Episcopal Church, formed. The congregation's size remained small and they rented space for worship at the Odd Fellows Hall.[40] A German Methodist Episcopal Church also organized in 1849. Like its Catholic counterpart, Immaculate Conception, it catered to the spiritual needs of a growing German immigrant population.

By 1860 Baptists surpassed the Methodists in numbers and made up the second largest single congregation in the town, after Catholics. Like the Methodists, the size of the Baptist congregations reflected the strong influence of southern religious denominations and practices. The First Baptist Church organized in March, 1845. Elder William Worley led the first services. Early meeting places included private homes and the log church constructed by the Presbyterians. The Reverend James Robinson became the first of a long line of pastors for the St. Joseph congregation over the decade and a half before the Civil War. During the early 1850s the congregation constructed a large brick church and boasted that a thousand Baptists inhabited the city.[41]

In 1844 a Christian Church began to hold meetings, with Elder Duke Young preaching the first sermon in the private home of one of the congregation. Not until 1850 did the Christian Church formally organize in St. Joseph. That congregation held services in a room of the county courthouse throughout the 1850s. The town of St. Joseph also had a Protestant Episcopal Church, formally organized in 1854, but without a permanent sanctuary prior to the outbreak of the Civil War.[42]

Like most other southerners, the Protestant denominations of St. Joseph, in general represented people of strong conservative religious beliefs based on a literal interpretation of the Bible. The sermons of several town ministers appeared regularly in the city's two weekly newspapers, often on the front page. Morality and the avoidance of sin and vice peppered most sermons. The political-social issues of slavery or the morality of taking Indian lands or the rights of women never appeared in the sermons or print media. The issue of slavery did lead to open splits in some St. Joseph congregations as the Civil War approached, just as it did elsewhere in the South.[43]

Members of the Jewish faith made up part of the religious tapestry of early St. Joseph. It is thought that the first Jews arrived in St. Joseph as part of the gold rush emigration of 1849. By 1850 the names of Jewish merchants began to appear as suppliers to overland emigrants. The name Westheimer appeared as one of the first Jewish families among the town's merchants. Brothers Samuel and Ferdinand operated a grocery supply on Felix Street, under the Odd Fellows Hall. The community grew, joined by the family of Aaron Kahn, in the clothing and dry goods business, and by other families named Oppenheimer, Epstein, and Schwabucher. Prior to 1859, they held religious services in homes or at a rented hall. In 1859 the congregation Adath Joseph formally organized under Rabbi Sigismund Kaufmann. The first temple occupied a former Presbyterian Church, but a fire destroyed it that same year. In the spring of 1860, construction of a synagogue began at the corner of Sixth and Jule Street. Though small in number, the Jewish community in St. Joseph became quite prosperous, with a number of the earliest merchants making large fortunes from the western trade.[44]

Schools represented another important institution for any growing town. In St. Joseph the attitude toward education reflected the southern viewpoint. Most southern states, Missouri included, "neglected the education of their poor people."[45] Education was for those young ladies and gentlemen who needed it, who would become the professional and merchant class. Public officials in the South gave little thought to education for the masses, an idea that had developed in the New England region and spread fairly consistently across the northern tier of states by the time of the Civil War. Prior to 1860 there had been no attempt officially to organize a public school district for the town. From its inception, though, a number of private schools served St. Joseph. The closest thing to an elementary school consisted of an operation, usually set up by an itinerant schoolmaster, in some available space. There, parents paid a tuition for a course of study lasting three or four months. The schoolmasters frequently advertised in the local papers. Typically, an ad that appeared in the *Gazette* in 1846 read:

> "ENGLISH SCHOOL   The citizens of St. Joseph and its vicinity are respectfully informed that JAMES O. DONOGHUE, will on Monday 16th November next, commence to teach the usual branches of English Education, at the Brick Cottage lately occupied by Mr. Robidoux."

The basic course of study consisted of "Spelling, Reading, Writing and Arithmetic," and cost $3.00 for a three month quarter. The advanced course, which included "English Grammar, Geography and History, as well as Geometry, Measuration, Trigonometry, Surveying, Etc., if required," would cost the parent $3.50.[50]

Those types of schools catered primarily to young men, and opened and closed at the whim of the schoolmaster, who might decide there were greener pastures over the hill in the next town. As time passed, a number of grammar schools opened and closed in St. Joseph, but the advertisements showed a marked change over the years, as tuition increased. In an 1853 advertisement, a schoolmaster named Dunlap listed his tuition at $8.00 per quarter for the basic course in the three R's, with his advanced course costing $12 per quarter. The ad was also quite gender specific: "Those who intend to send their sons; would do well to give me early notice as only a limited number will be taken."[51] To appeal to those parents seeking an even more upper class education, a man calling himself Professor Charles S. Raffington, advertised a school known as the St. Joseph Classical Institute, which lasted only a couple of years.[52]

To meet the needs of the German immigrant sector of St. Joseph society, the German School Society, Deutscher Schul Verein, opened a grammar school in 1855, under the guidance of headmaster Joseph Dreis. Though it catered primarily to the sons of the leading German immigrants, some young ladies also attended. By 1860, the German Catholic church, Immaculate Conception, had opened a parish school that also accepted girls, and the Sisters of Charity provided nuns to teach at a parish school.[50]

Of course, if you had a daughter, there were alternatives. From the beginning of the town's history, there were schools conducted by ladies in their homes, and there also appeared a number of so called "female academies." The use of academies for the training of young ladies had developed and become widely popular throughout the South. As early as 1845, Mrs. Israel Landis, wife of a prominent attorney and city official, opened a school for girls, which she operated from her home for a number of years. Mary Stone, "a Roman Catholic lady of culture," also conducted lessons for young ladies in her home.[54]

Like those schools opened for young men, some schools for girls advertised to get students. The St. Joseph Female Academy frequently sold itself in the *Gazette* as a "Young Ladies High School," taught at, "the house now occupied by Mrs. King." The course of academic study would be, "thoroughly and systematically inculcated." Particular attention would be paid to, "the manners, carriage and deportment of the Pupils," enforced by "Calisthenic Exercises" and "all kinds of fancy needle work," which, according to the ad, "will be attended to, two evenings each week." At the end of the term there would be, "a public examination and exhibition" including "music played by those Young Ladies who practice that branch" and "specimens of the Young Ladies' painting, embroidery, composition, Etc.." As with nearly all the schools for girls, limited boarding accommodations were advertised.[55]

Churches other than Catholic provided educational opportunity. Besides "Sunday" schools, the Protestant churches offered some elementary schooling, either in the church building, unused during the week, or in the pastor's home. But the parochial system that followed the arrival of Catholic brothers and sisters from various teaching orders provided the most substantial educational development prior to the Civil War. The Religious (Sisters) of the Sacred Heart built a convent school to serve the town, establishing a long standing and highly regarded relationship that lasted well into the twentieth century. Because of the strength of the Catholic community in St. Joseph, news of the convent school created a lot of excitement: "We learn that Madame Galway of St. Louis purchased one day this week of Mr. Morris 30 acres of ground; one mile east of this city for which she paid the round sum of $3,000, for the purpose of establishing a female academy, under the supervision of the 'Ladies of the Sacred Heart.' The main building, which we understand will be commenced next summer is to be 350 feet long and 3 stories high. Three of the Sisters are now in the City and two more will be up next month. The school has already commenced with about 20 pupils."[56]

The first attempts at introducing higher education into the new city came from the religious sector as well. Father James Powers, an assistant pastor at St. Joseph's Parish, worked to get a men's college built in the city. In 1858, donations raised enough money to build a three story brick building on a lot at Thirteenth and Henry Streets. Father Powers then asked the Christian Brothers to take charge of the facility and provide teachers. In 1859, they agreed, but the onset of the Civil War delayed the opening of the college until 1867.[57]

THE ARTS AND ENTERTAINMENT

What did people in the mid-nineteenth century, in a rapidly growing urban setting, do for fun, or intellectual stimulation? In St. Joseph, there were plenty of places for men to get a drink, socialize, and discuss their world of business and politics. For women, particularly ladies who would not be caught dead in a dram shop or tippling house, there were visits to a neighbor's home, reading groups, sewing or quilting circles, visits with the local pastor and his wife, or other church related work. Because of St. Joseph's position on the frontier, many men and women who lived in or near it were still too busy taming the earth to have much free time. When they did, they could find a number of outside sources of entertainment, including the theater, circuses, lectures, and band concerts. In that aspect of social development St. Joseph remained close to its southern roots.[58]

From the time the town formed there appeared an interest in theatrical production. The St. Joseph Thespian Society organized in the summer of 1845 and presented its first production on November 3, 1845. The double bill included the comedies "The Prisoner At Large" and "The Man and The Tiger." A character list, in the local paper, named the actors and actresses, identified only by their initials. The admission for the local troupe cost 30 cents, children, "half price."[59] Later productions of the local troupe included musicals and even Shakespearean plays. Traveling theatrical companies visited St. Joseph frequently during the ante-bellum period, and were generally promoted by the local newspapers. An editorial statement, regarding the pending visit of the "Varieties" company from St. Louis typified the support.

"As will be seen from a notice in another part of today's paper, our citizens will have the opportunity during the next week of witnessing the performances of a very superior Corps of Theatricals. This company is composed of performers of superior talent, and of more effective strength and superiority than any company that has ever visited this region of country."[60]

If the theater was not one's cup of tea, then the circus presented another option. Circuses visited St. Joseph on a fairly regular basis. Among the earliest arrivals, Spalding's North American Circus boasted:

"This Monster Establishment, comprising nearly 200 men and horses." They would visit St. Joseph for one day only, with two performances at "2 1/4 and 7 1/2 P. M.". It's promotional ad in the *Gazette* also claimed that it "contains the largest troop of performers in the United States, and the best *Band on this conti-nent*, composed of 15 picked Musicians, and led by the Lion Bugler of the World, the immortal Kendall, whose fame on his magic silver Bugle, has penetrated every circle to which Music has access."[61]

Other forms of traveling entertainment included professional dance troupes like the Sager family and Smith Sisters, magicians such as Professor Barton, called the "equal of the leading prestidigitators of the day," as well as assorted comedians, ventriloquists, singing groups, troupes of Negro minstrels, and even

Swiss bell ringers. The Odd Fellows Hall accommodated a large enough stage and seating for most productions and, in lieu of a proper theater, served that purpose well. Occasionally someone from the elite artistic centers of the nation, New York or Boston, might pass through the rapidly growing frontier town and offer a private reading to friends or a select audience of those high up on the social ladder. The artistic quality of many of the traveling acts remained questionable, but as in most towns with a strong southern fiber, that quality could be quite "low brow" and still draw a crowd.[62] The people of St. Joseph loved music and supported a number of bands that gave regular public concerts. Popular band leaders in the city included Professor Cruft and his American Brass Band; Professor Otto Behr, who led an orchestra and chorus; H. Rosenblatt and the City Brass Band; and J.L. Smith, who led the St. Joseph Musical Association.

As the dark storm of the Civil War approached, St. Joseph could rightly claim to be the most cosmopolitan place west of the city of St. Louis. It boasted all the trappings of a growing urban center and an attractive alternative to the surrounding rural hinterland. However, the strong southern filament of its fiber proved to be the thread along which the entire social fabric of the town ripped once the war began, leaving a tattered, disunited populace to deal with the problems the conflict brought to it.

CHAPTER 5

_____

A Bridge Too Far
1861-1870

On the face of history, the role of St. Joseph during the American Civil War seems neither illustrious nor of great military significance. Though situated on the bend of a great river, like Vicksburg, it never had a siege laid to it nor received bombardment from opposing fleets of river ironclads. The town served as a transportation crossroads, like Gettysburg, Chattanooga, or Manassas, but it never had a great battle fought there. Even though it was of economic importance, it never became the focus of a great military drive, like "on to Richmond" or a "march to the sea" from Atlanta. But like those cities which have become hallowed place names in the history of the war, St. Joseph also suffered. The war changed the course of the city's history as much as or more than any of its more famous counterparts.

Abraham Lincoln's election in November 1860, did not sit well with the residents of St. Joseph. Of the nearly 3,500 votes cast, Lincoln tallied only 410 from within the city limits. John Bell of Kentucky, leading the Constitutional Union party ticket, received the most votes, but only narrowly over Stephen Douglas of Illinois, the mainstream Democratic Party candidate. John Breckenridge, the candidate of the bolted southern Democrats, also received more votes than Lincoln. The results of the election touched off a furor within the city between union men and secessionists that would go on through crucial years. The *Gazette,* having taken a pro-Southern position, initiated trouble when it published a partial list of the citizens who voted for Lincoln, hoping to shame or embarrass them. The *St. Joseph Free Democrat,* an upstart, short-lived paper that published under the banner, "Organ of the Republican Party for Western Missouri," responded by publishing a complete list of the "Four Hundred and Ten." The tongue in cheek headline proclaimed: "HERE WE ARE! Let the Misrable Black Republicans Read and Tremble!" According to the accompanying story, the *Free Democrat* office filled from floor to ceiling with requests to: "Publish a full list. Put my name in capitals. Tell them where I can be found. Wonder if they think we are afraid of our own shadows."[1] The animosity ran strong and deep through every social and economic level of St. Joseph's

95

population. The town appeared to have split vehemently, a true case of brother against brother, citizen against citizen. However, those who actually stood toe to toe, shouting their political disagreement, comprised only a small vocal minority on the extreme of either position. As in most civil disputes, that can become more bitter than conflicts with outsiders or foreign powers, most either sat on the fence or sought to mediate.

The final vote count actually demonstrated that the citizens of St. Joseph opposed any intent to abolish slavery, which had been connected with Lincoln's Republican candidacy, but that they were not secessionist by a majority either. By supporting Bell and Douglas they indicated they still favored some type of compromise settlement to the issue of slavery.[2] In 1860 there were about 2,000 slaves in Buchanan County and the city, and the economic loss from setting them free, assuming Lincoln scored a victory, overwhelmed most voters. The vote also revealed that the vast majority believed they had a constitutional right to own and control their own property, even if that property were another human being.

When Missouri's newly elected governor, Claiborne Fox Jackson, took his oath of office on January 3, 1861, he gave an indication of the direction the state, and subsequently the people of St. Joseph, would take in the impending conflict. By that date, South Carolina had already declared, "The Union is Dissolved," and other slave states of the deep South were queuing up to follow her lead. Missourians demonstrated by their vote that they were not as deeply tied to southern sectionalism. Breckenridge, who swept the southern states during the election, only finished third in Missouri.[3] Jackson nonetheless stated his position in his inaugural address, making clear that any radical response to the question of secession or the abolition of slavery would not play well in the state. He said Missouri's people were devoted to the Union, but "Her honor, interests and sympathies, point alike in one direction, and, determine her to stand by the South." Jackson then added, "If the Northern States have determined to put the slave-holding States on a footing of inequality, then they have themselves practically abandoned the Union, and will not expect our submission to a government on terms of inequality and subordination."[4]

As the chance for compromise slipped away during the spring, and the litany of state names leaving the union increased over the first three months of 1861, Governor Jackson made it clear that he anticipated Missouri joining that

The Famous Flag Incident. *Courtesy of the Boder Collection*

list, though he never had the full backing of the state's legislature. State militia companies formed and began drilling, while leaders made secret plans to seize the federal arsenals in the state. The governor called for a convention, as had been done in other seceding states, to decide the issue in Missouri. All of Jackson's moves were well received by a vocal faction in St. Joseph, led by former mayor, M. Jeff Thompson. But just as Jackson had misread the extent of secessionist support within the state, so too did a number of St. Joseph leaders, among them Thompson. Missouri had never had a "plantation" economy, and by 1860 the immigrant population, particularly the Germans, who tended to be pro-Union, had grown substantially. Farm and business interests saw serious economic isolation and losses coming if they left the Union. The railroads had, in a very brief but important period, attached much of Missouri's hinterland to northern cities and markets, like Chicago. Because of the Hannibal and St. Joseph Railroad, most St. Joseph merchants faced disaster if a war severed transportation and commercial ties with the free states, particularly Illinois, through which most eastern connections existed. Ultimately, in their hearts they might be secessionist, but in their heads and pocketbooks they stood for compromise and the economic benefit of union.

With the first shot of the Civil War, fired on Fort Sumter in Charleston, South Carolina, the rip in the nation's fabric of life reached all the way to the northwest corner of Missouri. M. Jeff Thompson loudly supported Missouri secession and took a commission in the state militia [later reorganized as the Missouri State Guard] where he quickly rose to the rank of brigadier general. The Missouri State Guard, under Governor Jackson formed the backbone of pro-Confederate forces in the state, while Missouri Home Guard units [later called Missouri State Militia] formed the pro-Union equivalent. Contrary to popular belief, Thompson never received a Confederate commission, though he is still often referred to as a Confederate general by local historians.[5] Two companies of M.S.G. formed in Buchanan County commanded by Thompson and John Thornton, and camped near the Patee House Hotel on the southern edge of St. Joseph in April 1861. Members of those units took part in the raid that month on the federal arsenal at Liberty, Missouri, about forty miles from St. Joseph. Some of the 1,500 muskets and powder from that raid came into the city, and was apparently stored in the cellars of secessionist sympathizers for a while. Thornton also made verbal threats to deal with any "Lincolnites" he found in the city.

Because of Missouri's position as a border state, President Lincoln took immediate steps after Sumter to see that it, like Kentucky, western Virginia, and Maryland, did not have the chance to secede. Through May and into early June, Lincoln attempted, through his military commander in St. Louis, to convince Jackson and newly appointed Missouri State Guard commander Sterling Price, that he would try to negotiate the most peaceful methods for keeping Missouri in the Union. He even fired a Union general, who had commanded the Missouri district, to placate them. But that general's replacement, Nathaniel Lyon, wanted nothing to do with secessionists like Jackson and Price and by the middle of June 1861 moved against them. Federal forces from surrounding states rushed into Missouri, and for all intent and purpose the whole state came under martial law. In St. Joseph conditions likewise deteriorated, splitting the city and leading to its occupation.

The most notorious event during that tumultuous period involved the assault on the Union flag flying over the city's post office. The action, taken by a few, haunted the city for decades to come. John L. Bittinger, the newly appointed postmaster, a Republican and a strong Unionist, refused to take down the stars and stripes, even though he had been repeatedly threatened by pro-Confederate townsmen led by Thompson and Thornton. In May 1861, Thompson led a group of armed and mounted men galloping through the streets and up to the post office on Second Street. A mob of secessionist men formed to watch while businessmen hurriedly locked up their establishments. Thompson and his followers tore the flag from the mast of the post office, trampled it under foot, and replaced it with a Confederate ensign. The desecration of "Old Glory" further cleaved the city into two camps, even more deeply divided than they had been over the fall election. The city council responded by passing an ordinance to prohibit the flying of any flag within the city, even over the town hall, in an attempt to pacify both sides. It failed, as gangs alternately ran up or tore down the stars and stripes and the stars and bars. There could be no more sitting on the fence. Bittinger called for troops to protect the post office, a federal property, and to maintain order in the streets of the openly divided town.[6]

On May 20, 1861, a company of federal dragoons rode into the city, and nearly four years of occupation began. In June a regiment of Iowa volunteers arrived to occupy St. Joseph, and shortly after they left, different regiments from Illinois and eventually various battalions of Missouri Home Guards replaced them.

The city became a district headquarters for Northwest Missouri, with an officer of general's rank usually in charge. During brief periods of 1861, when federal troops left the city for maneuvers elsewhere, area Confederate forces, comprised of marauding bands of mounted raiders, visited the city, striking terror in the heart of the business district. They carried off as much merchandise as they could as a "tax" to support the cause. While federal troops occupied the city, the Confederate marauders lurked about the hinterland, on both sides of the river, practicing what they called guerrilla warfare. In reality, it often took the form of cold-blooded murder, or as the public came to call the activities, bushwhacking. One of the most blatant acts of terrorism performed by the bushwhackers took place on the night of September 3, 1861, when they burned down the trestle railroad bridge over the Platte River, just east of town. Without any warning, the Hannibal and St. Joseph passenger train, scheduled to arrive in the city at 11:00 p.m., reached the burned-out bridge and plunged into the riverbed. The cars piled in on each other, crushing to death dozens of passengers. The action outraged the citizenry of St. Joseph and bolstered demands for Union protection.[7]

In response to that disaster, federal authorities increased the level of occupation in St. Joseph and beefed up security all along the route of the Hannibal and St. Joseph Railroad. When General Benjamin Prentiss arrived to occupy St. Joseph, he issued orders that passports be carried by anyone leaving or coming into the city. The military trusted no one, suspecting that any number of pro-Southern sympathizers living within the city could be responsible for the terrorism. No one ever claimed responsibility for the bridge burning, but a number of local pro-Southern sympathizers remained suspect. Out of fear of growing anarchy, St. Joseph bowed to complete control by the army.

Prentiss also suppressed the pro-Southern press in the city. That meant shutting down the *Gazette* and its editor, J. R. Cundiff.[8] To replace it, and admittedly to try to repair much of the public relations damage done by the secessionists the previous year, the *Herald* went to press in February 1862. Over the next four decades, the paper would undergo some name changes—the *Morning Daily Herald*, the *Morning Herald*, the *Daily Herald*, the *Gazette-Herald*—but throughout it would remain a faithful supporter of the Republican Party. Charles Brownell Wilkinson published and edited the paper, taking a clearly pro-Union position. Though a new arrival to the city, only two years before, he strongly promoted his new home. Born in Waterville, New York, in 1827, Wilkinson was a descendant

99

of an English family of seventeenth century colonial stock. In his early years he was inclined to becoming an artist, but his father wanted him trained as a lawyer and found him a position in a local firm. Uninterested in the law, he became editor of the Waterville *Journal* for a time before investing in a milling and distillery company. When aspirations for public office failed, he moved west, through several states, finally coming to rest in St. Joseph. He brought to his paper the natural oratorical talent of a trained attorney and consummate politician, as well as artistic writing skills. Wilkinson supported Stephen Douglas of Illinois during the 1860 presidential campaign, but when the war broke out he settled completely into the Republican camp as a supporter of Lincoln and the Union.[9]

MARTIAL LAW

By early 1862, the Union forces had clapped a nearly complete lid on secessionist activities in St. Joseph. They built a fortified camp on Prospect Hill, the river bluff overlooking the city, both for their own protection and to impress the citizenry below. Benjamin Loan, formerly a prominent attorney and city official, commanded the town, having replaced General Prentiss, who moved on to other theaters of operation. Loan had been given the rank of brigadier general in the reorganized Missouri State Militia, and he ruled the town as a dictator through a series of general orders. The first and most succinct of those general orders, No. 5, dated February 4, 1862, stated: "In pursuance of Special Order No. ___ issued by order of Brig. Gen. Prentiss, I hereby assume command at St. Joseph, Missouri. BEN LOAN; Brig. Gen., M. S. M."[10]

The city's provost marshal, in charge of the military police, exercised wide authority under Loan. General order No. 4, dated January 28, 1862, outlined the function of that official in keeping St. Joseph reasonably safe and in Union hands. The order specifically enjoined the provost marshal to "keep the streets, alleys, public squares and all other thoroughfares in the city cleared of all drinking or disorderly persons. They will arrest and confine all persons who are in any way disturbing the public peace." The order also stated that soldiers were not to carry their arms through the streets unless under the command of an officer and to be unarmed when off duty. Loan did not want to incite the pro-Southern part of the population with an openly armed occupation force, although he could bring armed force to bear at a moment's notice.[11]

On February 15, 1862, Loan imposed a curfew on the city: "All persons within this city are required to retire to their respective places of abode by the hour of 10 o'clock P. M., each night." That meant all "Saloons, Bar rooms and Gaming establishments," had to shut down as well. General Order No. 6 proved highly unpopular to say the least. Besides the nighttime curfew for all individuals, St. Joseph business establishments felt the pinch of martial law through numerous restrictions imposed by Loan's orders: "April 21, 1862, all persons are prohibited from ferrying across the Missouri River from this city, any horse, mule or cattle, without written permission, therefore from the Provost Marshal."[12] In August, as the war had not progressed that summer in a favorable fashion for the Union, the restrictions tightened. One restriction warned: "No shipment of goods will hereafter he made from this city to any point, without permission from the Provost Marshal." The army completely prohibited certain goods from being shipped at all, including: "Pork, Bacon, Hams, Beef cured or dried, Flour, Crackers, Beans, Coffee, Tea, Sugar, Salt, Molasses," among food stuffs, and all kinds of clothing, leather goods, harness and saddles, and horse shoes.[13] Another order followed closely, that shut down all stores in the city at six o'clock. Soon after, Loan issued another more restrictive order that closed all stores at four o'clock, but allowed them to reopen after 6:30 P. M.. Drug stores, bakeries, and the city market were exempted, but it hurt nearly all merchants. To make sure no one had any fun, the provost marshal even issued an order stating: "All horse-racing of every kind, under any pretext whatever, will hereafter be prohibited within this district. All persons violating this order will be promptly arrested."[14]

Both the army and the newspapers targeted anyone who might be secessionist. Deep division had appeared at all levels of the city's social structure, but particularly damaging rifts occurred among the class of city leaders and promoters. General Loan forced openly pro-Southern sympathizers to take an oath and post a cash bond to insure their good and loyal behavior. If they did not, they went to jail. The local paper periodically described the roundup of secessionists and printed lists of their names. When brought before the provost marshal they were given the opportunity to "keep step to the music of the Union." Most did so reluctantly, or as the local editor saw it, "Truth compels us to say that they came up rather unwillingly, in fact with about the same alacrity a red squirrel manifests to come out of a hollow log, when pursued with a ramrod, or a cat

101

extracted from an ash hole, tail foremost."[15] Among those arrested and lambasted in the *Daily Herald* were men of standing in the community before the war. The paper described them as "a few men who have long been here as *tolerable* patriots," referring to their questioned loyalty. Among the many named in the paper were Israel Landis, whose son John served as a Confederate officer; James Millan, and Robert Donnell. All were prominent in business and city government, and all refused to post the required bond. The paper crowed, "Our readers will see that treason cannot be longer sported in St. Joseph."[16]

M. Jeff Thompson, the former mayor, remained the favorite target of the pro-Union press. His sympathy for the South was well known and he had won military honor for the Confederate cause in southern Missouri and Arkansas. In the press's attempts to defile his reputation, it exposed the true conditions that St. Joseph faced as the war continued. The political and economic leadership of the town had been torn apart. Because of Thompson's zeal as a promoter of the town and railroads, his defection left a void in the city's leadership cadre. He stood alone as the visible symbol of what had happened. Other leaders and promoters had "gone South," left town for better market places, or stayed dormant

 under martial law. The city of St. Joseph suffered severe economic trauma during the war. An editorial lamented in 1862: "The West Wind [a river steamer]has been the only boat touching at St. Joseph for the past two years; and her cables the only ones which have ruffled the grass growing on Jeff. Thompson's levee. Fated is the city of the Black Snake Hills. Thompson has gone—Jeff. the king is with them no more, and the little locomotive on the "great Pacific Road" lies idle and still, and the ties laid by the ex mayor are rotting in the sand. Secession has breathed upon St. Joseph, and prosperity has withered with the blight."[17]

Brigadier General,
M. Jeff Thompson.
Courtesy of the Boder Collection, St. Joseph Museum

Former governor, and champion of St. Joseph's efforts to secure railroad connections with the east in the previous decade, Robert M. Stewart visited the city in March 1862, and spoke at a public meeting in Corby Hall. Stewart remained a strong unionist, well respected in the city even by those with differing opinions. In his speech he openly chided the secessionists in the audience, saying they "deserved to be hung higher than Haman and lower than Hell. Beware of such men, for you have them among you. Let them meet the indignant frowns of every lover of his country." Then he addressed the economic depression that had settled over the city since the beginning of the war the year before. "I ask you mechanics of St. Joseph, I ask you farmers, I ask you merchants what is the cause of the stagnation which now prevails here? We have a city which, as the termination of a Railroad to the Pacific, over the path marked by our Omnipotence, has not an equal in geographical position, or natural facilities for greatness. Where is the emigration that one year ago filled your streets with men and your stores and shops with bustling activity?"

And the cause and effect of St. Joseph's sorry state? Stewart continued: "I told you last spring you were converting your city into a solitude. What has been the effect of the action on Secessionists in hoisting a dirty secession rag in St. Joseph? Since then the click of a hammer has not been heard in the city; the streets are covered with grass; children are growing up in ignorance; your bonds are worthless; town lots are almost valueless, and owners cannot pay their taxes."[18]

If St. Joseph had kept its dirty laundry to itself, or settled quickly and completely into the Union camp, it might have faired better, but that proved impossible. As the pro-union editor lamented in an editorial condemning secessionist activities in the town: "Emigration over the plains was turned to Omaha. No sane man would risk his property and life in a rabble that could be guilty of such indignities to the flag that they were born under. The town was paralyzed. Business sought other channels. Everything came to a standstill. Thus we now find ourselves."[19] Word had gotten out about St. Joseph and reached to the halls of political power in Washington, D. C., as well as the halls of financial power in other major east coast cities. They saw the city adrift. And to make matters worse, its chief competitor did not let a chance to attack St. Joseph's sad situation go by. "They are having a terrible time in St. Joseph," reported the Kansas City paper, *Weekly Journal of Commerce,* during the summer of 1863. "We learn enough to know that a reign of terror has been prevailing there." Pro-Southern men harassed Union troops stationed in the town, broke windows, tore down flags, and "pistols were freely fired, and men were pursued and knocked down in the streets, and terribly beaten. Several persons were killed, and more than fifty families left the place."[20]

103

At the same time, the Kansas City paper boasted about the patriotism of its own citizens. Its editor boasted: "Kansas City is today as thoroughly and *radically* loyal as St. Louis, or as any town in Kansas. As an evidence, we point to our recent city election, in which a radical Anti-slavery, Unconditional Union ticket was elected by over three hundred majority, over, not a pro-slavery ticket, but a conservative Union one."[21] St. Joseph had also elected a pro-Union administration by that time, but the tight reigns of martial law made attempts by the city government to rebuild its image and control its own streets a moot point. And the area around St. Joseph remained a sympathetic haven for pro-Southern bushwhackers, who harassed militia patrols and particularly the companies made up of primarily German immigrants. The cry, "Hurrah for Jeff Davis, and hang the d—d Dutch," echoed through town frequently.[22]

While the situation appeared to be improving in Kansas City by the middle of the war, the overall depression and air of conflict continued to hang over St. Joseph. A newspaper correspondent from Kansas City visited the struggling city in the fall of 1863 and gave a depressing report: "This place has probably done an immense amount of business, in days gone by. Those days will never return, for St. Joseph. She is dead, dead; past resurrection. When I first came here, I quickly saw the difference between this place and Kansas City. I saw here no streets crowded with wagons. No hoarse voiced 'carriers' bellowing to their teams that were dragging tons of freight across the great plains; no steamers unloading goods at the levee; no Southern Kansas wagons loading with groceries; but on the contrary, silent, and almost deserted streets, stores, ditto, &e."[23] Politically St. Joseph had not stabilized after two and a half years of war, even with the major Union successes during the summer of 1863, at Gettysburg and Vicksburg. Strong factions of radical Unionists and copperheads kept the city in political turmoil. An editor reflected that the "public excitement is kept up all the time by one party or the other, and we have narrowly escaped a collision several times." The collisions referred to involved armed companies of men, often ragtag bands of pro-Southerners, riding into the town, picking fights with union state militia men, then riding out before reinforcements could be brought against them. Sometimes the pro-Southern forces even charaded as Union men, just so they could get fresh arms and munitions from the local quartermaster.[24]

104

THE RAILROAD AS THE KEY

Writing from St. Joseph in late 1863, a correspondent for a Kansas City paper remarked in one of his columns: "The people here are beginning to look with jealous eyes at the Missouri Pacific Railroad. Go on with the good work; the first whistle of the cars at Kansas City, will be the death knell of St. Joseph."[25]

Prophetic, but true? The key to St. Joseph's rebound could only be found if the city reconnected and advanced its transportation links with its hinterland. The wagon trails leading from the city, which had built it up in the first place, lay as only memories, overgrown with prairie grass. Steamboat traffic had been reduced to a trickle, the town levee lay eroded and unattended. The Hannibal and St. Joseph Railroad kept a regular schedule when the bridges were repaired, but bushwhackers constantly harassed the line, to the extent that the army had to patrol nearly every mile of track across the state to keep it open. Despite those difficulties, the railroad remained the main economic artery into St. Joseph.

But the war, and the situation it created in the city, had brought St. Joseph's railroad prospects to an utter standstill. Nothing advanced from the city in any direction. The Marysville and Roseport, which was to have been the initial link to the great Pacific Railroad, lay, as Stewart said, rusting and decaying across the river in the Kansas bottoms. That dream of becoming the eastern terminus of the transcontinental road had died abruptly with the first glimmer of rebellion in the town, and more importantly, with the possibility that the whole state of Missouri might end up in the Confederate camp. It is an overstatement to say that Jeff Thompson's flag incident at the post office alone killed the future of St. Joseph. Too many other political and economic factors have to be considered. Primary among those, in the context of events in 1862, stood the belief in Washington that a transcontinental railroad had to be built, and it had to terminate in a city where the certainty of it remaining in the Union could not be questioned. Californians clamored for a rail connection. Before the war, the congressional delegations haggled over the advantages of a southern, central, or northern route. With the South taken out of the discussions, the Northern congress could decide more quickly. As confident as Mr. Lincoln may have been about preserving the Union, Missouri represented an uncertain political situation, whereas Chicago and Omaha did not.

105

Still, as late as early June 1862, the St. Joseph press published reports that the Pacific Railroad would start from the city, clinging to the belief that had been so prominent just two summers before: "Our dispatches bring the gratifying intelligence that the Pacific Railroad bill which has passed the House describes the route to be run as follows: the road will start at St. Joseph, and run gradually and directly North and West from this city to the South pass near the 43d parallel, thence to Salt Lake, from which point it will run to California in a Southerly direction, entering that State above Sacramento." At the same time, the pro-Union editor Charles Wilkinson reminded the citizens of the town that "there is much bogus loyalty here yet," and only a clearly union position led to benefits. "The sentiment that we must have a whole country or none, and that in no event, must Missouri be permitted to falter for a moment in her obligations to the Union, is rapidly becoming the dominate feeling in St. Joseph."[26]

Two weeks later, news of senate alterations to the bill fell like a hammer blow on the city. Wilkinson and the *Morning Herald* reported: "By our telegraph dispatches, this morning, it will be seen that the Pacific bill has passed the Senate, with an Omaha, Sioux City, and a Kansas branch, with the privilege extended to the Hannibal & St. Jo Railroad Company to build a line to the Kansas branch." The editor added wishfully: "This bill cannot pass the House as it is at present. Indeed, we shall not be greatly surprised if the bill is defeated this session."[27] But he was wrong. Some in the House may have favored St. Joseph, though Kansas City or Leavenworth actually elicited more support. However the Senate version of the bill specifically spelled out where the transcontinental road would begin, somewhere between "the south margin of the valley of the Republican River, and the north margin of the valley of the Platte River, in the Territory of Nebraska."[28] That meant Omaha. On June 6, 1862, editor Wilkinson lamented after reporting the passage of the Senate version of the Pacific railroad bill: "This [bill] is as favorable to St. Joseph as could be expected unless this city was especially provided for, by its provisions."[29] The Hannibal and St. Joseph Railroad would be allowed to build a line connecting to the transcontinental Union Pacific line at Fort Kearney, but the company would have to provide its own financing. It was also authorized to build south and west, connecting with the proposed line going west from Kansas City, for which a subsidy would be paid. All depended on favorable legislation from Kansas.[30]

The news of the transcontinental railroad starting from Omaha instead of St. Joseph, left a horrifically bitter taste. The town leaders felt they had been betrayed not only by the national government but also by their sister cities, which they called "sister" in only the most loosely literal sense. Wilkinson espoused the view that if the railroad could not be built from St. Joseph then it should not be built at all. "Our Representatives have decided—in a time of unusual embarrassments, when the nation is overwhelmed with a crushing public debt, when the republic is fighting for an existence among the powers of the nineteenth century—to expend millions upon million of dollars in opening up a highway to the Pacific, and spanning the Western hemisphere with an iron girdle." And, if it must be built, then the Congress should reconsider St. Joseph, for it represented "the most direct, cheapest and most practicable route." What about those "sister" cities? Wilkinson indicted them saying: "Every article yet published, in St. Louis, Kansas City, or elsewhere, bases its arguments against St. Joseph upon the fact of this city possessing every one of those advantages over each of its rivals, and urges those rivals to make Herculean efforts to prostrate so formidable a competitor."[31]

Clearly, the intense, intrastate urban rivalry that had begun two decades earlier with competition for the overland trails had merely moved on to the next level. But there were powerful influences being exerted on the city's situation from outside the state as well. Eastern capitalists who had made Chicago the Midwest's leading rail hub, pushed to secure a north central route to California, further expanding that city's huge hinterland and overshadowed St. Joseph's feeble efforts while delivered another blow to urban arch rival, St. Louis. The Forbes brothers and other investors in their group looked to systematically expand their railroads in Iowa and Missouri westward into the Plains and eventually tie in with the proposed transcontinental line. St. Joseph's leadership rightly accused its rivals of playing politics and courting big money to win favor, but they should have realized that competition for economic hegemony and hinterland was no friendly game of marbles.[32]

St. Joseph, 1868, showing Union Fortifications on Prospect Hill. *Courtesy of the St. Joseph Museum*

THE CHALLENGE FROM KANSAS CITY

While St. Joseph lay prostrate under martial law, in a deep economic coma, Kansas City to the south stirred. The St. Joseph correspondent for the *Western Journal of Commerce* wrote in December 1863: "I notice by the public prints that your town—the little "played out" town of Kansas City—is making rapid strides towards the completion of several of her railroads." The most important of those "several" roads, the Missouri Pacific Railroad, connected with St. Louis. Before the war that system had been beset with construction delays, cost overruns, and corruption, allowing the Hannibal and St. Joseph to beat it to the

108

western side of the state. While the war completely stalled any further expansion from St. Joseph, the Pacific line kept creeping along, a few miles being added at a time, when funding became available. Political instability within the state precluded the legislature from offering much assistance. Like St. Joseph, Kansas City had been visited by much turmoil and depredation during the first two years of the war. Nevertheless, it became clear to many that Kansas City had begun gaining ground on St. Joseph. The editor of the *Weekly Journal of Commerce* chirped: "If any town in the West deserves success it is Kansas City. She has been chastened by fire and flood until she is merely a wreck of her former self; still having strength enough left to gird herself and bend all her energies in the race which she is now engaged in with her rivals. But she is every day gathering strength and might, and will soon throw off all opposition and stand proudly preeminent and successful, all the stronger for the thorny path over which she came."[33]

It was an elegant, even heroic statement, not unlike all the other halcyon descriptions of towns and cities that appeared in the favorable press of dozens of places battling for urban growth and greatness. But if the truth be known, eloquence of press built nothing without capital investment. There would be no railroads unless the leadership of Kansas City could generate that capital. As the progress of the Missouri Pacific lagged, Kansas City leaders looked in a different direction to get their rail connection. That direction took them toward the line that had brought St. Joseph to initial hegemony over them, the Hannibal and St. Joseph. If a line could be completed from Kansas City north to the town of Cameron, 35 miles east of St. Joseph, then rail contact could be established between Chicago and the growing population and markets in the Kansas River Valley region. The possibility that the Great Plains, south and west of Kansas City, might fall into the hinterland grasp of Chicago because of rail connections, could help spur the financial powers in St. Louis to accelerate the building of the Missouri Pacific Railroad to protect their own economic interests.[34]

An article in the *Western Journal of Commerce,* published by one of Kansas City's greatest promoters, Robert T. Van Horn, outlined the potential influence of Chicago and the city's strategy to entice St. Louis capitalists to act: "The aspect of things at Jefferson City does not give us great hopes for any legislative action which shall secure the early completion of the Missouri Pacific Railroad. Nor can we place much reliance upon Saint Louis to put the road through, in the absence of favorable legislation. True, that city is perfectly able to do it,—and her very life in the future depends upon it, but the business men and capitalists are an old fogy set, who have hitherto made their money very easily, and who have but little notion of that sagacity and enterprise, which in the gigantic rivalry for the commercial supremicy [sic] of the West is so characteristic of Chicago. Chicago would build the road in six months, were it as necessary to her growth and prosperity as it is to that of Saint Louis."[35]

If the legislature in Jefferson City could not offer funding, then business leaders and the press of Kansas City would shame, cajole, or threaten St. Louis' economic leadership into action. The same article hammered home the issue: "We must have an eastern connection. The Cameron road offers it at a moderate expense." That type of public pep talk represented an important characteristic of leadership, present in Kansas City at that time, but lacking in St. Joseph. That characteristic was unity, a single- mindedness of purpose: *The business men of Kansas City must take hold of this matter themselves and push it through.* They can do it. The amount of money necessary to make the road a success is fully within the capacity of our citizens to raise. We only need to take hold of the matter unitedly and with determination, and the work will surely be accomplished. Shall we not do it?"[36]

Kansas City did it, but not entirely on its own. First its delegation in the state legislature, consisting of Robert T. Van Horn, Milton Payne, and E. M. McGee, worked tirelessly to get legislation though the state house, financing the continuation of the Missouri Pacific. On February 13, 1864, the Kansas City press heralded their success with the headline: "Rejoice! Rejoice! Kansas City All Right! The R. R. Bill Passed!"[37]

Many in Kansas City expected the link with St. Louis to be completed by the summer of 1864, but late war maneuvers by Missouri's Confederate general, Sterling Price, delayed construction. Not until September 1865 did the Missouri Pacific link with St. Louis reach completion. In the interim, the Kansas City press kept reminding the community of the importance of the rail link with the Hannibal and St. Joseph at Cameron. That link, more than the connection with St. Louis, provided the most staggering blow against rival St. Joseph to the north. To accomplish the task of building the road to Cameron, Kansas City needed help. And just as important as building the road itself, would be the bridge across the Missouri River, to run the line directly into the city on the south

110

bank. That help came from the real financial power brokers of the Hannibal and St. Joseph Railroad, the eastern capitalists who controlled the line. It is ironic for St. Joseph that the Boston capitalists, with the financial resources to build railroads, at first made her a star on the railroad map of the nation, but later made a decision that would profoundly impact the course of her history in the opposite direction.

THE POSTWAR RECOVERY

By the time the Civil War drew to a close in April 1865, the economic recovery of St. Joseph had begun. It came on the backs of beef cattle and hogs over the tracks of the Hannibal and St. Joseph Railroad. Beginning as early as 1863, the livestock market of Northwest Missouri revived, and both brokers and packers within the city began to bustle again with activity. The railroad that connected with the Chicago, Burlington & Quincy Railroad, by ferry across the Mississippi river in Illinois, began hauling thousands of hogs into the Chicago's packing plants. Chicago rapidly grew into the meat packing center of the nation during the Civil War, and St. Joseph served as the tip of one of its major supply tentacles. Cattle, for the most part, were driven the opposite direction, toward Colorado, where demand had been created by the mining and ranching boom. Farm credit and the supply business gradually revived, as well as the demand in the area for wholesale supply. By March 1865 martial law lifted, the army presence diminished, schools reopened, and again the talk of the town centered on railroad expansion. But capital remained scarce, to say the least.

Promoters of the city, lead by the editor of the *Morning Herald*, had not given up on St. Joseph as a railroad center for the nation, despite having lost the fight with Omaha for the starting point of the Union Pacific transcontinental line. Important connecting lines could still be built and exploited by the city's business houses. Those same lines could also be used to promote manufacturing in the city. Money needed to be raised, and that meant city bond proposals and stock subscriptions would have to be presented to the public. "We must have manufacturing if we would have a large city," wrote the editor of the *Herald*. "Without cheap fuel, manufacturing cannot be had. Our sole business now is the selling of dry goods and groceries. This alone will not maintain a continuous and permanent growth of our city. Give us the St. Louis and St. Joseph Railroad and the richest regions of the State are reached at a distance of only sixty miles."[38]

Besides the St. Louis and St. Joseph line, a number of other roads had been proposed, or were in various stages of work. They included: the Missouri Valley Railroad to Leavenworth; the Kansas City, St. Joseph, and Council Bluffs Railroad; the St. Joseph and Denver City Railroad; as well as roads to Des Moines and Atchison. While some local capital could be found to help promote those lines, the real money had to come from the East. Geographic determinism remained alive and well in the minds of many civic leaders who believed that St. Joseph's location could not help but bring her to the forefront again economically: "It is but rational," wrote editor Wilkinson, "to expect from our favorable situation that St. Joseph will, being the center of the continent also become the central point of this web work of railways. The main leaders shall converge to St. Joseph, while other cities shall hold connecting branches from point to point in connection with these radiating hues."[39]

During the spring of 1866, over 25,000 head of Texas longhorn cattle arrived in St. Joseph, for shipment to Chicago packing plants via the Hannibal and St. Joseph Railroad. That the city benefited from this at all was due to the fear of central Missouri farmers that the Texas cattle might be carrying Spanish fever which could infect local herds. The fearful farmers forced the Texas cattle drivers to divert from their intended railhead at Sedalia, and push on northward to St. Joseph. The event had important overtones for the future of St. Joseph as a major livestock center and transshipment point to the eastern markets. Texas cattle were beginning to be driven northward along the now famous cattle trails—the Sedalia, the Chisholm, the Goodnight-Loving and the Western—to towns in Kansas with rail depots. But the Kansas Pacific road pushed west from Kansas City, not St. Joseph, reaching toward Abilene and Salina, major cattle towns. At those points, the overland trail drives ended and direct shipment by rail to Chicago and the East began, all funneled through Kansas City. Cattlemen had no incentive to push on north past the Kansas Pacific because little of the St. Joseph and Denver line had been completed west of St. Joseph, and no railroad bridge had been built there yet.[40] Drovers still had to put cattle on the ferries, a slow and costly process, to cross the Missouri River to connect with the trains there. No bridge over the Missouri existed at Kansas City either, in 1866, but the Missouri Pacific line could route cattle east through St. Louis where they were still ferried across the Mississippi. It was a circumspect route, and only marginally accept-

112

able to shippers. The first of the two rival cities, St. Joseph or Kansas City, to get a bridge over the Missouri, thus making the most direct rail connection with Chicago, would win the contest to become the major livestock center of the Great Plains and gain regional hegemony.

By early 1868, prospects looked better in St. Joseph. The postwar boom had hit a peak. In March of that year the *Herald* crowed: "In all the history of St. Joseph, we do not recollect a season when the prospects of a splendid trade, in all branches of mercantile business, were so favorable as now." Manufacturing facilities, one of the recognized keys to urban development, began to appear alongside the warehouses of the drygoods dealers. "Woolen factories, flouring mills, boot and shoe factories, tailoring establishments, tin shops, sawing, planing, and scrolling mills, machine shops, &c., &c., looming up all over the city impress us with the conviction that St. Joseph is an important emporium for manufactures for the West."[41] In May 1868, readers of the St. Joseph *Herald* found on the front page a list of the town's wealthiest citizens, published under the headline, "Our Financial Exhibit." The list had been compiled from figures given to the United States Assessor for the year 1867. From the nearly one hundred men one could glean a handful of names that formed the economic elite of the city, men with reported incomes in the five figure range. Among the notables were Simon Adler, Armstrong Beattie, John Corby, Milton Tootle, and William Wyeth, all in banking, dry goods, or light manufacturing.[42]

Shortly after the war ended, steamboat traffic on the Missouri increased dramatically. St. Joseph's levee boomed again, with multiple daily arrivals and departures and regular packet service connecting with Omaha, St. Louis, and points in between. During the navigation season's 1868 peak, a dozen or more boats came and went in a single day. The local editors waxed frequently and eloquently about the Missouri River, its character, and its inevitable economic value to the city: "The river—the Old Muddy—the Mighty Missouri—has altered its opinion as to its condition lately, if we may be allowed the ideas of attributing opinions to such a fickle being as the Big Muddy." Despite the expansion of the railroad network, the "Big Muddy" still provided an important artery of commerce for St. Joseph. Not unlike the merchants and businessmen of St. Louis, who believed that the rivers were still superior to the railroad, St. Joseph business houses routinely still shipped by river. The *Herald* described a typical landing: "The steamer Girard B. Allen came in about noon from the up river ports, and left very soon after taking for—Daneron & Bro., 64 bundles of rags, 670 sacks of corn; J. McEntire, trunk: C. Peper, 5 craddles tobacco: H. Folsom & Co., case of guns; Edgerhill and Eaton, 497 sacks of corn; Lewis Manson & Co., 331 sacks of corn; F. Whittaker & Sons, 7,976 bulk shoulders, 500 sides, [pork]."[43]

The economic offshoot of that commitment to the river resulted in a number of business leaders in St. Joseph ignoring railroad promotion. In the short term, the rebirth of the steamboat era held promises; however, as history had shown, the glory days of the steamboat had passed and would never return. But what about the bridge over the Missouri River? There appeared nothing of note in the St. Joseph papers calling for funding or editorializing in support of immediate action to secure a bridge from the railroad companies. Had the economic and political leadership of St. Joseph fallen asleep or been blinded to the need to push for a bridge to connect their western hinterland? The leaders of Kansas City had not, and while their urban rivals in St. Joseph reveled in a substantial postwar recovery, they seized the bridge.

THE BRIDGE TAKEN

In August 1865, the Kansas City *Journal* reported a story under the headline: "Kansas City and Cameron Railroad." Contained in the story ran an ominous report for the future of St. Joseph and a joyful one for Kansas City. The story began with the announcement that the board of directors of the proposed connection to the Hannibal and St. Joseph line had assured the people of the city that it would be "speedily" built. Then it continued, "Either this or the coming week, an engineer will be here to make a survey of the river with a view to the location and estimates for a bridge over the Missouri at this city."[44] But obvious questions arise. Why, if the Hannibal and St. Joseph Railroad wanted to bridge the Missouri, to open the Kansas hinterland, did they not do it at St. Joseph, where the direct east-west line terminated, already hard against the river bank? Why would the railroad directors wait and go to the expense to build a spur to the river bank someplace else?

The answer to those question, which had so profound an impact on the future of both St. Joseph and Kansas City, may be sought in many places. And it would make "darn good" dramatic western history if the story could be told in the context of groups of town fathers and promoters, battling it out tooth and nail to gain the prized bridge. Some of that may be true enough, but on closer examination, the decision to build the bridge over the Missouri at Kansas City instead of what appeared the more obvious choice of St. Joseph, or even the highly touted point at Leavenworth, lay not completely with those cities, but within the board rooms of eastern capitalists. Financier James F. Joy proved to be a central figure in the fateful decision.

In all fairness to St. Joseph, the brutal period during the war had left it in a poor third place in the eyes of those contemplating the Missouri River bridge by 1865.[41] In view of the more solid Union position Leavenworth had maintained during the war, and its position further south with easier access to the Kansas Pacific line, that town received greater consideration from company offices for the bridge than did St. Joseph. Kansas City, already established as the primary eastern terminus of the Kansas Pacific line, lay south of the Missouri River and had to have a bridge to make the Chicago connection. When, it appeared that Leavenworth might take the bridge, over both St. Joseph and Kansas City, only Kansas City leadership rapidly responded. Kersey Coates, a prominent Kansas City promoter, led a delegation to Boston to meet with James Joy, then chairman of the Hannibal and St. Joseph and president of the Chicago, Burlington and Quincy line that connected it with Chicago. Joy represented the visible power contact for those Boston capitalists already introduced as the Forbes group.[46]

Coates, as well as Joy, knew they had to obtain congressional approval to bridge the Mississippi or Missouri rivers. Kansas Citians lobbied hard through the Missouri delegation, of which their champion, Robert T. Van Horn was a part, but so too did the financial powers of the Forbes group, lead by Joy. Besides Kansas City's earnest public appeal, the promise of personal financial gain moved James Joy to support that city over St. Joseph or Leavenworth. In early 1866, he had bought stock in the West Kansas City Land Company. The property developed by that land company became the site of Kansas City's first stockyards, which benefited enormously by having a direct rail link, over the bridge, with the eastern markets, particularly Chicago. In July 1866, Congress approved the Kansas City location for the bridge. Joy quickly moved the financing through company channels to finish the Kansas City and Cameron Railroad and organize the Quincy Railroad Bridge Company, which built not only the Kansas City structure, but another bridge over the Mississippi at Quincy, Illinois, to create a non-stop route

115

to Chicago. The question about what the leaders of St. Joseph were doing at that time, why they weren't in Boston lobbying company officials, remains unanswered and open to speculation. Regardless, they were too late.[47]

The "Hannibal" railroad bridge at Kansas City opened on July 3, 1869, and the St. Joseph *Herald* began its coverage of the event with a paragraph that carried the tone of a scolding for its readers: "The inauguration to-day of the first railroad bridge over the Missouri is a triumph not for Kansas City alone; it demonstrates the practicalibity [sic] of the enterprise, it teaches the lesson that railroad systems may be independent of rivers."[48] Thousands watched from the bluffs, the papers estimated at least 20,000, as a ceremonial train chugged across the structure at the head of a procession of railroad and public dignitaries. Speeches were made and the celebration lasted late into the night. General James Craig, a railroad official and citizen of St. Joseph, spoke at the occasion. The *Herald* reported he "declared that he was heartily proud as a resident of a neighboring city of the great triumph of the Kansas City Bridge—the people of Kansas City

Opening of the Kansas City Railroad Bridge 1869. Courtesy of the Boder Collection

had labored hard and earnestly, and poured forth their money with a lavish hand, and they well deserved success. He justly rebuked the lethargy of the residents of St. Joseph [declaring that he would give twenty of our prominent men, worth

116

$500,000 each, for five men fired with the energy and enterprise that character-izes Congressman Van Horn]."[49] Within a short time, 500 trains a month were crossing the bridge in and out of Kansas City.[50]

James Joy and the other Boston capitalists had not completely forgotten about St. Joseph, though they felt no compulsion to build their bridge there. Joy saw the need to connect the new rail center he had helped create in Kansas City with the new transcontinental line, the Union Pacific, at Omaha. To that end, he pushed the creation of the Kansas City, St. Joseph and Council Bluffs Railroad. Chartered in July 1867, the new company absorbed the St. Joe and Council Bluffs road that had been started by local subscription in 1859. In May 1868, a promi-nent delegation of railroad men, wheeling powers to make or break towns, like the pantheon of gods on Mount Olympus, passed through St. Joseph. "Last evening," as the *Herald* described the scene, "a party of Boston capitalists, largely investors in our railroads, arrived by special train from Quincy and took quarters at the Pacific House." The Pacific House carried at that time the reputation as the best hotel in the city. "The object of the visit is to make observations in reference to their interests in this section of the country, and to consider the visibility [sic] of taking hold of the railroad leading west from this city." The article listed the noted capitalists: "All hail from Boston; are Hon. Nathaniel Thayer, Henry Whitney, G. B. Bigelow, E. Austin, Sidney Bartlett, and Joseph Jasage. One of them alone, Mr. Nathaniel Thayer, is worth over fifteen million." Accompanying the capitalists were western railroad officials: "Among them we noticed Hon. James F. Joy, President, and Mr. Robert Harris, Superintendent of the Chicago, Burlington, and Quincy Railroad."[51] The excursion of the capitalists provided them with an opportunity to see first hand where their money had gone in completing the line between Kansas City and Council Bluffs. The complete line opened in late 1868, after an infusion of Boston capital to finish laying track through Iowa. As such, St. Joseph became another station along what became known in railroad history as the "Joy line."[52]

A DAY OF EMBARRASSMENT

Financing for a bridge or additional investment to extend a railroad west from St. Joseph across Kansas or into Nebraska was not forthcoming from the Boston group. Part of the rejection of St. Joseph as a major east-west rail termi-

117

nus can be attributed to Joy's overall strategy of railroad development, and part to the public perception of the city that had dogged it, both during and after the end of the war, as a politically and socially unstable place to invest. Unfortunately, that perception received reinforcement when General Ulysses S. Grant, Republican presidential candidate in 1868, arrived in the city for a brief visit. The accounts of his reception, widely discussed in public, prompted the editor of the *Herald* to run the headline the next day: "St. Joseph Disgraced."

Grant and his touring entourage, which included his good friends and Union heroes Generals William Tecumseh Sherman and Phil Sheridan, arrived in St. Joseph at nine o'clock on the evening of July 28, 1868. A crowd of about 6,000 people gathered at the Council Bluffs and St. Joseph Railroad depot on Second Street to welcome the prominent guests. The *Herald* described the arrival: "The visitors were met by a committee of the G. A. R.[Grand Army of the Republic] and escorted through a line of old soldiers to the carriages, and hastily drawn through the surging crowd to the Pacific House. During the reception a national salute was fired, whilst bonfires blazed and signal lights loomed up in all directions. Grant and Sherman were seated in Cundiff's open barouche, drawn by four spirited horses; the crowd clinging closely to the carriage from the depot to the hotel." After arriving at the hotel, Grant, Sherman, and Sheridan made appearances on the second floor balcony and attempted to speak briefly to the crowd. But as Wilkinson reported: "At that time it was discovered that quite a number were present, with the determination to insult the visitors."[53]

The political ruptures of the war had not healed. Many in the crowd who were ex-Confederates still despised the Union cause and vehemently hated the three living symbols of the South's greatest defeats—Grant, Sherman, and Sheridan. "The speech of General Grant, brief as it was, was interrupted by the most boisterous applause, mingled with hootings, groans and cheers for Seymour and Blair." [Seymour and Blair were the Democratic presidential ticket in 1868.] A battle of noise raged in the street below the hotel balcony. Old southern sympathizers with still open wounds, blew whistles and yelled to drown out the notables, while others, hoping to impress the next president with the town's hospitality, tried to shout them down. Grant went inside, not to return. Sherman came out on the balcony briefly, only to be greeted by the same tumultuous and conflicting noise. As the *Herald* reported, he tried to speak: "Gentlemen: I return thanks to you for this hearty reception. General Grant did not choose to speak, as he was worn out by travel." Loud cheers for Seymour and Blair interrupted Sherman. "I do not desire to advise violence, but if I was a resident of St. Joseph, I would duck that fellow in the Missouri river. There was a time when people who wanted to fight could be accommodated; we gave them all they wanted." That remark brought more hooting from the ex-Confederates. "When you learn to behave yourself, I'll continue my speech." Sherman then went back inside, also not to return.[54]

Republican city leaders and the *Herald's* editor, shamed and red faced, wasted no time responding. In an editorial the next day, Wilkinson laid it all at the feet of the old divisive elements within the city's population: "Citizens of St. Joseph, men who have property and valuable interests here, what has been, and surely will be, our reward for all this? We lost the initial point of the Pacific Railroad, the overland mail and express, custom house and other public buildings, because of that rebel rag which floated defiantly here when Schuyler Colfax, Chairman of the committee on post offices and post roads visited us in the spring of 1861. Our Senators declared that they could make no headway, in the Senate of the United States, against the charges of disloyalty and insubordination so truthfully made against the citizens of St. Joseph. Such insults as were heaped upon Grant and Sherman last Tuesday night, will lead surely and effectively against us, in every endeavor of ours for favor with the next administration, or the present Congress."[55] Though Wilkinson's Republican political beliefs were well known, his lecture to the citizens carried some well taken-points, regardless of party affiliation. St. Joseph's dirty linen had been waved across the nation and noted in the eastern halls of political and financial power.

It is fair to say that St. Joseph never completely controlled its own fate in regard to key railroad decisions. Failure to secure the starting point of the transcontinental can be blamed as much on the situation within the whole state as it can the perceived disloyalty of the city alone. Financially, the necessary private capital and entrepreneurial leadership needed to complete its own bridge and expand westward may have existed but never came forward during that decade. Many St. Joseph businessmen who could have invested in the railroads did not, because of conflict with their connections to the overland freight companies and the riverboat captains. St. Joseph remained void of private "venture" capital, even though the general populous often voted to support city or county bond subscriptions. Capital to build railroads had to come from the power centers of the East, and they saw other cities as more viable investments. The lack of vital leadership from the city, with the exception of Robert M. Stewart and the pre-war activities of M. Jeff Thompson to recruit needed investment, now seems glaring. A broad based civic spirit had built the city as the premiere jumping off point for the western trails, established it as one of the prime Missouri river ports, and initially given it the lead in western rail expansion into Kansas. That spirit had been crushed by the Civil War, and it never really completely recovered. The federal census showed St. Joseph had more than doubled its 1860 population, despite the dramatic losses during the war years, to 19,565. Kansas City, however had swept past it, rising during that single decade from about 4,000 to over 32,000.[56] Yet a cadre of leading citizens of St. Joseph went undaunted. Prospects for economic prosperity still existed, if only for those who pursued their private empires.

A DAY OF SADNESS

On the same day that the Boston capitalists passed through town in 1868, carrying the fate of St. Joseph and so many other cities in their wallets, the *Herald* carried a somber proclamation from Mayor George H. Hall: "Joseph Robidoux, the founder of the city of St. Joseph, Missouri, is dead. As a tribute of respect to the memory of Joseph Robidoux, whose name is inseparably connected with the city of St. Joseph as its founder, it is hereby requested that the citizens of St. Joseph close their houses of business from two o'clock till five o'clock P. M. on Thursday, the 28th day of May, 1868, during funeral services."[57]

The old man, known by nearly all of the almost 20,000 people who inhabited his town, had died quietly. Infirmed, almost completely blind, and nearly broke, he had lived out his last days in an apartment in one of his rented row houses. The astute old businessman had given away most of his money and property late in his life to family and friends. He had long ceased to be a political or economic force in his town, but his unassuming grace, friendliness, and generosity remained a model to all who knew him.

The *Herald* reported: "At noon, all the places of business were closed, and in all parts of the city there was a general suspension of business during the remainder of the day. Edmond street, in the neighborhood of the residence of Jule Robidoux, sr.[sic], was densely crowded during the early hours of the

120

afternoon by the old and young—all anxious to take a last look at the remains of the old pioneer." Simeon Kemper, William Fowler, Robert Carter, E. W. Welch, Judge Schreiber, and Gov. Robert M. Stewart officiated as pall bearers. A procession of family members, city officials, and citizens escorted the town founder to his resting place. "The remains of the deceased were taken to the Catholic cemetery and there consigned to their final resting place with all respects."[58]

CHAPTER 6

A City of Private Empires
1870-1900

A widely held, but never truly documented, part of St. Joseph's history in the late nineteenth century stated that there were more millionaires per capita in the city than anywhere in the United States.[1] And, as the story went, those millionaires manipulated the future of the city to suit their own needs and devices. They manipulated the economy, the start up of new business and industry, the labor market, the banks and availability of credit, and the city government, all the things that give a city economic prowess and allow it to compete successfully against urban rivals. If someone asked a twentieth century resident of St. Joseph why the city developed the way it did, more than likely they would repeat that often told story. Others would say that it could not be true and attribute the city's condition to other economic, social, and political forces.

The concept of the wealthy controlling the destiny of cities has some historical-sociological grounding.[2] In the course of American urban history, one has to ask the question, would there be any great cities if it were not for the wealthy? Who provided the capital to build the businesses, the banks, the industry, the rail connections, the stockyards and packing plants that built New York, Chicago or New Orleans? Why did people of all economic classes and social backgrounds move into the cities, particularly during the urban surge of the second half of the nineteenth century, if there were no jobs, products, services, or cultural inducements? Without wealthy capitalists to provide those inducements, the nation might have remained as Jefferson envisioned, an endless expanse of small farms and yeomen farmers from the Atlantic to the Pacific.

By supplying capital, the economically wealthy created new forces that not only built cities in brick, stone, iron and steel, but moved literally millions of people. In a real sense, the capitalists created the forces described by one of America's first and greatest urban historians, Arthur Meier Schlesinger. He wrote about the dynamism of change taking place in the urbanization of America following the Civil War, a change which created a "clash between two cultures, one static, individualistic, agricultural, the other dynamic, collectivistic, urban."

Specifically, in relation to the middle western region of the nation he said: "The migration from the country districts had attained a momentum that was fast giving the city a dominant position in the social organism. In 1880, one out of every five Middle Westerners lived in urban communities of four thousand or more inhabitants, ten years later one out of every three."[3]

During the period Schlesinger described, St. Joseph reached the peak of its urban development. By the turn of the century, it had the most people and the greatest concentration of wealth that it would ever have it its history. Regardless of the number of millionaires per capita, men of power and influence formed a cadre of economic and civic leaders, who guided St. Joseph through the last decades of the nineteenth century and into the next. Did those men, whose names blazed across the top of the city social registry—Tootle, Weyth, Krug, Goetz, and Davis—provided their leadership out of duty and civic pride, or was it merely to enhance their own financial empires? The nineteenth century ended for the city of St. Joseph with its promise still unfulfilled. If those men, who led the economic community are to blame, then understanding their motives may answer the question, why? Were they out for themselves only?

A BRIDGE AT LAST

In late 1869, the St. Joseph Bridge Building Company formed. Composed of thirteen investors, most of the board members had demonstrated interest in improving St. Joseph's railroad connections. Former Missouri governor and St. Joseph favorite son, Willard P. Hall, headed the company. Their objective was clear. If St. Joseph desired to maintain any area of hinterland west of the Missouri River, it had to have a railroad bridge. It could wait no longer. Congress approved a bridge franchise for the St. Joseph and Denver City Railroad, which in turn granted it to the bridge company. Initially the company's directors hoped to raise $1,500,000 for the project, through local stock subscription, selling shares at $100 each. But at a meeting of the newly formed St. Joseph Board of Trade, in early 1870, a new strategy emerged out of a perceived necessity.

Tight fisted St. Joseph businessmen, who could have carried the bulk of the bridge stock subscription, simply would not let loose of their private money. The only alternative remained to approach the taxpayers. James Matney, an investor and a member of the committee to finance the bridge, stood up at a public meeting and summed up the sad situation when he said "he believed that a subscription for $500,000 in the city, could be carried, because there was no use in depending on private subscriptions when it was notorious that many men who would be vastly benefited would not subscribe a dollar. The only way to get at the thing equitably was to vote a tax which would reach those persons. He could name ten men whose property would be enhanced 100 percent who would subscribe next to nothing."[4]

The bridge company, thanks to the influence of its president, Willard P. Hall, convinced the city to sponsor financial support in the form of an ordinance calling for a special election that authorized a city-held subscription of 5,000 shares of stock. Hall no doubt received assistance from councilman Robert Gunn and city attorney Jeff Chandler, both of whom were on the bridge company's board of directors. The ordinance passed at the end of December 1870, and set the special election date on January 25, 1871.[5] The proposed stock investment, backed by city bonds, would cost $500,000, and be paid off at 10 percent annual interest over 20 years. The vote by the citizens to support the bonds elicited a stirring headline in the *Herald*, "HURRAH FOR THE BRIDGE! Old Fogyism Dead!" Opponents to the bonds tallied only 20 negative ballots, with 1,836 voting in favor. The bridge across the Missouri River appeared to have suddenly captured everyone's imagination, everyone except those who still viewed the railroads as a threat to their overland freight businesses, but even those who would not invest a dime of their own, as Mr. Matney had put it, voted for the city commitment.[6]

On July 25, 1871, materials for the bridge building project began arriving in the city. The Detroit Bridge and Iron Works bid $716,000 for the project. Stonework began on September 26 of that year. Six huge piers, requiring 172,000 cubic feet of masonry supported the six iron trestles spanning 1,345 feet. The bridge actually carried three decks, one for rail traffic and the other two for foot and horse traffic on either side of the railroad track. By the end of 1871, noticeable progress had been made, enough for the *Herald* to crow: "A magnificent railroad, wagon and foot bridge is being constructed with all the speed and energy which the best bridge-builders of the nation can exercise and command. This colossal enterprise which has so long agitated and interested this community is now a fixed fact."[7]

124

As the completion date grew near, the *Herald* waxed eloquently on what the bridge truly meant to the city: "The vast domain of which St. Joseph is geographically, and may become commercially, the center, is being pierced and threaded with marvelous rapidity, by railroads, the great modern artificial arteries of the world of commerce, which naturally converge at this point. St. Joseph is just between the Great East and the Great West, and when holding the link uniting together these two mighty sections, she possesses the key that can unlock their commercial treasure and fill her coffers with gold. Without a bridge, she is neither with the East nor with the West. With a bridge, she is in close and controlling communion with both."[8] A stirring editorial, which would have been better taken to heart by city leaders a decade earlier.

By May 20, 1873, the first locomotive, an engine of the St. Joseph & Denver City Railroad, chugged across the bridge. The city planned a grand opening celebration for May 31, which coincided with a huge celebration by the German immigrant population known as the Saengerfest [song festival]. A massive parade, by the city's tradesmen touched off the combined celebrations. The *Herald* described the scene: "Such a sight was never seen in the West. The procession which traversed the streets of this city yesterday was never equaled West of the Mississippi. Every trade was represented. The cooper was hooping his barrels in his improvised shop on wheels, the shoemaker was pegging at his last, the axehandle manufacturers were using their drawing knives and turning out handles with the same celerity they would in their shop; lathes, looms, steam engines, collar factories, trunk establishments and an endless variety of other trades were in full blast in our streets. The procession in which this grand display occurred was fully six miles in length."[9]

But while the celebration of the bridge opening captured much of the news for that day, Wilkinson, the editor of the *Herald*, wrote a somewhat somber, but strikingly true assessment of what the struggle for the bridge had really meant to the city. In speaking of St. Joseph he reminded his readers that "every newspaper that was ever successful in St. Joseph has advocated a liberal policy with regard to great public improvements," and that "there are always a few men whose lofty instinct and superior insight are the tide-mark of the coming sea. St. Joseph had a few such." But as if to dampen the whole affair, he sermonized on how tardy the economic powers of the city had been and how the bridge, as glorious as it seemed on that day of opening, had come too late. Wilkinson understood better than anyone exactly what had happened to the future of the city. "Her citizens were generally prosperous and contented. They had very little genuine public spirit. They were sure that nature had destined this for a great city and they proposed to let nature do her own work in her own good time. The time was when St. Joseph could have been the eastern terminus of the Pacific railroad if her wealthy citizens had paid the expenses of five men to Washington. But they refused. The city lost every advantage by this inertness. It lost the Overland Stage, the Pacific Railroad, a bridge across the Missouri river, and millions of dollars of trade. Atchison took one, Omaha another, and Kansas City still another of these great essentials to our existence. Our rivals actually began to walk away from us, in the race for metropolitan supremacy."[274]

St. Joseph's railroad bridge over the Missouri river,1873. Courtesy of the BoderCollection

Within a year, the Missouri river span carried nearly 2,500 train crossings, each way, as well as over 10,000 horse drawn vehicles and 18,000 pedestrians.[275] St. Joseph's western hinterland, though flattened somewhat like a pancake between those of Kansas City and Omaha, could still expand into the growing agricultural area of northern Kansas and southern Nebraska. That expansion complimented the region of eastern hinterland that followed the route of the Hannibal and St. Joseph line east to the Grand River Valley and north to the Iowa

126

border. The city of St.   Joseph may have lost its race for urban hegemony, but the direct rail links to those agricultural products from the burgeoning Great Plains, over the completed bridge, made possible the building of personal fortunes and empires, in wholesale distribution, livestock, grain, and banking.

THE KINGDOM OF THE WHOLESALERS

Most of St. Joseph's wealthiest individuals during the late nineteenth century were wholesale merchants.   They often had roots going back to the beginning of the town, many of them had started in the dry goods and outfitting businesses for the overland trails.   More often than not, by the 1870s second generations assumed control of family firms, extended their business tentacles, and increased their private fortunes as they shifted from retail to wholesale operations, supplying the hundreds of small town merchants throughout St. Joseph's hinterland. The *Herald* confidently and optimistically boasted early in the decade of the 1870s: "The wholesale trade of St. Joseph, coupled with her immense retail business, has reached a standard unequaled by any other city of its size in the United States.   There are now in the city between forty-five and fifty large wholesale establishments, besides an infinitely vast number of retail establishments of all kinds." And, "St. Joseph, although comparatively a young city, has risen to a high standard of commercial importance.   But nothstanding [sic] her unparalleled increase in business, she is yet but in her infancy in this respect. Like Chicago and St. Louis, she will in the course of time grow to be the largest city and the most extensive business centre of the whole Northwest."[276]

The bulk of the city's wholesale business came from groceries and dry goods, but substantial amounts of other products passed through her warehouses. The following table from January 1, 1874, showing totals for the year 1873, illustrates the situation:

WHOLESALE TOTALS[13]

Groceries	$ 4,156,000.
Dry goods and notions	3,353,000.
Boots and shoes	840,000.
Drugs, paints, etc.	498,000.
Liquors	668,000.

127

Clothing	710,000.
Hardware	935,000.
Queensware	165,000.
Hats, caps, etc.	313,000.
Stoves, tinware, etc.	234,000.
Cigars and tobacco	285,000.
Confectioneries, jewelry, etc.	108,500.
Stationary and job printing	200,000.
Miscellaneous	840,500.
Total	13,333,000.

The table not only illustrates the range of products handled by St. Joseph wholesalers, but when compared to figures for years past and following, it can be demonstrated that St. Joseph business men continued to actively pursue growth. While the nation fell into a major economic depression in the year 1873, St. Joseph wholesalers held on despite a substantial one year decline. The *Herald* proudly pronounced in its year end summary, "Our City Occupies an Enviable Position. The Only City that Chicago Fears as a Rival. New Houses and no Failures During 1873." The middle headline stretched the credibility of the paper a bit, for Chicago did one hundred times the volume of trade, but as the following table shows, the wholesale business of the city bloomed into a nice recovery in the rather difficult financial times that staggered the national economy for nearly five years.

WHOLESALE BUSINESS TOTALS BY YEAR[14]

1870	$12,600,000
1871	14,519,000
1872	18,475,000
1873	13,333,000
1874	16,587,500
1875	19,829,000
1876	25,185,000
1877	28,258,000
1878	29,167,000

By the mid-1880s the wholesale figures reached $40 million and by the end of the century had topped out at about $62 million. It is significant that during the same period that St. Joseph's retail figures, representing what its merchants actually sold to individual consumers, stood far below those for its wholesale business. The retail figure for 1878 stood at $18 million and clearly demonstrates the extent to which wholesale dominated the St. Joseph economy. The total for manufactured goods from the city also pales in comparison, standing at about $12 million. No other economic activity, such as livestock sales and shipping, meat packing, brewing, milling, or banking generated anywhere near the figures for the wholesale trade.[15] It is that point that underscores the basic weakness in St. Joseph's ability to grow and compete with first rate cities. Manufacturing stood as the foundation of urban growth in the late nineteenth century, as Schlesinger described. Manufacturing created jobs which drew millions to cities like New York, Chicago, Pittsburgh, and St. Louis. In comparison to cities of that caliber, St. Joseph's manufacturing base remained minuscule in number of establishments, capital invested, and number of persons employed. The largest individual classes of manufacturing in St. Joseph were women's apparel and cigar and cigarette making. Overall, figures from the 1890 census show a total of 276 manufacturing establishments in the city, with total capital investment of $6.5 million, and just over 5,000 employees. By contrast, the largest city in the state, St. Louis, reported 6,148 manufacturing establishments, capital of over $170 million, and more than 94,000 employees.[16]

The driving forces behind the wholesale empires were of course the owners of the family dominated businesses, but their success and growth propelled itself along on the shoe leather and sample cases of an army of traveling salesmen. The "drummers" who traveled their routes by rail or buggy or on foot, stopping at every little town and station along the way, built the empires. That point is no better reflected than in the creation of the St. Joseph Commercial Traveler's Association in December 1874. It began with 100 members, with George G. Parry its first president. Referred to as the, "Knights of the Road," they served their wholesale "lords" by canvassing a vast territory for potential buyers, which included "the towns of Missouri, Kansas, Nebraska, Colorado, New Mexico, Montana, Dakota, the Indian Territory, Utah, Arizona and Texas."[17]

By 1880 the organization had grown to over 400 members, representing 50 wholesale houses. With continued growth through the decade and into the 1890s, it eventually reached over 1,200 members. Those traveling salesmen, or "keyster carriers," held in their satchels and sample kits, not only the keys to the private financial empires, but also the economic future of St. Joseph as well. The *Herald* boasted of the city's traveling salesmen saying: "It is not claiming too much to say that a large portion of the greatness which our fair city has attained is due to the energy and enterprise of her traveling men. All honor to them for a more intelligent, sober, energetic and honorable class of business men are not to be found in any profession of business than the gentlemen who bear the St. Joseph knapsack and spread far and wide the fame of the Queen City of the Missouri Valley."[18]

The association originated from the idea that it was important "to bring those representatives of commerce into closer ties of friendship, ideas and brotherhood, and elevate them socially." The life of the traveling salesman was no picnic. As an article in the *Herald* put it politely, "The commercial traveler's life is a varied one and is not by any means as enviable as might be imagined to the inexperienced." The job took them away from home and family for long periods of time. It involved long hours of travel, often lugging heavy, oversized sample and display cases, in all kinds of weather, that would challenge even the most ardent postman. To keep their expenses down, they got the poorest overnight or sleeping accommodations, often dozing in their train seats, ate questionable food, and faced fierce hinterland competition from drummers from competing cities like Chicago, St. Louis, and Kansas City. But as the paper also stated, "Our men are equal to the task and the mammoth commercial interest built up at this point and continuing to grow is the strongest proof of that assertion."[19]

Once a year, the great lords of the wholesale kingdom rewarded their knights errant with a grand reception and dinner. "Whatever also may create an interest in the social world of St. Joseph," wrote the editor of the *Herald*, "the grandest event of the year, beyond a doubt, is the Commercial Traveler's Association ball, given annually. No expense is spared in carrying it out and in it social gaiety culminates." The affair, held at various landmarks in the city, including the Tootle Opera House, the Tootle and McLaughlin Hall, and the Pacific Hotel, drew the cream of St. Joseph society to rub elbows for one evening with the hard working, shoe worn salesmen who brought them their wealth. The guest lists, published in the local papers, not only provided a "Who's Who" look at St. Joseph's wholesalers, bankers, and manufacturers, but something of a ranking of the economic elite of the city, detailed down to what the wives wore to the ball.[20]

130

Another important organization that grew out of the importance and influence of the wholesalers, the St. Joseph Board of Trade, became the forerunner of the city's modern Chamber of Commerce. Organized on April 19, 1878, wholesale businessmen dominated its membership list as well as its list of officers and board of directors. Of its 178 original members, which included retailers, manufacturers, millers, packers, and professional men, 62 were wholesalers. By 1883, the board had grown in both status and financial backing to the point that it built and occupied a fine new four story building which also rented space to the fruit, produce, and grain exchanges, railroad freight agents, and the clearing house for the local banks.[21]

If in the late nineteenth century St. Joseph had a king, and a royal family to rule over its wholesale empire, then that family's name was Tootle. While a number of other families could rightfully claim the title of "princes" in certain kinds of wholesaling—hardware, groceries, liquor, and though many were just as rich, the Tootles represented the epitome of St. Joseph's economic elite. The patriarch of the family, Milton Tootle, Sr., was born in Ross County, Ohio, in 1823. In the mid-1840s he established himself with his two brothers, Thomas and Joseph, as merchants in the town of Savannah, just north of St. Joseph. The lure of a fortune, made in outfitting for the Oregon Trail and the 49ers, brought him and his brothers south to the city to establish themselves in partnership with other bright, ambitious merchants. Milton came in to the dry goods firm of Smith and Donald as a junior partner in 1848. He quickly took control of the trading house through a series of restructures that saw the firm's name and list of partners change rapidly over the next few months. By July 1849, the original partners had all gone and Tootle had been joined by his two brothers, as well as William G. Fairleigh. The firm did business as Tootle & Fairleigh until 1873, though one brother died and another left to go into banking. A new partner, J. S. Ballinger, joined in 1865. Again, in 1867, Tootle added three more partners, Messieurs Craig, Masson, and Hosea. By 1870, the firm had wholesale orders amounting to $750,000 annually, making it one of the "big three" wholesale firms in the city, along with Nave & McCord and R. L. McDonald & Company.[22]

Milton Tootle epitomized the gentleman of culture, dignity and social correctness. Each day he dressed in a frock coat, clean white shirt and tie, trousers with a sharp crease in the legs, and donned kid gloves and a silk top hat before going into work. He continued to restructure his firm, allowing old part-

131

ners to drop out and adding new ones as the need for fresh capital dictated. Tootle & Fairleigh became Tootle & Craig, then Tootle & Hosea. Ultimately, with each restructure, Tootle saw growth and a more dominating position. As the *Herald* reported about one of Tootle's partnership changes: "This house has long been one of the leading wholesale houses of St. Joseph, and having made an entirely new arrangement, now promises to eclipse all others." Tootle's new firm boasted a doubling of warehouse space, capital doubled, new lines of products added, and "proposes to be the king of wholesale houses in the Great West."[23]

Tootle also established retail dry goods houses in several area cities, invested in a variety of companies both in and outside St. Joseph, and turned some of his fortune back to the city that had made him so successful, in the form of a grand opera house. Various charitable events and grand parties sponsored by his wife and children blazed like a comet over the city's social calendar [discussed further in Chapter 7]. When he died on January 2, 1887, he left his fortune estimated at between three and five million dollars, most of it in the form of various partnership agreements and real property, to his wife and three grown children. His stock portfolio contained a variety of holdings, including an insurance company, a stove company, a bank, the stockyards and grain exchange, a railroad, a blanket manufacturer, and stock in a local natatorium, a posh indoor

swimming pool club with limited membership. The total value of the portfolio amounted to $55,290, a small and financially cautious sum for a man of his resources. The amount of $89,412 remained outstanding as debts owed to his estate. John S. Lemon, Issac Hosea, and John Logan, all of whom had been in the dry goods business with him, served as administrators of his estate. The bulk of the fortune he left to his children existed in the value of his ongoing wholesale business, the largest in the city at that time, with gross receipts of approximately a million dollars per year. Milton Tootle could

Milton Tootle Sr. "King of the Wholesalers."
Courtesy of the Boder Collection

rightfully be called a millionaire and one of St. Joseph's richest men.[24] His sons, John J. and Milton Tootle Jr., became dominant figures in St. Joseph wholesaling and banking and expanded the family fortune.

MONEY ON THE HOOF

The growth of cities across the nation, particularly in the northeast, following the Civil War, had increased the demand for both fresh and processed meat. Local butchers found themselves unable to keep up with demand and the large slaughter houses of Chicago, Cincinnati, and eventually Kansas City found huge profits in supplying meat to millions of city dwellers who worked in factories and had neither room nor inclination to raise their own Sunday roast. That postwar boom in the meat packing industry had been partially stimulated by the arrival of inexpensive beef from Texas and later from the northern Great Plains region. Between 1866 and 1890, the label of "cattle kingdom" applied to the whole region. Railroads made the shipment of cattle to the packing plants and the eastern markets relatively economical, and the invention of the refrigerated car by Chicago meat packing giant Gustave Swift meant that fresh meat, no matter where slaughtered, would always be available. Kansas City's lead in developing a lucrative livestock market remained directly connected to its victory in the race for a bridge over the Missouri. Livestock buyers, meat packers, and interested investors in St. Joseph had some catching up to do, once their own bridge had been completed.

During the late 1860s, the Hannibal and St. Joseph Railroad operated a stockyards facility near its terminal on Walnut Street, just south of the city's main railroad station. It served primarily as a holding yard for cattle and hogs being shipped east over that line. Large numbers of hogs were still slaughtered locally for processing and shipment to the west, particularly Colorado. Drovers herded cattle from the St. Joseph area west to Colorado and beyond, both for meat and breeding. With the completion of the bridge, talk immediately turned to building a more substantial stockyard facility so that animals were not simply whisked through town but could actually be processed there. As one observer saw it and wrote in an editorial in the local paper: "Day after day great trains of cattle pass over the bridge and are whirled away to the East."[25]

In 1873, a group of investors formed the Union Stock Yards Company, and leased a five acre tract of land near the bridge and its juncture with other rail

133

lines coming into St. Joseph. The board of directors of the company included men from within and without the community. J. M. Walker, president of the Burlington line, and General James Craig, a St. Joseph resident and president of the Hannibal and St. Joseph line, brought in outside money, which again demonstrated a reluctance on the part of St. Joseph capitalist to invest in their own back yard. During its first year of operation it reported livestock shipment figures of 24,616 head of cattle, 69,000 hogs, and 1,100 horses.[26] Though seemingly impressive figures, the bulk of the cattle from Texas and the southern Great Plains passed through Kansas City, while the growing herds on the northern range passed through Omaha via the Union Pacific line. Because of the prodigious corn crops of northern Missouri and Iowa, St. Joseph's hinterland tended to favor hog production, as the figures indicate.

David Pinger, one of St. Joseph's prominent German immigrants, operated St. Joseph's most successful and growing meat packing operation from 1854 to 1865. After the war Pinger continued in the meat packing business with new partners, William Zook and J. C. Waterman, who showed interest in expansion. William Zook invested in the Union Stock Yard Company and served on its board of directors. The initial tie between stockyard operation and a meat packer had been established in St. Joseph. For a decade, Pinger & Co. stood as the city's leading packing house, though the Valley Packing Company, Hax & Brothers, and Hauck & Brothers also slaughtered hogs and shipped meat and lard to markets in Baltimore, Philadelphia, and New York.[27] While the total number of hogs slaughtered in St. Joseph, during the early 1870s, seems slight compared to figures for Chicago, it still meant St. Joseph had become an important regional packing center. For the year 1879, St. Joseph packers slaughtered 102,000 hogs compared to 1,315,000 in Chicago, but not far behind Kansas City with 124,000.[28] Joining the St. Joseph meat packing business in 1873, Henry Krug, of German immigrant stock, soon made a fortune from pork processing. and kept the St. Joseph pork packing industry growing steadily through the 1880s, as older firms, like Pinger's, eventually closed or sold out.

Cattle processing presented an entirely different story. St. Joseph had been bypassed as a major outlet for cattle produced in Texas and on the northern plains. Even cattle producers in northwest Missouri, who annually bred nearly 250,000 head of excellent and popular breeds of stock, shipped their cattle directly to Chicago for slaughter, or to the west to build new grazing herds.

Throughout the decades of the 1870s and 1880s, St. Joseph offered little or no incentive to cattle breeders or shippers, because of its small Union stockyard facility and no large scale beef slaughter plant. The most powerful influence in repressing St. Joseph's development of a beef processing industry had to be the major players in the "beef trust." Its members included the firms of Swift, Armour, and Wilson—powerful Chicago based meat packers—and the railroad monopolies that hauled the cattle. By charging more to haul cattle into St. Joseph than out, the city's major rail supplier, the Chicago, Burlington & Quincy, gave local breeders no other option than to ship to Chicago.[29]

Henry Krug, Senior. *Courtesy of the Boder Collection*

A remedy to that situation began to appear in the mid-1880s, when new rail lines, the Rock Island, the Grand Island and the Chicago Great Western, built connections to the city. Competition caused a dramatic drop in rail rates and St. Joseph became a more attractive place for transshipment. A further remedial action to expand the city's cattle business took the form of the new St. Joseph Stockyards Company, organized in November 1886. The primary promoter of the effort, James McCord, had already made his fortune as a partner in one of the city's largest wholesale grocery houses. He had become intimately aware that local butchers, not only in St. Joseph but across the nation, despite their protests, were being replaced by the big packers like Armour and Swift because of the convenience and quality of their processed meat. If St. Joseph kept up with the national trend, and hoped to exploit its position as a regional meat processing center, then the big companies would have to be attracted. The city needed a stockyard facility equal to the task of processing thousands of head of hogs and cattle every day. McCord approached one of the city's leading bankers, Charles B. France, and secured investment capital of $500,000. In June 1887, construction of the pens and an exchange building commenced on a 440 acre site on the

135

southern edge of the city. Six railroad companies agreed to build spurs to the site. By December 1887, the facility opened. France served as the stockyard company's first president. Henry Krug Jr. held a majority of the stock.[30]

Meat packers received free, 80 acres on the site if they would build a processing plant. But none of the big Chicago companies, like Swift or Armour, responded immediately. In the hope of protecting their investment and inducing outside interest, the company directors decided to build a packing plant from their own funds and eventually leased it to Allerton & Company of Chicago, a small scale packer, in 1888. It had the capacity to process 2,000 hogs per day. The *Herald* boasted: "It is well demonstrated that St. Joseph is the richest live stock connection in the United States, and it is a mere question of time when this will be the greatest livestock center in the West."[31] To further stimulate interest, the city of St. Joseph sold at public auction land on the south side of town and loaned the money to the stockyards company to build a modern, full scale beef processing plant. In October 1889, the Anchor Beef Packing Company leased the plant.[32] Unfortunately it failed within three years, and a New York consortium bought out its interest and formed the St. Joseph Packing and Transportation Company. The meat they processed found its way directly to eastern markets, representing a clear attempt on that company's part to circumvent the dominance of the Chicago based firms.[33]

Unfortunately, the *Herald's* 1889 boasting proved just that, and idle as well. Economic conditions across the nation turned sour again during the early 1890s, as another major depression seemed to follow the ten year cycle that had begun in the Panic in 1873 and revisited during the mid 1880s.[34] In 1892, another new packing plant for beef processing opened at the stockyards and was leased to the Moran Packing Company. But that company did not have the capitalization to develop a major operation like the Chicago-based giants, and along with the nation's economy in general, floundered along, well under production capacity. The St. Joseph stockyards moved large numbers of cattle and hogs, but the difference between the numbers received and the numbers shipped, equaling the quantity actually processed at the local plants, remained low. The Moran Company went out of business in September 1895, defaulting on a ten year lease and leaving the stockyards company with an empty processing plant and a $500,000 debt.[35]

The *Herald* lamented the situation of St. Joseph meat packers when in an editorial it stated: "Why hogs and cattle should not be brought here instead of

136

shipping them away is a mystery to the general public. There is no better point for packing in the whole West than here."[36] The paper put the blame on the stock yards, on the packing companies, on the railroads, and on the failure to advertise properly. But the actual problem could only be solved if a major packer could be attracted to set up shop in the city. John S. Donovan, a life long resident of the city and successful banker with interest in livestock brokering, fully understood the situation. Donovan convinced Gustave Swift, head of the Chicago based giant, to visit the city. Swift already appreciated St. Joseph's position as a major livestock transshipment point, because of its central location to numerous feeder operations throughout Northwest Missouri. Its rail connections provided more than adequate transportation facilities. Swift agreed to invest in the stock yards holding company, providing needed capital to reorganize and stabilize operations. In exchange, he became the controlling power behind the scene, able to direct the flow of livestock, by dictating the price and number of head, shipped to his packing plants, and also to a great extent controlling the supply to local packers. Ultimately, Swift committed to building a packing facility in St. Joseph, which opened on April 1, 1898. That facility proved the key to opening St. Joseph as a major national meat packing center, a position it had struggled to

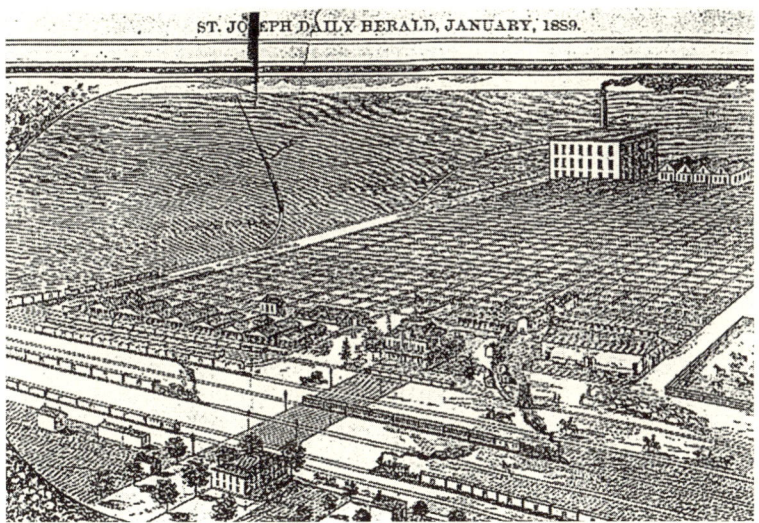

The St. Joseph Stockyards, 1889. *Courtesy of the Boder Collection*

attain for so long. Five years later, Armour & Company followed Swift's lead and a second giant of the packing industry made St. Joseph home.

By the end of the century, daily figures for livestock receipts placed St. Joseph among the top five livestock marketing centers and top ten meat processing centers in the nation. From a typical day in August 1899, the St. Joseph Stock Yards handled 4,613 hogs, 1,721 cattle, and 2,489 sheep. Of those numbers, Swift and Company bought more than half the total head for local processing, including over 3,000 hogs and 850 head of cattle. By comparison, on the same day, St. Louis reported receipts of 2,200 head of cattle, 4,500 hogs, and 2,600 sheep. Though it was a much larger city, the numbers are very close. Kansas City reported 8,600 head of cattle, 7,000 hogs, and 3,000 sheep. Omaha received 2,700 cattle, 10,200 hogs, and 800 sheep. And on the same day, the behemoth of the livestock world, Chicago, received by comparison, 1,500 cattle, 25,000 hogs, and 15,000 sheep.[37]

GOLDEN GRAIN

During the summer of 1873, the St. Joseph *Gazette* proudly announced, "The importance of having an elevator in St. Joseph has long been obvious, and some two weeks ago a company was formed for the purpose of erecting one." Thus began the bid by St. Joseph businessmen to initiate a new aspect of agricultural marketing in the city, following in the footsteps of Chicago, which had made grain elevators and the associated trade a mainstay of its booming economy.[38] Capital stock to build St. Joseph's first grain elevator amounted to $20,000. Within three weeks most of that had been subscribed to. M. M. Claggett and F. B. Kercheval, partners in one of the city's leading mills; Milton Tootle, the king of dry goods; and Louis Hax, a furniture manufacturer, purchased the majority of the shares. Claggett and Kercheval together owned 40 percent. The local market for flour and corn meal grew substantially after the war and area farmers produced greater yields from their fields each year. Having a central collecting point, an elevator, with a grain market close at hand, meant a great deal to local farmers who otherwise consigned their crop to the local railroad agent and hoped for the best once it reached market in some distant city. A local elevator and grain exchange would still rely on rail connections with the East, at favorable rates, and the fixing of the price of grain remained well within the inner sanctum of the big commodities brokers in places like Chicago and New York. People in St. Joseph knew that as well as they knew the power of the railroads as transporting agents. "The point for the location of the elevator has not yet been determined," the *Gazette* reported, "but it will be at some place easily accessible to all the railroad companies."[39]

Because St. Joseph stood on the edge of the Great Plains, a region rapidly becoming the recognized "grain basket" of the nation, its millers, like its meat packers, anticipated substantial success at becoming a great regional, even national processing center. No one believed that more than Randolph Truit Davis. Born in 1837, to one of the first families of Buchanan County, he grew up near Weston, south of St. Joseph in Platte County. A man with no advanced formal education, (he had to drop out of school due to family problems), he nonetheless proved to be ambitious. After a period of years trading in livestock, buying and selling farmland, and after having successfully operated a small mill in Platte County, Davis settled in St. Joseph in 1866. Davis sensed that the turmoil of the Civil War had not completely crippled the city's economy. In that year he bought half interest in a steam powered flour milling operation, owned by William Ridenbaugh, named the City Milling Company. It turned out a good quality flour, at 100 to 200 barrels per day. Under Davis' leadership and management, the mill soon expanded, producing 800 barrels of flour per day, and of vastly improved quality. By 1873 Davis had bought out junior partners in the firm and became the sole owner of City Milling.

Gradually Davis came to dominate St. Joseph milling by a number of different strategies. First, he captured the regional market by producing a superior product, called St. Joseph Number One white wheat flour, which by 1876 had achieved a national reputation for excellence. Second, he constantly moved within the circle of his fellow millers, forming partnerships, which he soon bought out, eliminating competition. Third, he experimented with new processes and products, always searching for better quality. An early type of research and development became particularly important to his milling empire. At the beginning of 1875, four major milling companies operated in the city: Star Mills, owned by J. Fairclough; Excelsior Mills, owned by Hauck & Brothers; Kercheval Mills, owned by F. B. Kercheval; and City Mills, owned by R. T. Davis & Co.. Together they processed 118,280 bushels of wheat and produced 58,154 sacks of flour, or 1.5 million pounds.[40] By 1876, Davis' firm stood "at the head of the list" of St. Joseph millers, and the *Herald* reported that his facilities "are the best mills in the city. In size—40 x 60 feet, solidly built of brick, four stories high. The building contains four runs of burrs and he has a grinding capacity of 1,000 bushels in 26 hours."[41]

Compared to the mammoth operations in other cities like Chicago and St. Paul, the capacity of the St. Joseph mills remained ˉelatively small. But St. Joseph flour sold widely throughout a four state area, thanks to its reputation for quality and its connections to St. Joseph's many wholesale grocery houses that promoted the hometown product. The best example of Davis's success in the milling business is tied to the development of a single product that well into the twentieth century remained a mainstay of American breakfast tables. It all began when Davis sold his first, and by then outmoded, mill to two St. Joseph business-men, Christian Rutt and Charles Underwood, in 1889. They proposed to manu-facture a specialty product, a pre-mixed, self-rising pancake flour, which had been developed in Rutt's kitchen and tested by a local librarian for content and nutritional value. The demand for such products grew from the ever increasing urban population in towns and cities across the nation. Working people, forced to live by the *time-clock*, wanted the convenience of foods which could be quickly prepared. Innovations in breakfast foods, like the corn flake, had already appeared, and pancakes had been popular on American breakfast tables since colonial times. Rutt concocted a mixture of hard wheat flour, corn meal, phosphate of lime, soda, and a trace of salt, which when combined with milk made an instant batter. While considering a name for the new product, Rutt happened across a cakewalk being performed at a black minstrel show in Chi-cago. The female performers strutted to the tune of "Aunt Jemima." Rutt liked the song. The sensation of a warm, inviting kitchen, presided over by a smiling mammy, caught his attention as being an attractive selling point; so he decided to christen his mill the Aunt Jemima Manufacturing Company, using the song's title for his new product as well.[42]

Davis saw the potential in Rutt's new product and purchased the Aunt Jemima facility in 1891. He then set about improving the pancake mix by adding rice flour, corn sugar, and powdered milk. That made the product truly "instant," for only water need be added. In 1893 Davis introduced his new improved product to the public at the Chicago World's Fair, which proved a splendid promotional setting. Davis had built a booth, shaped like a huge flour

140

barrel, and from it gave free pancake samples to thousands. A friendly African-American lady, named Nancy Green, worked at the booth. She wore the traditional costume of a southern plantation cook, with a long apron and her hair wrapped up in a bright bandanna. Green proved such a good salesperson that she received a medal and certificate from the fair's promoters for her showmanship.

Davis booked 50,000 orders from grocers for his product. More importantly, Nancy Green became Aunt Jemima, the famous image that graced millions of pancake mix boxes over the next century. Aunt Jemima became one of America's first great advertising icons and made the Davis family very rich.[43]

The flow of golden grain into the city of St. Joseph that did not find its way to the flour mills, went to the city's breweries, to become a deep golden liquid known as lager beer. Brewing activities in St. Joseph had started before the Civil War, coinciding with the arrival of the first German immigrant settlers. Fresh water springs that fed several small creeks coursing

R.T. Davis. *Courtesy of the Boder Collection*

through the city, most notably Smith's branch, proved attractive to beer makers. Joseph Kuechle, an immigrant who had recently passed though Louisville, Kentucky, started the town's first lager beer brewery in 1849.[44] Following the war, St. Joseph's most substantial brewing operation belonged to the Goetz family, headed by Michael K. Goetz. At first, a few local taverns consumed the brewery's total output. By 1870, the Goetz facilities at the corner of Sixth and Ablemarle Streets, on the near north side of the city, had to be expanded as the reputation for the beer's quality spread. As they did for other St. Joseph products, the local papers provided unwavering promotion. The *Herald* stated in an 1877 article: "This year they are making an article of beer that cannot be surpassed anywhere in the country. We would ask of our many saloon keepers in the city and neighboring towns to give this firm a trial, and we venture the assertion it will give more satisfaction to the lovers of good beer than that imported from other cities. Messrs. Goetz & Co., Brewers, do not intend to let foreign brewers surpass them in the make of good beer. Thousands of people who have drank this season of beer manufactured at the City Brewery pronounce it the best beer, *which is a fact.*"[45] One can only assume that the editors had done some free sampling at the brewery before writing the article.

St. Joseph boasted five breweries by 1880, with the Goetz operation clearly the largest. But competition between brewers to capture the "taste" market share remained fierce. The New Ulm Brewery provided close competition for the Goetz product from the mid-1870s on. The Ohnesorg family, doing business as Ohnesorg & Son, owned the New Ulm and had brought their brewing skills with them directly from Europe. A business report in the *Herald* stated: "Mr. Ohnesorg, is the grand centre and motive power of the New Ulm Brewery and he will not let any other institution in the same business surpass him in making a better beverage." The New Ulm boasted that its beer "is in every respect pure, palatable and in general favor as the Cincinnati or Milwaukee beer." Its yearly capacity of 5,000 barrels reportedly sold out early at the beginning of each brewing season.[46]

THE BANKER'S CLUB

Prior to the Civil War, the banking houses of St. Joseph had been private, and in many cases, storefront operations. Storefront in the sense that the city's wealthier merchants were also its money lenders, mortgage holders, and monetary exchanges. Following the war, a series of new financial institutions, both banks and savings companies, sought to bring a measure of stability and safety to those citizens wealthy enough to need more than the "tin can in the back yard" approach to personal finance and capital acquisition. However, those working toward developing a true banking industry in St. Joseph remained members of the city's mercantile elite, culled from the ranks of wholesale barons, meat packers, and millers.

Between 1870 and 1900, at least twenty banks operated at various times in the city, but within that group constant reorganization, closings, and consolidations took place regularly, as partnerships changed and as the economic cycle of the community, the state, and the nation produced an ebb and flow of both credit and hard currency. What emerged from the fiscal chaos of that age, for St. Joseph at least, was a small group of money men, who built their own private fortunes, and three or four institutions with the staying power to last into the twentieth century. First among the city's prominent bankers stood Able Saxton, who began his business career in dry goods and who by the early 1870s had helped create [at that time] the city's largest bank, the State Savings Bank. His protégé and former chief cashier in earlier banking operations, C. B. France, became the president of the institution as Mr. Saxton moved to the board of directors and eventually organized a new venture in 1883, as the Saxton National Bank. The State Savings Bank boasted of being the first city bank to have over $1 million in assets, by the early 1880s. As already mentioned, France used the assets of his bank to broker the deal creating the St. Joseph Stock Yards Company. Of the State Savings Bank's eight member board of directors, five were prominent wholesalers.[47]

JAMES NELSON BURNES
Courtesy of the Boder Collection

The Burnes family, headed by James N. Burnes, in business with his brother Calvin F., also held a prominent position in St. Joseph banking. In December 1874, they opened the Bank of St. Joseph, which nine years later reorganized as the National Bank of St. Joseph. It remained in family control until 1905, when it consolidated with the First National Bank of Buchanan County. By the turn of the century it had outstripped the deposits of all other city banks. The "Burnes ring," as the brothers were sometimes referred to, demonstrated an ambition bordering on ruthlessness in acquiring new business ventures, which at one time included the city's municipal waterworks.[48]

The German-American element of the city, periodically congregated in its churches, schools, social clubs, and businesses. Likewise it had its own banking. A German Savings Bank had operated for a short time during the period 1869-1870, when it had been founded and housed in a new building by pork processor, David Pinger. When Pinger withdrew his support, the Burnes brothers absorbed the bank building and assets, though the firm of Schuster, Hax & Company attracted many of Pinger's ethnic depositors. Another prominent pork packer of

143

Germanic immigrant stock, Henry Krug, organized the German American Bank in 1887, along with J. G. Schneider and other citizens of German decent. That institution generally ranked second among all banks in deposits and assets in the city, further demonstrating the strength of the German community. Not until 1918, when it became highly unpopular to be associated with anything German, did the bank change its name to simply the American National Bank.

One family already dominating the wholesale sector of the economy also became prominent in the banker's club. In 1889, the financial fortune of the Tootles merged with the also substan-

John S. Lemon. *Courtesy of the Boder Collection*

tial dry goods fortune of John S. Lemon to form the Tootle Lemon & Company firm, general bankers. Thomas E. Tootle, brother of Milton, represented their family interests in the beginning. When Milton Tootle Jr. came of age he moved into his uncle's position and became the more noted banker of the family. His brother, John J. Tootle, and their mother, Kate, remained primary operators of the wholesale business, though they also got into banking. All of the Tootle children, including their sister Frances, had inherited substantial fortunes from their father, wholesale magnate Milton Tootle Sr., and in turn invested and built large sums on their own. Routinely the Tootles and Lemon restructured their banking company, periodically taking in new partners to spread out the capital risk. For example, in 1896 Thomas Tootle and Lemon formed a partnership with James McCord and Samuel M. Nave, both wholesale giants in their own right. They capitalized their banking operation at $100,000, each of the four contributing $25,000.[49]

Two years later, in 1898, that partnership dissolved, with Milton Tootle Jr. and Lemon continuing their bank operation with Graham G. Lacy. Lacy came into the partnership without having to put up any capital. Tootle and Lemon each offered $50,000. Lacy had recently married into the Tootle family, and due

144

to an obvious bit of nepotism found himself in a lucrative situation, being named head cashier. By modern standards the bank partners agreed to pay themselves modest monthly salaries. Lemon drew $416.16 per month while Tootle took only $250 and Lacy $208.33 with an additional $500 twice per year [possibly a bonus for being nice to his in-laws].[50] Of course in 1898 dollars, they were by no means paupers, when by comparison their tellers and bookkeepers took home less than $100 per month, and general laborers barely $50. Their real income came in the form of dividends they paid themselves on their capital investments.

Nearly all the St. Joseph banks used the clearing house established by the city's leading bankers in 1877, to process their drafts, checks, and other paper transactions. During the mid-1880s those transactions averaged from $100,000 to $150,000 per business day. By 1899, that figure had reached as high as $600,000 per day. Total deposits over the period 1870-1900 rose steadily but never dramatically. In 1870, total deposits in city banks stood just under $40 million. By 1875, they were $48 million, and at the turn of the century twice that amount. Yet St. Joseph never escaped the dominance of the major banks in larger cities, particularly St. Louis, on which the smaller St. Joseph banks depended for backup invesment paper and cash.[51]

The State Savings Bank, 1880. *Courtesy of the Boder Collection*

Despite what appeared on paper as a healthy local banking industry, very little money appeared to be available for major industrial or other capital improvements in the city. Outside venture capital from St. Louis or Chicago or New York was nearly always sought for anything of size, be it railroad building or expansion, the stockyards, or the packing plants. St. Joseph banks held plenty of money, but the private financial empires that controlled it seemed reluctant to let it go for anything remotely risky. Diversification appeared attractive, but only if it seemed absolutely safe. In the financial game of cards, most of St. Joseph's elite, be they in wholesaling, milling, meat packing, brewing, or banking, tended to play their hands very close to their chests and abstain from bluffing. After all, it appears that their private empires and fortunes were so intertwined, maybe more so than in any other city, that they played with each other's money. Many of them were very rich for their day, but how many of them actually became part of the city's fabled clan of millionaires remains questionable. If there was a prototype of the entrepreneurs that St. Joseph's economic community produced, a good example would be someone like John S. Lemon. He may be no more distinguished than any other of his class, but fortunately many of his personal papers survive and can be examined to restructure a bit of his own financial world and illustrate how a rich man made it in St. Joseph.

THE FORTUNES OF A ST. JOSEPH MILLIONAIRE

John S. Lemon had southern roots. He was born in Bullitt County, Kentucky, in 1833. Industrious, but with little family money or formal education, he made his way to St. Joseph by 1850, and immediately found work as a clerk in one of the rapidly growing mercantile houses catering to the needs of the California and Oregon emigrants. By living frugally and turning his salary back into the company, he became a junior partner within two years. By 1861, he acquired enough capital of his own to open a dry goods house in partnership with William Hosea. That partnership lasted until 1871, when Hosea withdrew and the firm, renamed John S. Lemon & Company, came into being. In late 1873, due to ill health, Lemon withdrew from the wholesale jobber business and sold out to John S. Brittain [who continued as a leading dry goods wholesaler in the city, often only second to the Tootle concern in volume of business]. A balance sheet from April 1874, following the settling of accounts from his dry goods business, showed Lemon with a bottom line of $170,713.06, a substantial fortune for that period of history.[52]

After a couple of years of convalescence his health seems to have recovered, although there is no mention in his papers as to the nature of his illness. He turned his attention to a number of new financial interests, including the woolen industry, real estate both in and out of St. Joseph, pure bred cattle, a dairy farm,

146

and a dabbling of stocks. He served on the board of directors of several firms, held the office of secretary or vice president in several others, and even got himself elected to the St. Joseph city council for a term in 1880. A look inside his stock portfolio reveals the diverse interests of a nineteenth-century man of substance. From 1874 through the end of the century, documents and certificates show that Lemon owned shares of stock in the St. Joseph Fire and Marine Insurance Company, the St. Joseph Hospital Medical College, the Lake Park Club Association, the Merchants Insurance Company, the St. Joseph and Eastern Railroad Company, the Turner Coal Company, Commercial Bank of St. Joseph, the Benton Club House Company, and the St. Joseph Natatorium Association. His largest single stock holdings rested in the East St. Joseph Town Company, 200 shares, value $20,000, and the Chicago, Kansas and Nebraska Railway Company, 25 shares, value $2,500.[53]

Besides stock investments, some substantial, others quite minuscule, Lemon owned his own livestock company, which operated in Kearny, Nebraska. From that operation he traded in beef cattle from Texas to Colorado to Montana. He also had an interest in pure bred dairy cattle, including Holstein-Friesians and to a greater extent Jerseys, the breed from which he drew the name of his Jersey Park Farm Dairy. Lemon made a modest profit from fresh milk sold in the city.[318]

Having earned substantial "seed money" in the wholesale trade, Lemon added to the bulk of his fortune from three sources. Primarily he built his financial strength through his banking partnerships with Thomas E. Tootle and later Milton Tootle Jr., associations which he began relatively late in his life. Documents also indicate that for a time he owned stock in St. Louis banking concerns as well.[55] Additionally, he made money through woolens manufacturing. Lemon held a substantial interest in the Buell Manufacturing Company of St. Joseph, a major supplier of blankets, clothing articles, and bulk fabric to many dry goods wholesalers in the city. Among his personal papers can be found a handwritten notebook in which he kept track of current prices for all types of woolen goods produced by Buell. Documents indicate that he and a consortium of his personal friends and "financial" family gradually bought out the majority of the Buell family's interests in the manufacturing company by the turn of the century. Among those in partnership with Lemon in controlling Buell, Milton Tootle's widow, Kate, and children, Frances, John, and Milton Jr., as well as William and John Fairleigh and John Logan, all from families of substance in both wholesaling and real estate and all connected through marriage to other city elite. Yearly dividend checks from Buell to each member of the circle ranged up to $5,000. The relationship between the Tootle and Lemon families stood on more than just banking partnerships. They were personal friends and John Lemon served as one of the executors of Milton Tootle Sr.'s estate, helping his widow, Kate, conduct a number of business transactions. He also exercised power of attorney over John Tootle's estate as his health declined.[56]

Probably the most substantial part of Lemon's wealth lay in his real estate holdings. In the city itself he held stock in a number of real estate, or "town," companies. He also owned a number of tracts around the city, from lots in the older Robidoux Addition on the west side, where his impressive Victorian mansion still stands, to the upscale Brookdale addition on the east side. Besides town property he owned farmland outside the city, as well as real estate investments in Nebraska, Kansas, and Texas. One document reveals he bought 91 acres of land near Monique, Texas, in partnership with Milton Tootle Jr.[57] Included among his diverse real estate holdings were family plots in the Mount Mora Cemetery, which cost him $152.

A bank statement from his own institution, dated May 1901, indicated that from the beginning of the year Lemon had made total deposits in his personal account of over $83,000, yet the actual balance in the account on the day of the statement stood at just $7,098.65. A tidy sum, but hardly what one would expect to find in a "millionaire's" account. But he and his family lived well and traveled in the circles of the city's financial elite. His name and that of his wife and children graced newspaper reports of every major social event, and they traveled first class wherever they went. Among his papers one can find a pass from one of the railroad companies for a private coach to take Lemon or members of his family to and from the train depot. His wife and daughters traveled to Paris, France, stayed with personal friends there, and wrote him about the wonderful time they were having.[58]

During the last two years of his life, he retired from the day to day operation of his banking and real estate interests. John Lemon died on March 17, 1905. His family incorporated his estate in the amount of $50,000, divided equally between his wife Annie, and their four children, Florence, Mary, Hal, and Letitia.[59] If John Lemon made it to the rank of millionaire, then he had done so in the same fashion as Milton Tootle: through acquiring real assets, land and business holdings, and not through buying stocks and bonds or through cash accumulation.

The ultimate question about the number of millionaires living in St. Joseph is a moot point. Whether or not there were one or a hundred does not diminish the fact many men of substance lived in the city by the turn of the century. The best evidence of that can be seen in the number of fine Victorian mansions that dotted the hills of the city, ranging from Fifth Street just north of the commercial district, to the east, into the new suburbs along Felix and Francis Streets and Frederick Avenue. Those architectural wonders of brick and stone and wood, ornate and turreted, reflected an air of wealth that would have fit into the finest neighborhoods of the wealthy in St. Louis, Chicago or New York. Undeniably, men made money and built private fortunes in St. Joseph. And, as elsewhere in cities of size and importance, during the last three decades of the nineteenth century, one who looked for the reflection of America's "gilded age" could find it there.

CHAPTER 7

Becoming a Modern City
1870-1900

The historian many consider to be the father of American urban history, Arthur Meier Schlesinger, called the age between 1878-1898 the period of the rise of the city. He did so for a number of reasons: some demographic, some economic, and some simply dynamic. According to Schlesinger the growth of so many of America's great cities during that period, when urban populations doubled and tripled, was tied to the massive influx of both native and foreign born persons, attracted away from the farms and small towns, by jobs created as the result of the new industrial age.[1] In subscribing to his thesis, there are elements of it that fit St. Joseph, even though Schlesinger's focus tends to point more to the great metropolises that evolved during that age and became not only American urban behemoths but truly world class cities. Though not a great industrial center, St. Joseph's economy, firmly grounded in its wholesale trade, benefited from the vast array of new products made available to the consuming public as a result of the new industrialism.[2]

It is easy to get lost in nineteenth century urban history in the excitement of New York, Chicago, or San Francisco; yet the characteristics of urban development during that explosive period of growth, described by Schlesinger, share common threads with urban communities of lesser size, like St. Joseph. The rapid growth of urban populations created problems that overwhelmed the experience and abilities of those who attempted to run the cities. Sometimes the problems found solutions, sometimes not. Cities developed dynamics of their own; whether the people running them did their job well or badly. Cities still grew and spread and constantly reinvented or redefined their own boundaries, physically and socially. As Schlesinger said, because of the concentration of people, and of wealth, and inventiveness to deal with the problems of that concentration, cities became the cradle of modern progress in all areas of society: "In the city were to be found the best schools, the best churches, the best newspapers, and virtually all the bookstores, libraries, art galleries, museums, theaters and opera houses. It is not surprising that the great cultural advance of

150

the time came out of the city, or that its influence should ramify to the farthest countryside."[3]

The transformation of St. Joseph from a frontier town and mercantile outpost into a city with all the refinements of her larger counterparts reflected all the speed and ingenuity and progress of those bigger urban centers without some of the accompanying problems, such as immense immigrant populations, and subsequent slums, ghettoes, and political machinery. Like a teenage boy hitting a growing spurt, St. Joseph went on a building binge between 1870 and 1900. New additions of land to the city, doubling and redoubling the miles of streets, a new county courthouse, a new city hall, federal building, police station, numerous firehouses, a state hospital, and an opera house all fed the frenzy of the rush to become a modern city. But what made a city truly modern related to its ability to adapt to the basic needs of its population and supply such urban necessities as utilities, a safe water supply and sanitation, public transportation, schools, libraries, parks, police and fire protection, and public health. By developing those areas of urban life the city could attract new economic interests and possibly expand its hinterland. St. Joseph showed advancements in all those areas as it rushed to transform itself into a modern city in the last three decades of the nineteenth century and compete with other urban centers of the Great Plains region.

MODERN CITY SERVICES

In 1870, with a population just under 20,000, most of St. Joseph's streets remained unpaved, although periodic grading took place, and the laying of cobble stone and macadamizing had begun on business district thoroughfares. By 1880, the city had 112 miles of streets, of which only 24 had been paved with cobblestone. The quality of the stone used was reported as "frequently very inferior."[4] City residents repaired the streets in front of their own property or contracted with individual street repair companies to do the work for them. If the city had to order the repair work done, then the citizen received a corresponding assessment in that amount from the city. Apparently most of the property owners in St. Joseph liked that system over one in which the city provided all street repair services.[5] The city did own a steam powered rock crusher for producing gravel, but lacked a roller or much other maintenance equipment at that time.

151

Maintenance of sidewalks also remained the domain of the property owner with brick being the most popular paving material, as in nearly all other cities of that period. By the end of the century, the city had 51 miles of paved streets, primarily brick and macadam, but an additional 138 miles of unpaved thoroughfares.[6]

Little or no public transportation existed in 1870, with the exception of private horse cabs for hire and an omnibus line, started back in 1859. By 1880, the city had three horse drawn street railways, the Citizens Railway Company, the Union Railway Company, and the St. Joseph & Lake Narrow Gauge Street Railway, with a combined six miles of track, 32 cars, and 110 horses. The rider paid five cents for a ride between the suburbs, at that time as far out as Twentieth Street, and the central business district.[7] The Union Railway Company proved the most popular for a decade because it had the longest run of track and provided wintertime riders with a stove in every car. However, in 1887, the conversion from horse drawn power to electric power began when the former St. Joseph & Lake company reorganized under the leadership of Thomas Tootle and Joseph Corby as the People's Street Railway, Electric Light and Power Company. The conversion to electric motors heralded in a new age of transportation in St. Joseph and by the turn of the century over 32 miles of streetcar track had been laid and carried the bulk of commuters to and from work.[8]

In 1870, most houses in the city still used wells or cisterns for fresh water. Not until December 10, 1879, did the city council and mayor approve an ordinance to build a city water works under contract to the St. Joseph Water Company. By early 1880, installation of a powerful steam pump and the laying of mains throughout much of the city began. The growing population and the number of new homes and buildings mandated a new water delivery system for fire protection as well as for a reliable, if not always sanitary, source of drinking water. A principal part in the contract for water service required that 240 fire hydrants be installed. The initial system took water from the Missouri River at a rate of between two and five million gallons per day and pumped it into reservoirs north of the city and 300 feet in elevation above the river. Because the reservoirs stood over 100 feet above the highest point in the city, enough pressure existed to eliminate the steam powered pumpers used earlier by the city's fire companies. As far as purification went, the water flowed into two large settling basins and passed through a large copper strainer into an affluent well before flowing by gravity into the city mains. The municipal water system

152

produced an income of over $100,000 per year for its stockholders, among them prominent bankers, the Burnes brothers, and the city's largest saddle and harness maker, William Wyeth. They sold their local control of the water company to the American Waterworks and Guarantee Company of Pittsburgh, Pennsylvania, in 1889, a firm which managed the water systems of 31 other cities around the country.[9]

The city licensed a number of different gas works companies during the nineteenth century, which provided gas lighting for the streets. Several companies laid mains throughout the city as gas lighting for homes became more popular, replacing candles and kerosene lamps. Because of competition between suppliers, St. Joseph residents got bargain prices for the gas they used. By 1897, a number of small companies had been consolidated as the St. Joseph Gas Company, with its headquarters in New York City, but controlled locally by W. A. P. McDonald, one of the wholesale titans of the city. At the turn of the century, St. Joseph consumers paid about $1.25 per thousand cubic feet.[10]

St. Joseph's first electric company appeared in 1883, created by a consortium of local entrepreneurs headed by Joseph Corby. That company provided only arc lighting, which hissed and glared as the energy leaped between two open electrical leads. Though suitable for outdoor use such as street lamps or in a large industrial setting, it presented a danger when used within the confines of a smaller typical household room. After four years that company became part of the People's Street Railway, Electric Light and Power Company, the first to provide incandescent lighting based on Thomas Edison's model of power producing dynamos, overhead power lines, and household light bulbs. Though gaslights, with improved Wesbach mantles used to adjust the flame, remained the most popular form of lighting in nineteenth century St. Joseph, every year saw more miles of electrical line hung as the modern convenience of electric lighting eventually prevailed. In 1889, the city assumed the process of changing street lighting over from gas to electricity. The city built its own powerhouse and by the turn of the century had installed over 400 arc type street lamps.[11]

The world of modern, rapid communication began with the arrival of the telegraph in St. Joseph during the 1850s. The next step in the technological advance came in the form of Alexander Graham Bell's telephone, which appeared in St. Joseph shortly after its national debut in 1876 at the Philadelphia Centennial Exposition. In 1877, John Kenmuir, a jeweler installed the first telephone

153

line in the city, connecting his shop with his residence some seven blocks away. Quickly, the St. Joseph fire department adopted the telephone to call in alarms, wiring the chief's house to two stations that same year. By 1879, the St. Joseph Telephone company, headed by Kenmuir and Joseph Corby, began selling phone service to city residents. Within a few months they had set up a central office, a switchboard, and had attracted 150 subscribers. The monthly charge amounted to two dollars. Shortly after, the Western Union Telegraph Company began a short-lived venture into the telephone business, as did the National Bell Telephone Company, which absorbed the latter two fledgling company's subscribers. Two other local companies tried to compete with the Bell giant through the 1890s, but by the turn of the century the Bell monopoly appeared well on its way to closing them out of business. Like elsewhere in the United States, most of the subscribers were in the business or professional community, with less than one in fifty private homes wired for service in the city by 1900.[12]

As American cities burgeoned during the late nineteenth century, drawing in millions of new people, they developed as centers of economic and social advancement; but they also produced, as a result of that advancement, all the less desirable by-products, tons of trash and refuse. While huge cities like New York, Philadelphia, and Chicago presented apparently insurmountable problems of cleanliness, so too did smaller cities like St. Joseph. Early in its history, the city government had in its power the right to call citizens into the streets for cleaning and grading. By 1880, the city had given up on that premise and assumed the duty. The office of street commissioner oversaw a small force of sweepers, who did all the work by hand. The annual budget stood at about $10,000. The central business district received a cleaning about every two weeks, with the refuse dumped directly into the Missouri River. The cleaning, "done very poorly," benefited only a small but politically influential part of the community. A census bureau report stated, "the whole system is very defective." [13] By the turn of the century the street conditions had not improved much, as the *Herald* lamented in an article from early 1900: "At the present time the paved streets are covered with several inches of mud and filth. The city wagons were busy yesterday trying to clear the crossings but the mud was soon carried over them again by the vehicles which passed to and fro and the efforts were practically in vain."[14] When it became apparent the small force of city sweepers and wagons could not possibly keep up with the task, the Business Men's Association hired twelve of its own sweepers, called the "white wings" because of their white duck coats and caps, to supplement the city workers.

Sewerage presented an old and continuous problem. Private homes for the most part, still had a privy in the back yard, but business and industry, particularly the breweries and meat packing plants, required much improvement in handling their volume of waste. Prior to 1870, open creeks served as sewers with the resulting nuisance of noxious odors and an ugly view. By 1880 a system of sewer mains had been initiated, built of brick and ranging in diameter from five to ten feet. The mains generally followed the routes of natural drainage, meaning the formerly open creeks that crossed the city, running toward the Missouri River. Sewerage dumped into those mains trickled untreated into the river, but if the water level rose during flood stage, it backed up through the mains and went nowhere. Periodically, heavy rains flushed the system as water rushed into a few street inlets or basins which also served as vents for the system. When no rain came and the system grew too foul smelling, the fire department opened their water mains to flush it out. Lateral lines to new residential districts and businesses appeared as construction boomed, but apparently the city had no concise plan for its overall sewer layout, nor any organized plan to connect homes to it.[15]

Numerous city ordinances dealt with removal of private garbage "before it became offensive, but the law was poorly enforced," resulting in a system that, "was poor and indifferently executed."[16] The city apparently provided some garbage removal in the process of street cleaning, and some private haulers or scavengers picked up dry waste, trash and garbage from the alleyways behind private homes. Liquid sewage, from newly installed household water closets, baths, and kitchen drains flowed into the city sewers, from the few homes connected to the very limited system. Other homes and businesses had their own cesspools, dry wells, or old cisterns no longer used for fresh water, but when those got full they simply overflowed into the streets or created foul little swamps in yards. Some people whose homes were not actually connected to the sewer system carried their garbage and bed chamber slop to locations where there were sewer inlets or basins for storm water and dumped it directly in. That practice, though it apparently provided a good dumping site for the individual residents, proved to be a nuisance when too many started taking advantage of it. In 1885, the *Herald* published a report on the practice saying: "The people residing near the point on Main street where the sewer crosses Blacksnake creek, are complaining terribly of the stench arising from the accumulation of filth and rubbish thrown into the creek. A large pool of stagnant water there is covered with a thick, nauseous scum that is very offensive and obnoxious, rendering the whole surrounding neighborhood almost uninhabitable. This manner of complaint will not only apply to this point, but also to many other points along various sewers in the city, and should be looked after by the city authorities for the protection of the health of all citizens residing adjacent to the sewers and inlets."[17]

City ordinance required privy vaults to be at least eight feet deep, but enforcement proved lax and the cleaning and maintenance of vaults remained at the discretion of the property owner. Seepage into the subsoil could contaminate a neighbor's well from which fresh water for drinking might still be drawn right next door. Even in 1880, hogs still provided the valuable service of consuming sewage and slop. Some dead animals, particularly horses or cows, that lay in the streets eventually got hauled to the glue factory near the stock yards, but anything smaller, like dogs or cats, were collected by the street cleaners and dumped into the city's main sewer. In fact, all garbage collected throughout the city, from whatever source, wound up usually dumped in the Missouri River which carried it off to St. Joseph's sister cities down stream.

St. Joseph had established a Board of Health in the 1840s, and by the 1880s, its role had changed little. It consisted of a board member from each of the city's wards, a health officer, and a hospital steward. Except during an epidemic, its yearly expenses barely reached $4,000, of which $500 went to the salary of the physician appointed as health officer. One to three nuisance-inspectors worked the streets, making rounds of the city during warm weather, but during cool months responded only when requested. Their primary job involved looking for sewage disposal violations and checking out reports of contagious diseases, like small pox or scarlet fever, but they were also called on to do such jobs as check for open wells and cisterns what might swallow up children or livestock. An editorial in the *Gazette* aimed at city health inspectors called for action: "Open wells in exposed places within the city limits should be looked after by city authorities. Yesterday a valuable cow was lost in one of those traps on Highly street,—On Eighteenth street, near Jones street, there is another well, completely open, and is just in the way of the children attending the Webster school, and a more sad accident than the loss of a cow may any day occur at this place."[18] They could not arrest anyone, but had to report the complaint to the city attorney, who made the decision whether or not to file a formal charge.

At the beginning of the 1870s the city owned a hospital building, a filthy two room shack on the bluffs north of the city, referred to as a "pest-house".[19] The city used it for the isolation of indigents or persons who could not afford the care of a private physician or hospital accommodations. The city eventually put up a brick structure, 20x40 feet, to handle the sick, and added a second story to it by 1880. However, financial support for the city hospital came from of all things, a dog license tax, and it remained grossly under funded and woefully lacking in both the quality and quantity of caring treatment. In the case of infectious diseases, the health officer could order a house quarantine. Vaccination against small pox was compulsory in the city for school children but apparently enforcement lagged far behind. Health record keeping remained a hit or miss proposition as many of the people in St. Joseph "have not yet learned the benefits of statistics, and look upon laws requiring statistical information as an invasion of individual rights," according to a report published by the census bureau.[20]

For anyone who could afford to pay for medical treatment the number of doctors proved quite adequate in St. Joseph. Not only were there plenty of practicing physicians in the city, but it also boasted several ongoing medical schools, turning out new doctors. They included the St. Joseph Hospital Medical College, founded in 1876; the College of Physicians and Surgeons, 1879; the Ensworth Hospital Medical College, formed by the merger of the latter two; and the Northwestern Medical College, which began training doctors in 1881 and merged into another school around 1895. Nearly all of the city's prominent practicing physicians served on the faculties of those colleges at one time or another.[21]

Those ill of mind and not necessarily of body could also find treatment in St. Joseph. Beginning in 1874, the state operated the State Lunatic Asylum, Number Two, in St. Joseph, after the only other state facility for the mentally ill at Fulton became over- crowded. A wooded, gently rolling site of 120 acres had been selected just east of the city limits for the hospital, and the first frame structures to house inmates quickly opened. Those earliest buildings burned to the ground in 1879, and subsequently larger brick structures took their place. The hospital grew throughout the rest of the century, housing most of the hundreds of the state's inmates suffering mild to moderate symptoms of mental

157

illness, while the Fulton facility took in the more desperate or criminally insane.[22]

The burial of deceased persons received only minor regulation from the board of health, and that concerned itself only with the provision of a death certificate from the attending physician. The city had embalmers and a well-established mortuary business, but many who did not want the expense or could not afford it prepared the body in the home. Mount Mora, the major cemetery, covered about ten acres just east of the business district, on Thirteenth Street. The city's Catholics, Jews, Baptists, and even the Freemasons had their own smaller private cemeteries.[23] The Board of Health had no required annual report, and the health officer's report to the mayor rarely found its way into print.

The city of St. Joseph attempted to provided its people with fire protection as both the population and physical size of the city grew. By 1870, volunteer companies gave way to a paid professional department, which at first consisted of only two men and two horses to operate a steam powered engine. Subsequently a hook and ladder and rescue company formed, stationed in the heart of the business district. With the advent of a central water system, the city retired or sold its old steam engines, began filling in the cisterns, and added hose reel companies as strategic sites. By the turn of the century the department had grown to 68 regular members and 36 horses manning eight full time stations, with 15 hose reel apparatus holding 14,650 feet of hose. The city could boast one of the lowest rates of fire loss of any of the nation's 100 largest cities.[24]

Public protection from crime lay in the hands of the city police force. Until 1887, the city marshal, who was appointed by the mayor and city council, headed the police force. Twenty uniformed patrolmen guarded the city, serving patrol tours from 7 P.M. to 7 A.M. The city provided them with their navy blue uniforms, fashioned similar to police uniforms in other American cities of the period, and gave them night sticks, but the patrolmen had to bring their own revolvers. Two special policemen, early plainclothes detectives, who reported to the major and city marshal only, worked independently of the patrolmen. City police recorded over 1,700 arrests in 1880, most for public drunkenness, prostitution, and disorderly conduct. There were also more serious crimes and an occassional murder in St. Joseph. The most noted of the nineteenth century took place in April, 1882. It involved the death of the outlaw Jesse James, who was shot by a fellow outlaw named Robert Ford. [25]

After the city adopted a new charter in 1885, a push began to organize a metropolitan system.[26] The city instituted that system in 1887, with the appointment of three police commissioners, by the governor, to manage the police department. The office of chief of police replaced the town marshal. William Tullar, the last town marshal, became the first chief, simply by changing his title. Besides the chief, a captain and two sergeants oversaw the duties of about fifty patrolmen, detectives, and drivers by the end of the century. Besides the policemen on the street, the city also employed a humane officer, a matron, an engineer, and three telephone operators to handle calls. Most of those taken into custody went before the police court to pay fines or post bail. The adoption of a metropolitan system stood out as an attempt at reform in most cities, but it did not stamp out corruption completely. Police officers and judges received a set salary under the new system, as opposed to the old fee system frequently abused by unscrupulous patrolmen or town marshals of the past.

Ultimately, how well the city provided services depended on which end of the socio-economic spectrum a person occupied. If Milton Tootle could afford all the latest utilities and a private street cleaner, then his position differed from that of someone who lived on an unpaved road with no sewer or water line, and to whom the telephone still lay another century away. As in all other American cities during the late nineteenth century, there existed in St. Joseph clearly defined class lines, based on the ability to acquire wealth and the visible trappings of happiness that went with it.

GAIETY AND LIGHT

On the evening of December 9, 1872, one of the great social events of St. Joseph's nineteenth century society calendar blazed in like a comet. Milton Tootle, the city's leading wholesale merchant, decided in late 1871 that St. Joseph society needed a proper opera house. Work soon began on the building, located at the corner of Fifth and Francis streets, in the heart of the business district. Designed by architect Walter Angelo Powell, the project cost Tootle $165,000. Seats on the orchestra floor, designed for comfort, had ample leg room, and there were two balcony levels. On each side of the orchestra pit were large boxes, two on each side at both levels. The Tootle family reserved the front right box for themselves. One of the largest chandeliers in the state hung gracefully over the orchestra pit, glittering crystal, yet utterly modern. Lighting came from gas with an electric ignition. Only two other opera houses of that advanced technology existed in the United States.[27] Tootle could afford it.

When the Tootle Opera House opened on the evening of December 9, 1872, it elicited rave reviews, including the claim to being the grandest opera house west of St. Louis. The next morning the *Herald* described the scene: "The largest and most brilliant audience that ever assembled in St. Joseph gathered at the Opera-house last night, to witness the opening of this magnificent temple of amusement by the peerless Maggie Mitchell. Miss Mitchell herself, with her wide popularity and splendid reputation, was enough to draw a rousing house, but everybody in the city, except a few old fogies, wanted to get a look inside the splendid structure when lighted by gas and filled with people. Both these causes contributed to bring out the entire city."[28]

Of course, Milton Tootle attended the opening of his grand palace and did not go unrecognized for his contribution to the city's culture. The article in the *Herald* continued: "Before the play began, one of the actors appeared before the curtain and read a long dedicatory poem. At the close of the recitation, Milton Tootle's name was spoken and as soon as it was announced a loud cheer arose from all parts of the house to hear a word or two from the man whose munificence and enterprise had reached such a large and beautiful edifice. In response to the general call made upon him, Mr. Tootle came out upon the stage and made a speech of welcome."[29]

The *Herald's* editor heaped further praise on Tootle saying: "Milton Tootle has prospered in this community: here in St. Joseph he has accumulated a vast fortune, and here he has expended a large sum to ornament our city and to advantage of our people. It is a noble example that should be followed by a number of other wealthy residents. For this magnificent temple our citizens are solely indebted to Milton Tootle, a debt of gratitude that can not be paid in this generation."[30] The occasion turned out to be a fitting opening in St. Joseph to a period known in American history as the "Gilded Age." The name represents a period of opulence and splendor that fitted the new found fortunes of a prosperous nation and prosperous cities, and a prosperous upper and middle class charging headlong into the new industrial age.

160

An Ad for Tootle's Opera House, 1881. *Courtesy Boder Collection*

Socially speaking, St. Joseph may not have been confused with Newport, Rhode Island, where the great industrial and banking barons like the Vanderbilts kept palatial mansions as "summer houses," only open two months out of the year, while their likewise palatial townhouses along New York's Fifth Avenue aired out. But there were a number of rich people in St. Joseph who formed a clique or exclusive social registry consisting of about forty families. Their taste for high society and the good life could only be called slightly less refined than their eastern counterparts, if that. Their refinements could be seen not just in gala events, like the opening of the opera house, but in their homes, their fashion, their entertainment, and in general the way they spent their money.

161

Great, grand Victorian houses still dot the city of St. Joseph, a reflection of the wealth and influence that ruled the city's economy during the late nineteenth century. Monuments of brick, cut stone, ornate terra cotta entrance ways, soaring turrets, stained glass windows, and gray-blue slate roofs, with grand porticos and carriage houses, the homes of the city's wealthy stood as the physical symbol of opulence and a distinct style of living. The genius behind the style of nearly all the great homes built during the late nineteenth century lay in the mind, the vision, and the drawings of the renowned St. Joseph architect, Edmund J. Eckel.[31] In a real sense, the style that a modern day visitor sees in historic St. Joseph is a reflection of Eckel.

Born in Strasbourg, Alsace, on the French German border, in 1845, he studied architecture and design in both Germany and Paris. At an early age he demonstrated a talent for art and an understanding of how to build buildings. As a teenager he worked for three years under the city architect of Strasbourg. Accepted for a course of study in 1866, he graduated in 1868, from the prestigious Ecole des Beaux Arts architectural school in Paris. Later that year he immigrated to the United States, landing in New York in October 1868. Though eminently qualified to work at any firm, he stayed in that city only a short time before traveling west, first to Cleveland, Ohio, where he had relatives. By July of 1869, Eckel found himself again moving west, heading toward Kansas City. But his train took him to Omaha first, and to reach Kansas City he had to pass through St. Joseph. He had a layover in the city for a night and, liking what he saw, decided to stay permanently. Eckel immediately received an offer of employment as a draftsmen with a St. Joseph firm, Stigers & Boettner. Within two years his talent commanded promotion to that of a full partner, and by 1880, following several personnel changes, the company bore his name first, Eckel & Mann. That firm continued until 1891, before breaking up. Eckel continued to design from his St. Joseph office, and eventually the firm of Eckel and Aldrich, with his son George as a partner, succeeded it in the early twentieth century. Eckel's work dominated not only the gracious chateau style of many of the city's mansions, but also its churches, schools, public buildings, commercial buildings, as well as buildings and homes in other cities across the nation. His reputation for excellence and style received nationwide attention. Among the names of the St. Joseph economic elite for whom he designed are those of Tootle, Lemon, Wyeth, Nave, McCord, Lacy, Brittain, and nearly all the princes of wholesale and banking.

162

Between the grand homes of the rich traveled a steady stream of carriages as one social season gave way to another and an endless round of parties, dinners, wedding receptions, or simply the return from a New York shopping spree elicited the getting together of the city's grand social clique. The society pages of the *Herald* and *Gazette* never lacked for stories and the descriptions of the events, no doubt, inspired the wonder, envy, and even disgust of those ordinary folk who read the articles. The social reporter left nothing to the imaginations of those who would never be invited, as they described in fine detail the events, such as a party given by one of the city's princes, described in the *Herald*: "Milton Tootle Jr. gave a brilliant ball last Thursday at the Lake Contrary clubhouse in honor of Miss Florie Lemon and her guest, Miss Duckworth. The guests were conveyed to the lake by a special train. The clubhouse was decorated with palms and plants and the orchestra stationed in the central hall was screened by a wall of palms."[32]

Besides the exclusive setting, a private clubhouse on a small recreational lake south of the city, the reader could find descriptions of the beautiful dresses worn by the ladies, dresses that would have cost the average wage earner three to six months salary. "Miss Duckworth wore a handsome trained gown of heavy white satin under tulle. Low corsage entirely covered with gold embroidery. Long white gloves and pink roses." And once the grandeur of the reception line had been described, a list of the invited guests, appeared, with the usual clique of family names; McCord, Fairliegh, Davis, Enright, Smith, McDonald, Landis, Burnes, Hosea, et al, and out of town guests such as 'Miss Courier of New York'. One need not wonder what those people did at such a grand party, for "Dancing began at 10 o'clock and an elaborate supper was served at midnight."[33]

A few months later, in November 1892, Milton Tootle Jr. married Miss Lillian Duckworth, the guest of honor at that grandiose party. The wedding, announced in the *Gazette* by Mr. and Mrs. George King Duckworth of Cincinnati, took place at the Plaza Hotel in New York City, and was attended by an exclusive entourage of St. Joseph blue bloods who took the opportunity to mingle with their east coast counterparts. It appears from the society stories that many of St. Joseph's rich frequently traveled to the East for vacation, shopping, and social engagements. While the Tootles honeymooned at the Plaza, Henry Krug Jr., son of the meat packing and banking Krug magnate, had only recently returned from a wedding trip to New York and other "prominent Eastern cities."[34]

163

The children of the rich had their own social calendar as well, with engraved invitations and special entertainment, as an article on the *Gazette's* society page revealed: "About a week ago the relatives of Master Duckworth Tootle received tiny cards engraved; G. Duckworth Tootle, XMAS, 1894. Sugar Plums at 3 o'clock." The children of all the "best" people also got invitations and "promptly at the hour named a merry party assembled at the Tootle home which was even more beautiful than usual with its decorations of Christmas greenery and flowers. In the sitting room on the third floor was an immense tree laden with toys, and handsomely decorated with novelties purchased in New York for the occasion."[35]

When not entertaining at home the wealthy congregated at various social clubs, the most prominent being the Benton Club. Named for the famous Missouri senator Thomas Hart Benton, and formed by forty charter members in 1887 to, in their own words, "furnish facilities for bringing together, as often as may be, gentlemen in commercial, manufacturing, and professional pursuits in the city of St. Joseph." The initial focus of the club, as stated in the preamble, stressed education, a place for "discussion of all general education and scientific subjects and the reading of papers, magazines, periodicals and books of scientific literary and financial character," with the goal to "stimulate and develop the mental and moral faculties of its members," and "for the higher and better education of inhabitants of the city."[36]

The club became the meeting place of the economic elite of the city. Housed in a rambling two story brick house adjoining the downtown business district, its dining roomed served the finest European and American cuisine for a business lunch or a formal evening meal. After business hours, men gathered to play cards in the spacious lounge or to discuss the latest business news. A two story porch surrounded the building and became a favorite gathering place on warm summer evenings. The club sponsored at least four major balls, one for each season, giving the social elite another place and opportunity to gather. In 1894, the club expanded its membership limit to 250 so as to encompass more of those gentlemen and families wealthy enough to purchase stock and pay dues.

The Lotus Yacht Club, built just before the turn of the century, proved another popular place for the business class of the city to congregate. Unlike the Benton Club, it made no pretense about being anything educational. Housed in a luxuriant frame building, with a rambling verandah, grandly columned entrance, and a half dozen turrets with cone shaped roofs, it served as the centerpiece of a recreational complex and amusement park on the beach of Lake Contrary. Built by the St. Joseph Railway, Light, Heat and Power Company, the Lotus Club had room accommodations for its members, a casino, and soon became the popular after business hours "watering hole" for nearly any man in the city's commercial club.[37]

The wives of the wealthy spent a lot of time overseeing their huge households and probably had less free time than their husbands. Servants, cooks, and cleaning ladies needed direction; the daily wardrobe required arranging; shopping, either personally done or delegated; and children had to be looked after. If they had free time after that, then numerous committees for charity balls elicited their support, as did church functions and some women's clubs. The Married Ladies Euchre Club, founded in the 1880s, provided an opportunity for ladies of the community to gather at private homes for an afternoon of games, discussions, or casual conversation, followed by tea and refreshments. As the society page writer described it: "Each meeting was such a charming party that hostesses usually made preparations weeks in advance."

WHAT DO THE SIMPLE FOLK DO?

The rich seem to wield so much power and influence in relationship to their actual numbers, that it becomes easy to focus on them and forget how the rest of the people, who made up the true character of the city, lived. Those were the people who made a living, often at low pay for long hours, whose sweat and toil provided the physical labor that created the fortunes of the rich. Across the nation, the last three decades of the nineteenth century proved a brutal time for those attempting to organize labor into unions. And in larger cities the horror stories abounded of the abusive conditions of women, children, and men who worked in the textile mills, clothing sweat shops, mines, and steel mills of the burgeoning industrial giant their nation had become.[38]

165

Because of St. Joseph's light manufacturing base, the conditions of her working class reflected a more benign situation. Most of St. Joseph's laboring class worked in small plants or shops, with a few exceptions such as the packing plants, and wages, though not high, kept most workers from the desperate squalor of living in tenements and slums. The city did have its ethnic neighborhoods. Numbers of Poles, Ukrainians, and Irish immigrants moved in to work on the railroads and at the packing houses. The formation of St. Joseph's later Catholic parishes are a good reflection of those neighborhoods. The city's small African-American community had its own neighborhood as well, typical of cities across the nation with de facto segregation.

St. Joseph's working class neighborhoods sprouted "shotgun" bungalows, one story frame houses of three or four rooms, on narrow 25 foot wide lots, on poorly paved streets. But no matter how poorly furnished or how small, in most cases the homes belonged to the workers. The *Herald* proudly pronounced in an 1893 review: "More people own their own homes in St. Joseph than in any city of its size in the Union and fewer of them are shaded by the poor man's spectre in the shape of a mortgage."[39] The city boasted more craftsmen and skilled mechanics than sweat shop workers and a middle class larger in proportion to the whole population than most other cities. Organized labor, in the form of specific trade unions, ranging from bricklayers to boiler-makers to barbers, found St. Joseph a place more readily accepting to them. Wages varied, and periodically the papers published in their year-end summary editions, with some pride, the average salaries for a number of trades. Throughout the 1870s and 1880s, persons who worked as masons, millers, plasterers, printers, teachers or wagon makers made from $25 to $45 per month. Skilled machinists made from $2-3 per day.[40]

When not rolling cigars, scraping hog carcasses, running a weaving machine, or manufacturing horse harnesses, the people of St. Joseph did the same as people in other cities. They tried to make the most of their time off in the evening, as working hours shortened to a ten hour day, or on Sundays and Saturday afternoons; time that increasingly became popularized as leisure time. Of course they had no television, radio, or movies yet, and most still did not have electric lighting or telephones by the turn of the century, but surprisingly there seemed to be plenty for even the simplest of working men and their families to do.

If getting out of the house for some exercise seemed the solution to one's problems, then going for a walk along one of the city's boulevards or avenues, like Lover's Lane, immortalized by the poet Eugene Field, or visiting one of its parks might have been inviting. By the end of the nineteenth century, bicycle riding had become popular nationwide and St. Joseph had plenty of streets and lanes to provide safe and enjoyable cycling. However, St. Joseph had few parks during the period, only four scattered though the city, and none of those larger than a city block. South of the city lay Lake Contrary, a popular place for swimming, rowing, and fishing; it also became one of the most used sites for fairs. It eventually had an amusement park and some private clubs built near its beaches.

Not until 1889 did the city acquire anything resembling the large parks in big cities like New York or Chicago as places to escape the hum-drum of close urban living. Apparently because of the uncrowded living space in the city, municipal leaders saw no need. But when the city received, as a donation from the Krug family, ten acres on its northern outskirts, the site immediately became popular, even though for most, reaching it required a ride on the streetcar. By the turn of the century, Krug Park had become a city showplace under the skilled hands of Superintendent Rudolph Rau, a talented landscaper and florist. Rau not only planted marvelous beds of roses and other flowers, but also instituted pony rides for children, started a small zoo, oversaw the construction of walking paths, a carriage way, a beautiful steel and glass botanical conservatory, and an imposing turreted gateway, that reflected the medieval flavor of his native Germany.[41]

Fairs, or expositions, provided a fairly regular and popular form of entertainment and recreation for the working-class family. Nineteenth-century expositions could best be described as a cross between the traditional county fair, a circus, an amusement park, a science and technology exhibit, and a trade show. In large cities like New York, Chicago, or St. Louis, they often carried the title, "World's Fair" or "World Exposition." Because large expositions took time and substantial capital outlay to organize, companies or associations had to be formed to cover the cost. The first major exposition slated for the city following the Civil War took place in 1873. Unfortunately for the organizers, a tornado ripped through the site, just south and west of the city, demolishing most of the buildings. Nonetheless, an exposition took place in late September after a major push to rebuild. Subsequent yearly expositions took place on that site until 1877, but lack of money or interest led to a period when they were few or of very limited scale.

167

Not until 1889 did the city again attempt a major exposition, then to be called the New Era Exposition. Many of the city's prominent entrepreneurs invested in the venture, assembled under the guidance of H. D. Perkey, who had organized a major exposition for the city of Denver. The organizers leased a massive two story, 80x960 feet building from the Steel Car Company for the main hall, and dozens of smaller pavilions sprang up around it. The entire site glowed late into the night with the new electric lighting. Organizers had installed a huge amphitheater for mass presentations and lectures, created an artificial lake with a waterfall, and rebuilt an old grist mill with rotating water wheel. Stressing the importance of agriculture in Northwest Missouri, "Korn is King" splashed across the exposition grounds as the organizer's motto. Beginning on September 3, 1889, the exposition got off to a good start, but the number of patrons waned after ten days, and on September 15 a massive fire destroyed the main building, which regrettably for the investors, had been grossly under-insured. The exposition ended with a whimper on October 3.[42] Later fair organizers stayed away from the grand exposition theme, and for a number of years during the early 1890s various organizations successfully operated a horse racing venue near Lake Contrary, which reportedly drew tens of thousands of spectators and betting folk to watch some of the nation's leading trotters.

Circuses, from small companies to Barnum and Bailey, visited St. Joseph during the late nineteenth century. Traveling theatrical troupes also frequented the city. Ticket prices were usually within the range of the average working man. Tootle's Opera House, though sometimes reserved for the social events of the upper class, played host most of the time to the middle and working-class families with shows that ranged from Mr. and Mrs. W. J. Florence presenting a two person comedy titled "Uncle Bob" to huge productions like the London Specialty Company's "Cinderella; or, The Little Glass Slipper." Admission prices for even those grand productions stayed at $1 for the dress circle and 75 cents for the balcony. Matinee performances could be viewed for as little as 25 cents.[43]

Sports began to provide growing leisure time activities for the people of St. Joseph. The upper class took a liking to lawn tennis, sailing, and shooting, but for the "average Joe" baseball rapidly became the favorite warm weather recreation. As early as 1868, baseball scores and stories began to appear regularly in the St. Joseph press, as the game that had been the pastime of so many Civil War soldiers caught on nationally. Clubs of various levels and caliber of players formed across America, with the appearance of the first professional teams and numerous city leagues. The Germania Base Ball Club formed one of St. Joseph's first major teams, and drew a city-wide following. As the *Herald* reported on a late July day in 1868: "One of the most noteworthy events of this season to the citizens of Atchison was the match game of base ball between the Germanias, of St. Joseph, and the Ad Astra of their city." The *Herald* didn't give a score but did say: "We offer them our sympathy and have already donated them a scoop [sic] for the laurel we plucked from their midst."[44]

By the 1880s, St. Joseph had city leagues, like the Commercial League, made up of teams sponsored by the big business firms. The names of those sponsors included Tootle, Hosea, Wyeth, Buell, McDonald and Richardson. They played at fields all over the city, in parks, and sometimes on vacant lots between businesses. Besides major clubs sponsored by nearly every big company in town, there were dozens of neighborhood teams, or "nines," that played regular schedules. The pride of St. Joseph rested with a professional club known as the Saints, that played teams in Kansas City, Topeka, and Lawrence, Kansas, in the Western League. Like professional teams of the twentieth century, they generated a big fan following, and not just among men and boys. As the *Herald* commented after one game against Kansas City: "The attendance was large, especially by the ladies."

BASE BALL

3-Champion Games-3

KANSAS CITY

—vs.—

ST. JOSEPH,

Wednesday, Thursday and Friday,

July 6th, 7th and 8th.

Admission, - - - - - 25 Cents.

Topeka—July 9th, 10th and 12th.

Courtesy of the Boder Collection

The daily papers gave play-by-play highlights of the games and didn't pull any punches when the performance did not meet expectations. "To help out their lame pitching department the Saints put in young McDonald, a clever local southpaw, and he came near equaling Cunningham's clever work," wrote the *Herald's* sports editor after watching the St. Joseph team take an early drubbing by one of Kansas City's better pitchers. But if you were a fan, you could follow all levels of the sport, for the daily papers printed the results of all the major games in

169

town as well as scores and standings from the National League and American Association [later called the American League].[45]

St. Joseph also had a team called the "Black Wonders" that played in an eight city "colored league." The team's long-term local manager, Bud Fowler, proved popular even with white fans, according to the *Herald's* sport reporter: "All of the local fans are delighted to see manager Fowler at the head of the 'Wonders.' He is probably the best Negro manager St. Joseph has ever had and for the past ten years he has maintained a good team which promises to be better this season than in any previous year."[46]

Next to playing baseball during the warm months, bowling provided many with a leisure time sporting activity in the winter. Bowling alleys appeared around the city, usually single lanes located in saloons, with the Donovan Hotel Bowling Alley being the largest. Because of the locations, "proper ladies" did not have much chance to participate. St. Joseph's premiere bowlers played teams from Kansas City, Lawrence, and Topeka in the Inter-City Bowling League. The papers gave full coverage to the games. Based on the scores and stories published, some pretty good rollers made up the five man St. Joseph team, as the report of a championship match with Kansas City indicated. "All the St. Joseph bowlers scored over the 500 mark with the exception of Siemens, who made a fatal miss in his last frame. Tolman made the highest individual score, 626 pins, with the remarkable record of no misses in thirty frames. The score of 626 is the alley record." According to the paper, "a very good attendance watched with interest the game," and afterward "the players were treated to a Dutch lunch."[47]

One of the most popular ways to spend time out of the house for a St. Joseph man or woman during the last three decades of the nineteenth century involved active membership in one of the secret or fraternal societies, the numbers of which exploded during that period. As historian Arthur Schlesinger said about this nationwide phenomenon: "For the average person no use of leisure so well suited his taste as that afforded by the ubiquitous fraternal orders which sprang up during the last quarter of the century." Some secret societies, like the Masons, had been active in St. Joseph from the beginning in 1843. But following the Civil War, as in nearly all towns and cities across the nation, "Americans turned with furious zeal to the creation of secret societies cut to their own pattern."[48] St. Joseph proved no exception, and by the turn of the century the city had dozens of societies and brotherhoods. The *Directory of St.*

Joseph for the year 1899 listed 39 different secret societies, 14 benevolent societies, and 26 others with either fraternal, military veteran, or religious affiliation.[49]

The names of some of the societies are still well known, but many have long since disappeared. Most conjure up some romantic age or purpose, while some seem almost comical. Among those prominent in numbers in St. Joseph during the period: the Masons, with seven lodges; the Oddfellows, five lodges; the Knights of Pythias, 400 members in nine lodges; the Catholic Knights of America; the Independent Order of Foresters; the Independent Order of Free Sons of Israel; Sons of Herman; the Ancient Order of Hibernians; the Knights of the Maccabees; Woodmen of the World; and for the ladies, the Daughters of Erin and the Daughters of Liberty. African Americans in St. Joseph also had lodges, the most popular being the Knights and Daughters of the Tabernacle.[50]

Why did so many join the societies? Companionship and camaraderie, or the building of personal and business connections outside the family, certainly contributed. Most societies also offered practical benefits to their members, such as life insurance, or financial assistance in case of an accident, a disability, or just falling on hard times. As Schlesinger wrote, the societies also replaced the neighborliness of the small towns that no longer seemed to exist in larger, impersonal, urban settings. The societies, "filled a compelling human need. Moreover, the romantic opportunity to posture before a mystic brotherhood in all the glory of robe, plume and sword restored a sense of self-importance bruised by the anonymity of life amidst great crowds."[51]

Though most societies catered strictly to male members, family members could become active in such things as picnics, outings, lectures, dinners, and women's auxiliaries. Regular meeting times ran in long columns of the daily papers, but often in a code only members could decipher. Typical of the listings appeared one for the Improved Order of Red Men: "HUNTING GROUNDS OF ST. JOSEPH RESERVATION OF MISSOURI, WIGWAM OF LOGAN TRIBE NO. 27. Meet every Thursday's sleep of each moon at the seventh run, thirtieth breath, northwest corner 7th and Messanie. Harry Block Sachem, W. R. Womach, C. of R.."[52] Probably only an Improved Redman knew or cared what that meant.

171

One secret society that many wished had never come to the city, descended like a plague in 1868, and remained quietly active, though never as a hotbed, through the rest of the nineteenth century. That society, recognized by its initials, K. K. K., attracted an invisible but by some reports substantial following in the city. A reporter from the *Herald*, feigning interest, visited one of the early meetings of the St. Joseph "den" and reported: "Our advocacy of the plurality of the races was in accordance with their views. Our doctrine of non-sympathy with Indians, Chinese, Africans, Beduins, Aboriginal Australians, Lapps, Patagonians, & etc. suited them to a dot." And after witnessing the taking of the oath by forty-five new members of the city's hooded society, the reporter continued: "Having been properly initiated, the members of the "Den" took off their masks, and we recognized among them several prominent citizens of this city, whose names from prudential motives, we must be silent upon."[53]

Men seeking another kind of camaraderie, without the code words and swords, who wanted some time away from the wife and children, or just a good stiff belt, had no problem finding a place to go where "everybody knows your name." St. Joseph had literally a hundred corner saloons where beer and a sandwich could be had for a nickel or a dime, where a game of pool, a hand of cards, or even a few frames of bowling could be played. The city directory for 1890, listed 117 saloons in the city, and by the 1900 book, over 130 establishments.[54] It may be no wonder that one of the largest women's clubs in the city was the Women's Temperance Union. It was not that St. Joseph produced more than its share of alcoholics, nor had an inordinate number of saloons per city block. Neighborhood saloons became institutions, forums for the public voice of the common man, to talk about work, sports, or politics, just as the Benton Club provided a forum for the city's wealthy. Whether you were rich or just a working stiff, national and local politics made an excellent conversation topic, over a glass of imported wine or a frothy mug of Mr. Goetz' local brew.

CITY POLITICS

The rise of the city in American history produced a new kind of political creature and new and untried applications of what we so affectionately call American democracy. As the urban historian Schlesinger wrote: "From long experience Americans had learned how to rule populations scattered over large areas, but they had had little or no training in the management of densely packed urban centers. Yet every year a larger proportion of the people hived in cities, rendering all human relations more complex, creating new social maladjustments and requiring governmental service and safeguards unknown to the earlier and simpler days of the republic."[55] If men governed their cities badly then part of the problem rose from the fact that they had never done anything like it before. That, coupled with the possibilities of turning an uncertain situation to one's own financial gain, proved more than tempting to too many urban leaders.

The stories of the new breed of city political leader who emerged from the rapid growth of the urban setting in the late nineteenth century summons to mind persons of the caliber of Boss Tweed, George Washington Plunkitt, Richard Croker, and the whole Tammany Hall gang of New York City, who corrupted and looted that city of untold millions of dollars. A large number of cities, whether Philadelphia, Boston, Washington, New Orleans, Cincinnati, Chicago, St. Louis, or Kansas City, all had their own equivalents of Tammany. In an age of dynamic change at all levels of American culture and society, many cities found themselves governed by rings, or bosses, who raked piles of money from public coffers into their own accounts. They corrupted delivery of even the most basic services, like fresh water, gas or electric power, and public transportation. For personal gain they manipulated and sometimes ruined the financial standing, credit, and stability of the government of millions of city dwellers. As Schlesinger aptly described the situation: "It seems clear that there was a cesspool under nearly every city hall, dug secretly by politicians in the pay of respectable, or at least respected, business men."[56]

It does not appear that St. Joseph produced anyone of so prodigiously corrupt character as a Boss Tweed, yet the charges of corruption and mismanagement flew in the city, just as they did elsewhere during the later part of the nineteenth century. Clearly, St. Joseph did not have a single, all-powerful ring or boss or machine that dominated it over any long span. But like many other cities it struggled with the common problem of having a voting public clearly split along national party lines, with vehement partisanship in even its municipal elections. When the Republicans gained control of the city hall, the Democrats harangued and accused them. The same happened when the tables turned and the Democrats won an election. The result of being part of the political feast or famine appeared to be a willingness by political leaders to run rampant during

173

their time in office out of fear that when they were turned out of office, the gravy train would end. A number of other factors, including the structure of the mayor-council form of government, the accessibility of politicians to business leaders to pressure or influence them, and a type of "blind-leading-the-blind" approach to solving growing city problems, because so many new situations had evolved due to rapid growth, all contributed to the age of urban growing pains.

A common theme of corruption in St. Joseph, so similar to other major cities, involved the issuing of public utility licenses and contracts. The first of those conflicts appeared in St. Joseph in 1875 with the call for a public water system to replace the archaic and inadequate wells and cisterns that watered the city. Amid the sweet air of widespread public support, drummed up by both major St. Joseph daily papers, the *Gazette,* [pro-Democratic] and the *Herald* [pro-Republican], there arose the smell of a skunk in the form of what appeared to some as a corrupt bargain among certain water commissioners, the city hall, and the legislature in Jefferson City. Even the daily papers received reproach for supporting the deal, all in the name of progress.

A flier, widely circulated in the city in April 1875, carried the title "Public Opinion" with the banner "To be Issued Whenever the Emergency Demands." Never identified, the author[s] supported a slate of city council candidates who wanted the city to own the municipal waterworks. Their flier blasted both papers, the newly appointed water commissioners, and the state legislature for turning over to four prominent St. Joseph bankers and investors, led by James Burnes, the rights to control the city's water supply. The flier raved: "Down with the rings! The Burnes Ring. The *Gazette* Ring. The *Herald* Ring. The Water-Works Ring. The Metropolitan Police Ring. The Young, Bittinger and Wells Ring. Down with them. Let the people speak! The perfidious *Gazette*—a traitor to Democrats and the principles of Democracy. The lecherous *Herald*—treacherous alike to the Republicans and Republican principles."[57]

Whether the flier represented the honest political outrage of the people, or just the sour grapes of other investors left out of the waterworks decision, remains questionable. However, the Burnes brothers, general bankers, and their cohorts not only collared the positions as public water commissioners but at the same time were the major stock holders in the private water company licensed to supply the city. As such the "ring" set its own water rates at whatever level the public could pay and stayed in the good graces of the city hall as long as the required number of fire hydrants were installed and worked, while the obvious conflicts of interest became a political aside. Fortunately, competition among other utility vendors in the city kept rates reasonably low compared to other big cities where rings or bosses gobbled up and monopolized everything from street-car lines to public gas, coal, and electricity concessions.[58] In St. Joseph, similar charges of corruption followed the letting of almost every city contract for sewer mains, street paving and maintenance, or construction of public buildings.

Many accusations of corruption or favoritism simply stemmed from the swing of the political pendulum in St. Joseph, between the Democrats and the Republicans. From national elections down through state and local contests the battle along party lines raged during the last three decades of the nineteenth century. The following chart of presidential election results in the city, from 1872 to 1900, illustrates the party in favor among St. Joseph voters:

YEAR	REPUBLICAN		DEMOCRAT	
1872	Grant	1,870*	Greeley	1,629
1876	Hayes	1,748*	Tilden	1,849
1880	Garfield	1,920*	Hancock	1,898
1884	Blaine	2,701	Cleveland	2,629*
1888	Harrison	3,578*	Cleveland	3,250
1892	Harrison	4,205	Cleveland	4,552*
1896	McKinley	5,328*	Bryan	4,468
1900	McKinley	6,832*	Bryan	6,202

* Indicates winner of the national election.

Of the eight elections recorded on the chart, St. Joseph voters went with the winner six times. Overall, the city voted in the majority for a Democratic presidential candidate only twice. However during the same block of elections they supported Democratic gubernatorial candidates four times. Between 1872 and 1888, the city had five wards. The First, Second, and Fourth Wards voted consistently Republican during that period while the Third and Fifth voted Democratic. After 1888 the city expanded to eight wards. The Third and Fifth Wards shifted their majorities to the Republican presidential candidates beginning in 1892 while the Seventh Ward became the new Democratic bastion in the city, even voting against McKinley in 1896 and 1900 when he won substantial majorities in all other wards.[59]

In city council and mayoral elections, the ward voting patterns tended to vary somewhat from the presidential elections, with stronger Democratic showings. The First and Second Wards, composed from the older parts of the city, remained staunchly Republican, while the newer wards, made up of expanding working class neighborhoods to the east and south, tended to vote Democratic. After 1888 the number of voters in the older wards tended to remain static while the newer wards showed increasing numbers each election. For example, in 1888 the First Ward had 1,306 voters participating in the November general elections, but by 1900 had shown only a minuscule increase to 1,376. The Fifth Ward had 1,707 participating voters in 1888 but that number jumped to 2,226 by 1900. The Seventh Ward, which did not exist in 1888 polled 1,449 votes by 1900 surpassing the total of either the First or Second Wards.[60]

Between 1880 and 1900, the two parties swapped control of the mayor's office and city hall four times. Of the six men who held the highest office in the city during that period, four Republicans and two Democrats, none could ever be called a true political boss.[61] Four were businessmen with substantial private fortunes or held other governmental positions and two were practicing physicians. None of them seems to have developed the loyal party apparatus that was associated with some bosses, like Tweed's Tammany Hall in New York or Issac Rasin's Democratic machine in Baltimore.[62] Yet all stood at one time accused of heading rings, and the opposing dailies had regular field days lambasting each administration. As the Republican minded *Herald* said of one Democratic mayor, Dr. Peter Kirschner: "There are several hundred men of more or less influence who are really opposed to the present mayor and who would be glad to apply a knife to him if they dared."[63] Fortunately, no one took the article to heart and attempted an assassination.

The major political problem facing the city of St. Joseph during the last three decades of the nineteenth century involved its enormous debt. Succeeding administrations had for better or worse, pushed by the papers, influential promoters, and sometimes with public mandate from an election, supported the passage of bond issues. By the early 1880s, those issues included indebtedness to the tune of $2.25 million with the two largest, the Denver and St. Joseph Railroad and the city's railroad bridge each amounting to $500,000 each. Throughout the 1870s, other railroad companies had dipped into the till as well, with the Kansas City, St. Joseph & Council Bluffs, the Missouri Valley Railroad, and the St. Joseph & Topeka Railroad bond commitments amounting to another $410,000 at from 8 to 10 percent interest. As an observer of city government wrote: "In those days the council proceedings, instead of being dull and prosy accounts of resolutions ordering sidewalks repaired, were in nature of a meeting of railroad builders."[64]

On top of the huge bond debt, the city fathers found it difficult to collect taxes because of the depressed conditions caused by the Panic of 1873 and another depression during the 1880s. With an average of $150,000 in back taxes owed from each fiscal year, a cash flow problem developed and the merchant class began to vehemently complain when the city neared default on its bond payments. Mayor Joseph Piner found a temporary solution to the cash problem by convincing the city council to issue, as an emergency measure, $100,000 in St. Joseph script in denominations of one and two dollar bills. It could only be used in the city, but merchants accepted it from local customers, laborers took it in pay, and people could use it to pay their back city taxes. But merchants soon grew short tempered with the "funny money," because they could not pay their outside suppliers with it. They moved to have the script redeemed for real money by 1885, and over the next few years the bills disappeared from circulation.[65]

With financial default on the horizon, Piner's successor Mayor H. R. Hartwig in January 1885, approached the state legislature to allow St. Joseph to reorganize itself under a new charter for cities of the second class. The city's voters approved the transition in April 1885, and slowly the city began to climb out of its financial abyss. No more bonds were to be issued, no debts or contracts could be let, or city purchases made unless the money actually existed in the city treasury. The assessments in the city increased to $2 per $100 evaluation with half of that going directly to pay off the city debt. The situation presented a belt tightening that proved unpopular but necessary, and yet fifteen years later at the turn of the century the city's coffers still fell short of paying for many needed city services. Money wound up being moved from one account to another as every emergency that produced a shortfall had to be covered. Sometimes the transfer of funds between city accounts, for instance from the back tax fund to the street fund, for desperately needed repairs brought the ire of the opposing party and its newspaper. This was just another example of city corruption.

Typical of the political banter that flew back and forth in the St. Joseph press, the Republican organ, the *Herald*, delivered a tongue-in-cheek attack on the sad state of the Democratic party in the city: "The Democratic organization is

177

evidently poor. With so many city employees and such an utter disregard of the performance of public duty as the Kirschner administration has shown from top to bottom, it would seem that at least one or two Democrats could be kept at the headquarters of the party most of the time, but such does not seem to be the case, and if the man paid a dollar a day to guard the room should leave to take a drink—something no candidate is likely to ask him to do—any man with a wagon and a team could haul away all the equipment of the Democratic organization."[66] The *Gazette* could be just as glib in its attack on Republican administrations, and both papers at times, as the locals said, "got downright nasty." City money often found its way into the misguided hands of officials or contractors and public services suffered. How much of the mishandling of public funds could be proved in a court of law to be blatant corruption or outright theft remained as much in doubt as it did in any other city that suffered from ineffective, incompetent, or dishonest public officials. Despite the political heat constantly applied through the press, indictments of city officials went lacking. No doubt St. Joseph had its share of petty officials who, in the words of the noted New York grafter, George Washington Plunkitt, "saw their chances and took them."[67]

The major political question regarding St. Joseph to this day remains, just how much influence the wealthy residents exercised over those actually holding political office and did they use them as puppets to suit their own needs? There appears to be a correlation between what sociologists Robert and Helen Lynd found in the exercise of community power in the mid-size American cities they studied during the 1920s, and a city like St. Joseph in the late 1800s. They found that the truly wealthy rarely held public office themselves. On rare occasion they might run or "dabble" in elections, but they usually refrained from giving up the time, or they stayed behind the scene out of the fear of being "soiled" by politics. But the people who did hold office, generally from the middle class, or the ward healers who became councilmen, ultimately acted as purveyors of what the upper class wanted. Once in office they supported the ordinances or bond issues, and made deals that favored big business, even though elected by the votes of the middle and lower class majorities.[68]

As proved the case in so may burgeoning cities of the late nineteenth century, the ever swelling mass of people, bringing their industry, inventiveness, and culture, outraced their own urban governments into the next century.

STILL IN 2017!!

St. Joseph Union Station before it burned in 1895. *Courtesy of the Boder Collection*

CHAPTER 8

Unfulfilled Promise,
The Census of 1900

As the new century dawned, St. Joseph could rightfully claim to be a regional center for the meat packing industry, a center of wholesale distribution, the home of one of the nation's largest stockyards, and a rail junction for at least ten lines serving the American West. But it no longer legitimately competed for the position of regional metropolis of the Missouri Valley. As the calendar pages turned to the year 1900, the United States government took another decennial census to count the population of the nation. To the country's cities, it provided not only a count of their peoples but also a ranking, for whatever a town or city might have to offer to the American civilization, the number of people who inhabited its limits remained the number one measure of status. Everyone knew that New York would never be surpassed as the nation's largest city at the turn of the new century, and Chicago, with its phenomenal growth and regional dominance, stood firmly in second place. Statistically, to be included in the Census Bureau's classification as a Group I city, of which there were about a dozen with over 300,000 inhabitants, proved all important to any city claiming to be a great regional or industrial metropolis. Other cities in that group included places like Pittsburgh, St. Louis, Cincinnati, New Orleans, and San Francisco.

Group II cities ranked next with populations between 100,000 and 300,000 inhabitants, and if realistically Group I status stood beyond reach, then a ranking among the nation's top forty cities still represented a nice plum. The mark of attaining a population of 100,000 meant a city had true national status, at a time when nearly all of American society, liking it or not, viewed the "big city" as the showplace of the best American culture and industry had to offer. Having 100,000 inhabitants represented a superior status, and made a statement that a city had arrived and had importance. Civic leaders and commercial boosters sought the status of size as if it were the holy grail of urban development. In its competition for the position as the regional metropolis on the eastern edge of the Great Plains, St. Joseph needed a big population "bounce" if it hoped to keep pace with Kansas City to the south and Omaha to the north. A population count of over 100,000 meant St. Joseph could stay statistically close in the competition for another decade. In all reality, that competition had already been decided, as we have seen, decades earlier, but St. Joseph city fathers intended it to go on, one way or the other.

The federal census of 1890 counted 52,324 souls in the city of St. Joseph, and the accuracy of that census, did not bring forth questions suggesting anything unusual or inflated. But the census of 1900 proved something else. City boosters relished the idea that St. Joseph's population growth had accelerated since the 1890 count. Early in 1900, a new city directory, compiled and published by the Combe Printing Company of the city, drew the attention of the press when it showed an estimated population increase of over 10,000 persons in one year: "An estimate based on the canvass that has been made for the new city directory places the population of St. Joseph at 82,541, an increase of 10,816 over the last year, and it is estimated that within a year we will have passed the 100,000 mark."[1]

Now the reasons for the rapid population growth appeared perfectly clear, according to the article in the *Herald*: "The increase in the population of the city during the past two years has been rapid, but it has been a healthy growth, and not due to any boom conditions. The packing houses have been the means of bringing many people into the city, and the increased importance of St. Joseph as a stock center has been the cause of a corresponding increase in the industries already located here, and of bringing other large institutions to the city."[2] The same article went on to point out that the number of businesses operating in the city, the number of building permits, the amount of deposits in the city's banks, and enrollment in the public schools had all increased substantially over just the two previous years.

If the canvass made for the city directory had been reasonably accurate, showing a population of approximately 82,000 at the beginning of the year, it would have stretched plausibility to believe that another 20,000 persons would take up residency in the city by June of that same year. Nonetheless, that magical figure of 100,000 fixed in the minds of the city's boosters, centered in the St. Joseph Commercial Club, with full support of the city's press. So began a coordinated public relations campaign to convince the people of the city, the county, the state, St. Joseph's urban competition, and specifically, the United States Census Bureau, that it was not only plausible but entirely possible.

COUNT EVERYONE

In late March 1900, the congressional district supervisor for the Census Bureau, Mr. E. E. E. McJimsey, from Maryville, Missouri, visited the city to meet with his assistant supervisor for the city, Hathon G. Getchell. By coincidence or not, an article appeared in the *Daily Herald* the same day McJimsey arrived under the headline, "If We Had 100,000." It made several strong arguments pointing out the benefits of having that population: "If the census this

Caricature of Hathon Getchell, the man behind the Census of 1900.
Courtesy of the Boder Collection

year showed that St. Joseph had 100,000 people or more the city would be entitled to a charter of the first class. The city would then be conducted independently of the county and many advantages would result. The tax levy would no longer be controlled by the county and the city would be enabled to legislate for its own revenues, and, when it had been obtained there would be no sharing of the receipts with the county. St. Joseph is a city of too great proportions to be under the sway and control of a county court."[3]

The article simply presented another motivation, beyond the status question and competition with other regional cities for a "favorable" census. St. Joseph, like many other urban settings across the nation, found its interest at odds with that of the local county or township governments, and even state legislatures, which remained dominated by rural interests and had neither sympathy for cities nor any desire to understand the growing lists of urban problems and the cost of addressing or solving them. Also sticking in the "craw" of many St. Joseph promoters for fifteen years had been the demotion to a second class city to gain the new charter in 1885.

The day after McJimsey's visit another article appeared about the pending census, detailing the dates it would begin and close and how Getchell would be in charge, with 37 men working under him. Hathon Getchell proved the ideal man to appoint to get the job done and make sure the count came out the way it should. Getchell, born in Bath, Maine, in 1855, first operated businesses in Memphis, Tennessee, before coming to St. Joseph in 1884. He worked for the gas company for awhile, then formed his own roofing company which he eventually expanded into paving and general construction. Having made a sizable sum in that endeavor, he moved on to manage a loan company and a transfer company before starting the My Laundry Company in 1898. A true business jack-of-all-trades, he worked his way into the best social institutions of the city, became a high ranking Mason, served on the school and library boards, and held office in the St. Joseph Commercial Club. The article made the point to say how "the Commercial Club is prepared to assist the census taker in every manner possible and will do what it can to facilitate the work of the small force which has been allotted this city."[4]

To continue the reinforcement, the article added: "Local authorities who have investigated the present conditions in St. Joseph have no doubt but that this city will show over 100,000 inhabitants when the census is completed. This will make St. Joseph a city of the first class and will divorce the city from the county government to accomplish more than it can at the present time and will place St. Joseph in the class to which St. Louis and Kansas City now belong."[5] The authority that the paper quoted appeared to be the secretary of the Commercial Club, none other than Hathon Getchell, who estimated the population of the city at that point in time, two months before the official census, to be 105,000. Compared against the city directory canvass, that figure would have meant that the city's population had increased 23,000 in just three months. If that pace continued the city would have 200,000 people by the end of the year!

Census takers began their rounds of the city on June 1, 1900, ready to meet the June 15 deadline for filing their reports. Besides counting the people, they asked more than two dozen questions, gathering statistical information that not only helped determined representation in the Congress, but filled volumes of government reports and census bulletins. Getchell ran the census taking operation from his headquarters in a room provided by the Commercial Club in the Board of Trade building. On June 8, the papers reported that Getchell had phoned McJimsey in Maryville to ask for more help, as his 37 men were working day and night and could not possibly finish on time.[6]

On June 12, the *Daily Herald* published an article on the front page which gave the appearance of a proclamation from the Commercial Club. The wording made clear Getchell's concerns about the number of persons counted and that a number had been "passed over" by his counters. What Getchell proposed through the communication amounted to turning over the census process to the people themselves and making it a head count free-for-all. Getchell's announcement stressed that "there are now but four days left for this important work. The enumerators are working faithfully but they need the friendly assistance of our citizens. Every public spirited citizen should give some of his time and personal effort to the accomplishment of this important work. Personal inquiry among neighbors and friends, and sending names of omissions if they have been enumerated and of people who have left the city, to the supervisor will be of great value and assist materially in obtaining a complete census."[7] The communication also called for "businesses, manufacturing establishments, hotels, boarding houses, and families who have people making their homes with them, who are temporarily out of the city," to send their names into the Board of Trade building. The communication carried the signatures of the presidents of the Commercial Club, the Retail Merchant's Association, the Retail Grocers' Association, and the St. Joseph Clearing House Association.

Responding to the well-laid scheme of Mr. Getchell and the city's boosters, rolls of names came pouring in, no doubt from employers who did not ask if their workers had already been counted at home, and from hotel registers which listed anybody who had checked in or out over the past year as a resident. By one account in the *Daily Herald,* 500 names were brought in one day, simply by people off the street. So much for anything resembling an accurate count. On June 15, the last day of the official count, the morning paper carried another official-looking appeal from Getchell. "The deputy supervisor and members of the commercial bodies of St. Joseph further request every hotel and boarding house proprietor and every head of a family to see that every person in their house is registered." And to punctuate the urgency, Getchell added, "if the names are not sent in today it will be to the detriment of the city."[8] Getchell requested a two day extension before sending his final count to the Census Bureau in Washington. Then the waiting began.

When the census takers finished, they reported the population of St. Joseph at 102,979. That figure represented an increase of over 50,000 persons in ten years, an almost numerical doubling of the population. If accurate, the figure showed a percentage increase matched by only two others out of the top hundred cities in the nation, Los Angeles, California, and Portland, Oregon.[9]

Almost immediately eyebrows rose at the Census Bureau office in Washington. Where had all those people come from and what were they doing in St. Joseph? Obviously, statistics on manufacturing, industry, and employment for the years immediately before and after the 1900 census could not support a population growth of that magnitude over just ten years. The Census Bureau dispatched a special agent to the city to decipher the questionable numeration. Victor Olmsted's arrival in the city on September 27, after having been in Memphis to review their census figures, immediately made the headlines: "Victor H. Olmsted, a Census Official, in City on Important Business. Object of Visit Not Known."[10] Getchell, along with a delegation from the Commercial Club, scheduled meetings with the investigator and immediately went to work,

185

ostensibly for the good of the city, and to insure the count stood. Olmsted told a reporter at the train station that he had been sent by the bureau "to make a few inquires concerning the population of St. Joseph." He also said that he thought "the questions can be answered satisfactorily by Mr. Getchell and that he antici- pates no trouble concerning enumeration."[11] By chance, according to the paper, district supervisor McJimsey just happened to be in the city that day, and he quite unexpectedly ran into Olmsted in the lobby of the Hotel Donovan, one of the city's better hostelries.

Olmsted met with a reporter from the *Gazette-Herald* [the city's two main daily papers had merged on August 1,1900] in his hotel room at the Donovan. During the interview: "Mr. Olmsted had but little to say concerning the object of his visit to St. Joseph. He intimated that he was here to secure information without imparting it." The reporter "asked if any complaint had been made rela- tive to the manner in which the census of St. Joseph had been taken," but Olmsted "appeared to be surprised and wanted to know who there was to complain. He also wanted to know what the people of St. Joseph thought the census ought to show the population to be." The reporter responded that everyone anticipated at least 100,000. Olmsted then replied, "Figuring on the basis of the directory you only have a population of about 80,000 haven't you? Where do you get the other twenty or twenty-five thousand? The population of the city hasn't increased that much since the directory was issued has it?"[12]

The reporter responded by telling of recent annexations by the city and Olmsted did not appear the least bit ruffled. He told the reporter, "The work in St. Joseph and in this district was in the hands of very honorable gentlemen, and so far as I know bear no evidence of padding. There is no reason why the people should be alarmed at the delay in getting the returns." The population count for urban rival to the north, Omaha, had been published a full month earlier and nerves had grown a little frayed in St. Joseph, especially after Olmsted's arrival.

The next day, September 28, Olmsted toured the city with Getchell, "made inquires at several locations," and visited with Commercial Club members, after having spent the evening before at the Lotus Club, the swank private resort near Lake Contrary on the southern edge of the city. The paper followed Olmsted's every move and reported on the 29th, under the headline, "Result is Gratifying" that the inspector had found nothing out of order. "There is every reason to think that the investigations to be made by Mr. Olmsted today will be as satisfactory as those made yesterday."[13] At noon on the 29th, Olmsted wired his boss in Washington that "he need not finish his work here as he had found everything satisfactory so far as he had investigated." Within two hours the Census Bureau wired back that the official count of 102,979 could be released. "The ringing of fire bells and the blowing of whistles shortly after 3 o'clock yesterday proclaimed the arrival of the census returns and the fact that Greater St. Joseph contained a population of more than 100,000," crowed the *Gazette-Herald* the next day.[14]

Special agent Olmsted never made a report to contradict the initial count. So as far as the official government reports went, the city had reached a great plateau. But as the unofficial story goes, according to the locals who could recount the tale in a fashion not available to the newspaper, it is doubtful that Olmsted ever reached a state of sobriety the entire time he remained in the city. Drinks were provided on his arrival, at lunch and at meetings with Getchell and McJimsey, drinks with dinner at the Lotus Club, then after dinner drinks, and more drinks coming and going from every point on the agent's itinerary. During the height of the evening rush for home at five o'clock, during one of his "inquiries," the agent viewed the city's population first hand from the corner of Fifth and Edmond streets, the busiest trolley intersection in the city. His state of intoxication required that he be propped against a utility pole to remain in an upright position. It was after that he reportedly sent the telegram to the Census Bureau in Washington, reporting that there had been a "gross error" in the reporting of the city's population. However, the error had been in the transposing of the digits in the total of 102,000. According to the agent, the real population of St. Joseph stood at 201,000![15]

THE HEALTHIEST PLACE IN THE WORLD

Olmsted never disputed the 1900 census for the city, and as far as the government saw things, the figure found its way into print as fact. However, real questions remained. If the figures were not valid, then what was the actual population of St. Joseph at the turn of the century, and had the city really reached its zenith at that time? And how could it be proved? There are numerous statistical anomalies within the Census Bureau's own reports, emanating from that count and later estimates of population that indicate the 1900 figures must have received substantial padding. Surprisingly, the Census Bureau, in follow-up re-

187

ports during the next decade, continued to use the 1900 count as a basis to predict population growth. In one report dated June 1, 1904, it estimated that based on growth rate percentages, the total population of St. Joseph had reached 112,979.[16] Yet the Census Bureau's own statistical reports showed obvious contradictions and raised unexplainable questions and comparisons that could lead to no other conclusion than that the 1900 count and later estimates based on that count had to contain gross errors.

Besides the sheer percentage of increase, there appear too many other glaring gaps in the statistics to believe the population of St. Joseph had reached anywhere near 100,000 persons. And when put in comparison with other cities of nearly the same size, those caps became more glaring. Along with St. Joseph, the 1900 census showed eight other American cities with populations between 100,000 and 110,000. Those cities within that population range were as geographically diverse as Los Angeles, California; Memphis, Tennessee; Scranton, Pennsylvania; Omaha, Nebraska; and New Haven, Connecticut. In nearly every statistical field from census reports dated 1902-1903, St. Joseph's numbers did not compare with those cities, but more often than not, did so with cities with populations between 60,000-75,000.

In the category of policemen and firemen, the average number of patrolmen for those cities in St. Joseph's group [between 100,000-110,000] was 94. St. Joseph employed 62.[17] For regular firemen the average number was 112, while St. Joseph employed 68.[18] The average number of school children for the eight other cities reported at 15,520, while St. Joseph registered 10,695, with only Omaha having a lesser number in the statistical group.[19] One might justify those statistics in defense of St. Joseph by saying the city had less crime, fewer fires, and families with fewer children than those other cities. But remembering that St. Joseph purportedly had a population explosion second only to Los Angeles, California, around the turn of the century, a comparison of the number of permits for new buildings, consisting of new homes and business construction, might indicate whether that growth rate could be legitimized. For the year 1902, Los Angeles issued 3,739 permits for new buildings while St. Joseph issued 443.[20] The question is, where were all the new people in town living?

If those types of statistics—and there were a dozen other categories, ranging from the number of libraries to street lights, which do not match up either—did not convince anyone in the Census Bureau that the St. Joseph count had been inflated beyond belief, then a glance at the statistics on death rates would have. The figure for St. Joseph leaps from the mundane government chart with all the impact of a brick through a plate glass window. For the reporting year 1902, the death rate per 1,000 inhabitants, based on an estimated population of 107,000, reported in at 8.7, the lowest of all 175 cities with populations over 25,000 in the nation and less than half the national average! Lincoln, Nebraska, the next closest, reported 9.5 per 1,000. By contrast the average within its population class stood at twice St. Joseph's rate, nearly 17 per 1,000.[21] In the total numbers of reported deaths for 1902, St. Joseph had 936 from all causes, which compared it to most American cities in the 60,000 to 70,000 range of population.[22] One would have to draw one of two conclusions: either the 1900 count had been a work of fiction or that St. Joseph could rightfully claim to be not only the healthiest city to live in the nation, but considering the advanced state of American medicine even at the turn of the century, likely the healthiest in the whole world!

Finally, by the 1910 census, the big bounce of 1900 had become a deep pothole and confirmed the earlier anomalies. Census figures reported the St. Joseph population at 77,403, with talk that even that figure had been somewhat padded to keep the city within the 75,000 limit required for first class cities in Missouri.[23] What natural or economic calamity had so decimated the city, plunging its population by some thirty thousand? A great flood on the Missouri River? A massive earthquake along the New Madrid fault? Raging epidemics of unspeakable diseases? Those questions are facetious of course.

St. Joseph should not be labeled as the first, the last, nor the only city to pad its census report. Many cities, and for that matter whole states, practiced census padding for a number of reasons. Obviously, the status of numbers and the ranking they created made padding attractive, for with cities, largeness somehow equated with the power to attract more people, business, and industry. But there were other practical purposes as well. Census numbers determined representative districts at both the national and state levels, so the larger the population the more clout in Washington, D.C., or the state house. City populations also determined important factors such as the amount of self government permitted, the amount of land that could be annexed, the power to issue bonds, and taxing authority allowed by the state, depending on whether the urban area had been classified a First Class or Second or even a Third Class city. St. Joseph stood in the dock no more guilty of wanting to be a first class city than any other, and it's ardent over-zealous boosters, like Hathen Getchell, worked for what they believed was best for their town. St. Joseph's Nineteenth Century leaders can be accused of rampant boosterism, a not so horrible characteristic which would be missing during most of the twentieth century. The census of 1900 could be said to be St. Joseph's *fin de siecle*, an end of the century adornment or extravagance.[24]

In conclusion, St. Joseph lost its competition to become the regional metropolis of the Great Plains region. By not building its own "bridge legend" or being able to exploit its early economic and transportation advantages, St. Joseph ultimately lost its premier status among Midwestern cities. The Civil War years stand out as a turning point in the destiny of the city, a time of conflict when many events were beyond the control of St. Joseph's leaders and citizens. Following the war, a notable lack of vision, beyond their own private empires, by the economic elite of the city retarded St. Joseph's potential. That lack of vision, combined with the aggressiveness of leaders in Kansas City to solicit the support of eastern capitalist, seize the bridge, and claim the designation as the transportation hub of the Great Plains region, proved critical. St. Joseph did become a major center for the wholesale business and ranked as the fifth largest livestock market in the nation at one time. Its citizens early on benefited from the introduction of city-wide utilities, adequate police and fire protection, and the lack of any all-powerful political machinery or bosses which plagued other cities during the late nineteenth century. St. Joseph developed into a beautiful river city with great gothic mansions, many graceful church spires, spacious parks, and clean working-class neighborhoods, with a pace of life that encouraged the raising of families.

No single person, or for that matter cause, can be blamed, because during the nineteenth century cities evolved into such complex economic, social, and political organisms. It can be said that cities are made up of individuals, who ultimately, in demographic terms, submit to being part of a complex organism which develops dynamics of its own. The destiny of a city may travel in directions and to places and beyond limits where no individual citizen may want to go. The history of St. Joseph, Missouri, may be compared with the urban rise and fall of many other American communities; yet it is distinct in that maybe no other city west of the Mississippi River, began with such promise, a promise that went unfulfilled.

NOTES

BIBLIOGRAPHY

INDEX

PREFACE NOTE

Gharles N. Glaab, *Kansas City and the Railroads: Community Policy in the Growth of a Regional Metropolis* (Madison: State Historical Society of Wisconsin, 1962), 1-10.

CHAPTER 1 NOTES

[1] Tiernan to Willard P. Hall, published in the St. Joseph newspaper, *The Adventure,* 31 May 1850. Tiernan wrote the letter while in Baltimore, Maryland, to Hall in St. Joseph. In it he described the report he had made in Washington, D. C. regarding the Hannibal and St. Joseph Railroad survey he had recently completed. The quotation, presented as part of his official report to the Congress, would hopefully influence consideration of the grant of public land to the railroad company.

[2] *Campbell's Gazeteer of Missouri* (St. Louis: R. A. Campbell, Publisher, 1874), 78.

[3] Important discussions on the influence of urbanization in the development of the American West can be found in Richard Wade, *The Urban Frontier* (Cambridge: Harvard University Press, 1959), which spells out the theory of town placement in the vanguard of western settlement. For a more recent interpretation of the geopolitical urban influence on the West see D. W. Meinig, *The Shaping of America: A Geographical Perspective on 500 Years of History, Volume 2 Continental America 1800-1867* (New Haven: Yale University Press, 1993), 248-250.

[4] Statistical information from "Missouri Highlights," published in the St. Joseph *News-Press,* 21 January 1996.

[5] Some of the earliest written reports about the area around St. Joseph come from the Swiss artist Rudolph Friederich Kurz. He recounts the story of Robidoux's arrival there over forty years after the fact, based on oral reports and stories he heard. See J.N.B. Hewitt, ed., *Journal of Rudolph Friederich Kurz.* Bureau of American Ethology Bulletin 115 (Washington: Government Printing Office, 1937), 54.

[6] Very little of historical substance is actually written specifically about St. Joseph prior to it offically becoming a town. The local historical society, and its most prominent president, Bartlett Boder, have left some notes and manuscripts on the town's pre-history, but it is sketchy at best and difficult to document without having actual letters, diaries, maps, or written accounts. See Bartlett Boder, "Old Saint Jo," *Museum Graphics* 6 (Spring, 1954): 8-9.

[7] Meriwether Lewis, *Lewis and Clark Expedition*, 1814 Edition, Unabridged. 3 vols. (Philadelphia: J. B. Lippencott, 1961), 1:20.

[8] In the manuscript of an article written by Bartlett Boder for the *Museum Graphics* magazine, he refers to time and distance calculations made by members of the St. Joseph Historical Society, using the Lewis and Clark journals to show that the July 7 entry did match where the city is located and where Lewis and Clark would have been on that day. file 26, Boder Collection, St. Joseph Area Chamber of Commerce, St. Joseph. Also see Bartlett Boder, "Old Saint Jo," 8.

[9] Though written insights into Robidoux's personality are few, nearly all those that do exist,

written by business associates, allude to his ambition. In particular J. P. Cabanne's correspondence to the Chouteau brothers in St. Louis regarding his partner Robidoux are quite direct to that point. See Dale L. Morgan, ed., *The West of William Ashley, 1822-1838* (Denver: The Old West Publishing Company, 1964), 152-154. Also see Hewitt, *Journal of Rudolph Friedrich Kurz*, 66-68.

[10]The incident was related in a story by the artist Rudolph Friederich Kurz, who visited the St. Joseph area during the 1840s and 1850s. See Hewitt, *Journal of Rudolph Friederich Kurz*, 66-67.

[11] There are a number of good sources that document the western fur trade. In regard to the activities of Robidoux and his brothers I suggest, Merrill J. Mattes, "Joseph Robidoux," in *The Moutain Men and the Fur Trade of the Far West*, ed. LeRoy Hafen, 10 vols. (Glendale, CA: Arthur H. Clark Company, 1965) 8:288-303 Also see Orrel Messmore Robidoux, *Memorial to the Robidoux Brothers* (Kansas City: Smith Grieves Company, 1924). For general background material on the influence of the Chouteau brothers see, William Foley, *A History of Missouri, Volume I, 1673-1820.* (Columbia: University of Missouri Press, 1971).

[12] From a fractious English translation of an original letter in French, part of the Chouteau Collection, Missouri Historical Society, cited in Morgan, *The West of William Ashley,* 154.

[13] Licensing information for Indian traders of the period, 1824-1828, can be found in the records of the 19th and 20th Congress, *Senate Document 58* [Serial 146], *Senate Document 96* [Serial 165], and *House Document 84* [Serial 185], cited in Morgan, *West of William Ashley*, 157, 307-308.

[14] Morgan, *West of William Ashley,* 157. Morgan indicates that Cabanne paid Robidoux with company funds. The exact date of the consumation of that deal is not known but it was likely sometime after August, 1828, when Robidoux's initial license with Baptiste Roy had expired.

[15] 19th Congress, *Senate Document 58.* Also see Morgan, *West of William Ashley*, 156, and Hafen, *Mountain Men,* 8:300.

[16] A visitor to Robidoux's outpost in 1839 commented on Robidoux's Indian wives and scaffolds on which some of his Indian children's bodies had been laid after death. From an excerpt of Abel Paxton's, *Annals of Platte County* in "Historical News and Comments" *Missouri Historical Review* 11 (October 1916): 107-108.

[17] One of the best sources describing the early Blacksnake Hills post and its hinterland comes from the observations and recounting of stories about Robidoux by the Swiss aritist, Rudolph Freiderich Kurz. See Hewitt, *Journal of Rudolph Friedrich Kurz,* 54-68.

[18] Maxmillian, Prince of Wied, *Travels in the Interior of North America, 1832-1834*, reprinted in *Early Western Travels*, ed. Rueben Gold Thwaites, 32 vols. (Cleveland: Arthur H. Clark Company, 1906), 22:257.

[19] Ibid., 24:111-112.

[20] *Revised Statutes of Missouri, 1835.* 34.

[21] Letter from L.F. Linn to John Forsyth, cited in *History of Buchanan County, Missouri* (1881;

reprint, Cassville, MO: Litho Printers & Bindery, 1973), 107. This work is the earliest published history of the county and the city of St. Joseph. Though no author is given, its editors most likely were St. Joseph newspapermen. The accuracy of the material, printed less than 40 years after the founding, does not raise serious question, as much of it is told by the individuals who were actually there. The publisher thanked many of the "old settlers" for their first hand contributions. Its format became the platform for later histories of Buchanan County and St. Joseph, dated 1898, 1904, and 1915. During the early 1830s, Linn championed the goal of adding the Platte Purchase area to the state, among members of the congressional delegation. For further discussion of Linn's role see Perry McCandless, *A History of Missouri, Volume II, 1820-1860* (Columbia: University of Missouri Press, 1972), 116-117.

[22] The text of the treaty is reproduced in *History of Buchanan County, Missouri*, 109-111. For further information on the Platte Purchase see McCandless, *A History of Missouri*, 117. Also see Howard McKee, "The Platte Purchase," *Missouri Historical Review* 32 (1938): 129-147.

[23] It was the apparent belief of the Robidouxs that their influence with the Indians of northwest Missouri and northeastern Kansas territory, built through years of trade, was substantial. As a result, their ability to help bring about the peaceful acceptance by the Indians of the Platte Purchase deal should have been rewarded by the government. The correspondence with Senator Benton regarding Robidoux's request for land is described in Robidoux, *Memorial*, 96-97.

[24] There are a number of early geographical descriptions of the Blacksnake Hills area, including notes made by Lewis and Clark, Maxmillian, Prince of Weid, and Rudolph Kurz. One of the earliest geographic surveys consists of a bound atlas of early Buchanan County maps, in the reference room of the River Bluffs Regional Library, St. Joseph, Missouri.

[25] Nearly everything regarding the events of Joseph Robidoux's life appear to be anecdotal, including the family biography from 1924, Robidoux, *Memorial to the Robidoux Brothers*. Rudolph Kurz related stories about Robidoux's love of, and skill at poker play in his journal. Kurz met Robidoux at least once according to his writings and relates other stories as being told by old settlers in the area or other Robidoux contemporaries. See Hewitt, *Rudolph Kurz*, 67-68. Also in Paxton's *Annals of Platte County*, he relates how Robidoux was brought up on several charges of "gaming", card playing, and how the court let him off. See Paxton, 108.

[26] For immigration patterns into Missouri during the early nineteenth century see McCandless, *History of Missouri*, 37. Also see Meinig, *The Shaping of America*, 229-230.

[27] Names are drawn from the 1840 federal census report for Buchanan County, on microfilm at the St. Joseph Public Library. Exerpted from Bureau of the Census, *Federal Census Schedule, 1840* Microcopy No. 704, Roll No. 226. Also, what appears to be a fairly comprenhesive listing of the early settlers of the county, listed by townships, can be found in *History of Buchanan County*, 114-138.

[28] Buchanan County, Missouri, *Records of the Buchanan County Court*, Book 1:36. Robidoux was allowed the sum of $30 in December, 1839 for the use of a room for the court meetings. He is listed in records as drawing money for the room and fuel for several months after that and on several pages the house is listed as a designated polling place in Washington Township.

[29] Ibid., 73.

³⁰ From the journal of Richard Hayes McDonald, in the collection of the Library of the Commonwealth of Virginia, cited in Sheridan Logan, *Old Saint Jo* (John Sublett Logan Foundation, 1979), 21.

³¹ The names of many early craftsmen and businessmen in and around the Blacksnake Hills are listed in, *History of Buchanan County*, 400-401.

³² *Records of the Buchanan County Court*, Book 1:184.

³³ McCandless, *History of Missouri*, 48.

³⁴ The price of hemp and other commodities such as sugar, salt, or lumber could be commonly found in the first St. Joseph newspaper, the *Gazette*, which began publishing in April, 1845. Also in the paper appeared ads for the hiring of slaves to break hemp.

³⁵ Most of the events surrounding Robidoux's decision to finally lay out a town are based on the oral history passed on and published in *Memorial to the Robidoux Brothers*, written three generations after the fact. The stories are supported by anecdotal material drawn from Smith and Kemper in the first *History of Buchanan County*, 405. Smith's Addition became part of the town on January 13, 1845. Ibid, 408.

³⁶ Ibid. Also see Logan, *Old Saint Jo*, 24.

³⁷ For an excellent overview of the popularity of the grid system and early urban planning in America see John Reps, *The Making of Urban America: A History of City Planning in the United States* (Princeton: Princeton University Press, 1965). An original plat of the town can be found in the Recorder's Office, Buchanan County, Missouri, as well as the city clerk's office. A copy of the Smith plat and early city additions can be seen in a nineteenth century plat book, part of the Boder Collection, St. Joseph Area Chamber of Commerce, St. Joseph.

³⁸ Complete copies of the Declaration of the Proprietor, Certificate of Proprietor's Acknowledgement, and the promissory note to Chouteau may be found in the Recorder's Office, Buchanan County, Missouri, and in *History of Buchanan County*,, 405-411.

³⁹ St. Joseph *Gazette*, 25 April 1845.

CHAPTER 2 NOTES

¹ The importance of road building and the building and maintainence of a river landing are clearly reflected in the record books of Buchanan County and the City of St. Joseph. Numerous entries deal with the surveying of new roads to outlying towns and appropriations for riverfront development to handle the growing number of landings from steamers coming from St. Louis. See Buchanan County, Missouri, *Records of the Buchanan County Court*, Books 1-3, and City of St. Joseph, Missoauri, *Incorporation and Ordinance Book, 1845-1851*.

² *Records of the Buchanan County Court*, Book 4: 215.

³ St. Joseph *Gazette*, 12 May 1848.

⁴ That fact was often repeated by the St. Joseph newspapers and by word of mouth between emigrants. For an example of the promotional editorials see the St. Joseph *Adventure*, 16

February 1849. Also see, Joel Palmer, *Journal of Travels Over the Rocky Mountains*, re-printed in *Early Western Travels*, ed. Rueben Gold Thwaites, 32 vols. (Cleveland: Arthur H. Clark Company, 1906), 30: 261-262.

[5] For a general overview of the Oregon Trail see Ray Allen Billington, *Westward Expansion A History of the American Frontier* (New York: Macmillan Company, 1967), 525-533.

[6] From a clipping from the *Marshall County News*, 7 May 1935, file 570, Boder Collection.

[7] The complete articles of incorporation are found in *Incorporation and Ordinace Book, 1845-1851*, 1-7.

[8] From City of St. Joseph, Missouri, *Notes From the Board of Trustee Meetings, 1845-1851*, 15.

[9] From city ordinances 40 and 41, *Incorporation and Ordinance Book, 1845-1851*.

[10] Ridenbaugh's role as town promoter and local publisher was not at all unusual in the urbanization of the American West. Pride in their adopted communities, and the singing of the town's praises was often a common theme for newpapermen. See Lawrence H. Larsen, *The Urban West at the End of the Frontier* (Lawrence, Kansas: The Regents Press of Kansas, 1978), 5. Also see Meinig, *The Shaping of America*, 250. A number of biographical sketches of Ridenbaugh have been published in local histories of the city. See *History of Buchanan County*, 873-874, or Christian Rutt, *The Daily News History of Buchanan County and St. Joseph, Missouri* (St. Joseph: St. Joseph Publishing Company, 1898), 83.

[11] Excerpted from the complete editorial, St. Joseph *Gazette*, 9 May 1845.

[12] St. Joseph *Gazette*, 2 May 1845.

[13] Ibid., 6 March 1846.

[14] Ibid.

[15] The existence of at least four large ferry operations in the area explain St. Joseph's popularity as a crossing point on the Missouri River. See McCandless, *History of Missouri*, 51.

[16] St. Joseph *Gazette*, 19 March 1847.

[17] From the prospectus of the St. Joseph *Adventure*, 5 May 1848.

[18] St. Joseph *Gazette*, 3 April 1846.

[19] Excerpts from the *Expositor* were reprinted in a rebuttal article published in the *Gazette*, 28 May 1847.

[20] St. Joseph *Gazette*, 28 May 1847.

[21] Ibid., 25 June, 1847.

[22] St. Joseph *Adventure*, 15 December 1848. For an overview of the Gold Rush, see Ray Allen

Billington, *The Far Western Frontier, 1830-1869* (New York: Harper & Row, 1956), 214-242.

23 Gold seekers left from a number of towns along the edge of the Great Plains, including Independence, Weston, Leavenworth, and Council Bluffs, but if the claims of the number of wagons crossing on the town's ferries, published in the St. Joseph papers, are accurate then St. Joseph had become the clear leader. St. Joseph *Adventure*, 6 April 1849. Also see Billington, *The Far West Frontier*, 214-218.

24 From, "Missouri History Not Found in Textbooks," *Missouri Historical Review* 31 (1937): 120-121.

25 From the St. Joseph *Gazette*, 9 February 1849, and reprinted the next week, 16 February 1849. Also see Kate Gregg, "Missourians in the Gold Rush," *Missouri Historical Review* 39 (1945): 137-154
26 St. Joseph *Adventure*, 16 February 1849.

27 St. Joseph *Gazette*, 16 February 1849.

28 Ibid., 23 February 1849. Also see Gregg, "Missourians in the Gold Rush," 147.

29 The thermal zodiac was the invention of 19th century German geographer Alexander von Humbolt. A number of western visionaries and promoters used Humbolt's ideas to justify large scale town planning. For a further discussion of Gilpin see Larsen, *The Urban West*, 2-3. Also see Charles N. Glaab, *Kansas City and the Railroads: Community Policy in the Growth of a Regional Metropolis* (Madison: The State Historical Society of Wisconsin, 1962), 22-29, and Charles N. Glaab and A. Theodore Brown, *A History of Urban America* (New York: Macmillan Company, 1967).

30 St. Joseph *Adventure*, 22 April 1849.

31 Prices listed in the St. Joseph *Adventure*, 2 February 1849.

32 Ibid., 12 July 1849.

33 Hugh Williamson, "One Who Went West," *Missouri Historical Review* 57 (1963): 368-378.

34 The estimate is from the St. Joseph *Adventure*, 12 July 1850.

35 St. Joseph *Adventure*, 11 January 1850.

36 Bartlett Boder, "Missouri and the Latter-Day Saints," *Museum Graphics* 9 (fall 1957): 4-5. For an overview of the Mormon's western migration see Frederick Merk, *History of the Westward Movement* (New York: Alfred A. Knopf, 1978), 335-338, Billington, *The Far Western Frontier*, 196-200.

37Raymond W. and Mary Lund Settle, *War Drums and Wagon Wheels, The Story of Russell, Majors and Waddell* (Lincoln: University of Nebraska Press, 1966), 42-46.

38 St. Joseph *Adventure*, 30 April 1852.

[39] St. Joseph *Weekly Commercial Cycle*, 20 January 1854.

[40] City of St. Joseph, Missouri, *Ordinance Book, 1851-1857*, 107 F171.

[41] Billington, *Far Western Frontier*, 261-265.

[42] St. Joseph *The Weekly West*, 12 June 1859.

[43] It was long believed, but never confirmed, that Russell had also made a personal bet with a Wall Street consortium, amounting to $200,000, that he could pull off a ten day delivery to San Francisco. See, *History of Buchanan County*, 643. For an excellent view of Russell, Majors & Wadell see Raymond W. and Mary Lund Settle, *War Drums and Wagon Wheels, The Story of Russell, Majors and Waddell*, 111. Also see Billington, *Westward Expansion*, 639-641.

[44] Those concessions included access to ferrys, depots, and financial support. Ibid., 112.

[45] St. Joseph *The Weekly West*, 7 April 1860. The confusion over the role of rider Johnny Fry, may stem from the report that he was also the first rider to come into the city, bring mail from Sacramento, and supposedly racing the clock to beat a deadline on Russell's personal bet. Also see *History of Buchanan County*, 644.

[46] From an ad appearing in *The Weekly West*, 7 April 1860.

[47] Ibid.

[48] Settle and Settle, *War Drums*, 113-114.

[49] For a discussion of the competition for hinterland between Chicago and St. Louis in the midwest, see William Cronon, *Nature's Metropolis-Chicago and the Great West* (New York: W.W. Norton, 1991), 295-305.

[50] St. Joseph *Gazette*, 6 March 1846.

[51] Ibid., 23 May 1845.

[52] Ibid., 20 June 1845.

[53] *Board of Trustee Minutes*, 108, and *Incorporation and Ordinace Book 1845-1851*, Ordinance 40.

[54] *Incorporation and Ordinance Book 1845-1851*, Ordinance 39.

[55] *Board of Trustees Minutes*, 90.

[56] Ibid., 163.

[57] Ibid., 159-160.

[58] *Incorporation and Ordinance Book*, Ordinance 53.

59 Ibid., Ordinances 73, 82.

60 Ibid., Ordinance 74.

61 Ibid., Ordinances 51, 69.

62 From the Marine List, St. Joseph *Adventure*, 4 May 1849.

63 Ibid., 16 February 1849.

64 St. Joseph *Commercial Cycle*, 19 August 1853. Also see an original manuscript for an article by Bartlett Boder titled, "Captain Thomas H. Brierly," for the *Museum Graphics* magazine. file 622, Boder Collection.

65 Ibid.

CHAPTER 3 NOTES

1 St. Joseph *Gazette*, 6 November 1846.

2 For a biographical sketch of Stewart see, *History of Buchanan County*, 244-245, and Donald B. Oster, "The Hannibal and St. Joseph Railroad, Government and Town Founding, 1846-1861" *Missouri Historical Review* 87 (July 1993): 406.

3 *Laws of the State of Missouri, 14th General Assembly, 1st Session, 1846-47*, 156-157. A reprint of the entire charter can also be found in *History of Buchanan County*, 570. For the early history of the railroad see Homer Clevenger, "The Building of the Hannibal and St. Joseph Railroad." *Missouri Historical Review* 36 (October 1941): 33-34, and Oster, "The Hannibal and St. Joseph Railroad, Government and Town Founding, 1846-1861," 406-407.

4 St. Joseph *Gazette*, 13 November 1846. For a biogrpahical sketch of Corby see Bartlett Boder, "The Railroad is Built." *Museum Graphics* 10 (summer 1958): 9.

5 Oster, "The Hannibal and St. Joseph Railroad," 405, and Clevenger, "Building the Hannibal and St. Joseph," 34.

6 St. Joseph *Gazette*, 29 January 1847.

7 The entire report from the convention was printed the following week in the St. Joseph *Gazette*, 11 June 1847.

8 Ibid., 17 September 1847.

9 Ibid., 7 July 1848. The *Gazette*, quoting from the Weston, Missouri, *Democrat*.

10 Ibid.

11 An overview of the development and subsequent connection of the railroads of Illinois and Missouri, and the influence of Douglas can be found in, Richard C. Overton, *Burlington Route: A History of the Burlington Lines* (New York: Alfred A. Knopf, 1965), 17-21. Also see Oster, "The Hannibal and St. Joseph Railroad" 407.

[12] St. Joseph *Adventure*, 19 October 1849.

[13] Ibid.

[14] Ibid., 1 March 1850.

[15] From a letter from Tiernan to Hall published in the St. Joseph *Adventure*, 31 May 1850.

[16] Ibid., 4 October 1850.

[17] *Laws of the State of Missouri, 16th General Assembly, 1850-1851*, 266-267. Also see McCandless, *History of Missouri*, 146.

[18] Oster, "The Hannibal and St. Joseph Railroad" 407.

[19] St. Joseph *Adventure*, 15 July 1852.

[20] Oster, "The Hannaibal and St. Joseph Railroad," 408. Also see McCandless, *History of Missouri*, 148.

[21] St. Joseph *Adventure*, 1 June 1852.

[22] Ibid., 18 March 1853. For an overview of Duff's role in the construction of the railroad see Clevenger, "Building the Hannibal and St. Joseph Railroad," 39-40, and Oster, "The Hannibal and St. Joseph Railroad," 410.

[23] McCandless, *History of Missouri*, 149. Also see *History of Buchanan County*, 577.

[24] Stock subscriptions and payments on pledges lagged in many northern Missouri counties, including Buchanan County and St. Joseph. As a result the fear that control of the railroad would be taken from Missourians and transferred to Easterners became a reality. Oster, "The Hannibal and St. Joseph Railroad," 410.

[25] Arthur M. Johnson and Barry E. Supple, *Boston Capitalists and Western Railroads: A Study in the Nineteenth-Century Railroad Investment Process* (Cambridge: Harvard University Press, 1967), 163. Also in reference to Forbes see Clevenger, "Building the Hannibal and St. Joseph Railroad," 131, and Oster, "The Hannibal and St. Joseph Railroad," 408-409.

[26] Ibid., 188.

[27] Ibid., 166-167. In regard to Forbes and overseas investors also see, Cronon, *Nature's Metropolis*, 82-84, and, Oster, "The Hannibal and St. Joseph Railroad," 410-411.

[28] St. Joseph *Weekly West*, 25 February 1859. Also see Boder, "The Railroad is Built," 8.

[29] Complaints about Duff's construction techniques were well known not only to travellers but to the investors in the line as well. However, Duff's Boston based company actually did none of the work, as nearly the entire line went to subcontractors. See Horace Greeley, *An Overland Journey, From New York to San Francisco* (New York: C. M. Saxton, Barker & Co., 1860), 13. Also see Johnson and Supple, *Boston Capitalists*, 170, and Clevenger, "Building the Hannibal and St. Joseph," 39-40.

[30] Greeley, *Overland Journey*, 15-16.

[31] For an overview of all the small lines proposed for St. Joseph, see *History of Buchanan County*, 570-583.

[32] Ibid., 578-579.

[33] For an overview of the early transcontinental debate see Billington, *Westward Expansion*, 644-645, and Meinig, *The Shaping of America*, 161-163.

[34] Figures from a population table in, Bureau of Statistics, *Statistical Abstract of the United States, 1907.* No. 30 (Washington; Government Printing Office, 1908), 56-57.

[35] From an article reprinted in the St. Joseph *Weekly West*, 12 June 1859.
[36] Ibid.

[37] St. Joseph *Weekly West*, 5 September 1859.

[38] Glaab, *Kansas City*, 66-68.

[39] From an article in the Independence *Democratic Gazette*, reprinted in the St. Joseph *Weekly West*, 3 December 1859.

[40] Ibid, 25 February 1860.

[41] From the Washington correspondent of the Chicago *Press & Tribune*, reprinted in the St. Joseph *Weekly West*, 17 March 1860.

[42] Ibid., 28 April 1860.

[43] Ibid.

CHAPTER 4 NOTES

[1] Glaab and Brown, *Urban America*, 63-68.

[2] Federal census reports for St. Joseph, dated 1850 and 1860, both show that the vast majority of the heads of households reported their place or state of origin as southern. Besides Missouri, Kentucky and Tennessee were most frequently mentioned. The number of respondents listing European nations increased from 1850 to 1860, but remained under one fourth of native born citizens, with England, Ireland, and Germany as the primary places of origin for foreign born inhabitants. See *Federal Census Schedules 1850 and 1860, City of St. Joseph and Buchanan County*, National Archives Microcopy.

[3] *Incorporation and Ordinace Book, 1845-1851,* Ordinance 33.

[4] Ibid., Ordinance 19, sec. 1,4,6.

[5] Glaab and Brown, *Urban America*, 86.

[6] *Incorporation and Ordinance Book, 1845-1851*, Ordinance 62, sec. 8. For further discussion of the problem of hogs in early American cities see Glaab and Brown, *Urban America*, 86-87.

[7] *Ordinance Book, 1851-1857*, Ordinance 93, F158.

[8] Ibid., Ordinance 13.

[9] City of St. Joseph, Missouri, *Minutes of the Board of Trustees, 1845-1851*, 134.

[10] For a discussion of city health problems see Glaab and Brown, *Urban America*, 83-91. Also see Clement Eaton, *The Growth of Southern Civilization, 1790 to 1860* (New York: Harper & Brothers, 1961), 253-256.

[11] Outbreaks of cholera were common in St. Joseph during the late 1840s and early 1850s, evident from newpaper reports and stories passed on from emigrants. While the papers did admit to the presence of the disease they tended to downplay the number of people affected. However one traveller described cholera as "considerable" around St. Joseph in 1849. See Williamson, "One Who Went West," 374.

[12] St. Joseph *Gazette*, 25 July 1845.

[13] For an overview of how many towns and cities handled fire protection see Eaton, *Southern Civilization*, 256-257.

[14] St. Joseph's city laws regulating the building of chimneys and flues and open burning reflected those of many older towns in the United States. For specific ordinances see *Incorporation and Ordinance Book, 1845-1851*, Ordinances 17, 46, 80, 91, 105.

[15] *Minutes of the Board of Trustees Meetings*, 1845-1851, 127. Also see Eaton, *Southern Civilization*, 256-257.

[16] Glaab and Brown, *Urban America*, 95-96.

[17] *Incorporation and Ordinance Book, 1845-1851*, Ordinace 9, sec. 2,3.

[18] Ibid., Ordinance 9.

[19] Ibid., Ordinances 9, 22. Why the ordinance lists stallions and jackasses within the same sentence was not further explained. The reason may have been in regard to keeping individuals from promoting gambling on races by parading their race horses.

[20] *Ordinance Book, 1851-1857*, Ordinance 74, F139.

[21] Eaton, *Southern Civilization*, 289-293.

[22] St. Joseph *Adventure*, 15 December 1848.

[23] Ibid., Ordinance 6, F75. Also see Eaton, *Southern Civlization*, 289-291, for a discussion of drinking problems relating to the ante-bellum southern society.

[24] The duties of the constable were defined in the original incorporation document of the town and in subsequent odinances. See *Incorporation and Ordinance Book, 1845-1851*, Ordinance 24, for specific duties.

[25] Glaab and Brown, *Urban America*, 96.

[26] *Ordinance Book, 1851-1857*, Ordinances 68 and 71.

[27] *History of Buchanan County*, 645-646.

[28] The initial report is found in the St. Joseph *Adventure*, 25 September 1850. Also see Logan, *Old Saint Jo*, 42, and Rutt, *Daily News History of Buchanan County*, 247, for accounts of the event.

[29] St. Joseph *Gazette*, 19 December 1846.
[30] From an original hand written bill of sale, file 361, Boder Collection.

[31] St. Joseph *Gazette*, 5 April 1849.

[32] *Incorporation and Ordinance Book 1845-1851*, Ordinance 27. The ordinance covers a variety of restrictions on the behavior of blacks and is typical of ordinances and black codes found in other southern towns. For an example of those codes see Eaton, *Southern Civilization*, 252.

[33] *Ordinance Book 1851-1857*, Ordinance 76, F143.

[34] There exists for St. Joseph little in the way of African American written records for that period, and as of this writing no written documentation of underground railroad activity in St. Joseph, according to Mrs. Geraldine Robinson, currator of the Knea Von Black Archives Museum, an African American history repository for the St. Joseph area. Stories of possible underground railroad stations in the city have been passed on orally but none have ever been archeologically documented nor any physical or written artifacts presented to support the existence of an actual "station" on the railroad in the city. Geraldine Robinson, interviewed by author, St. Joseph, Missouri, 8 October 1996.

[35] *History of Buchanan County*, 473-474.

[36] The early history of the Catholic Church in St. Joseph has been recently documented in a fine work produced in conjunction with the sesquicentennial of the first parish in the city. See *St. Joseph Cathedral Parish, Our Story, 1845-1995* (Marceline, Missouri: Wadsworth Publishing Company, 1995), 2-5.

[37] Ibid., 5.

[38] *History of Buchanan County*, 476.

[39] Ibid., 477. Also see Logan, *Old Saint Jo*, 146-150.

[40] Ibid., 485.

[41] Ibid., 489-490.

[42] Ibid., 492.

[43] Religious practice in St. Joseph reflected the southern way as much as any other field of social endeavor. See Eaton, *Southern Civlization*, 314-315.

[44] The early history of the Jewish community in St. Joseph is nicely told by Bartlett Boder, "Arrival in St. Joseph" *Museum Graphics* 7 (spring 1955): 18-19.

[45] Southern ideas about education are nicely discussed in Eaton, *Southern Civilization*, 114-119.

[46] From an advertisement in the St. Joseph *Gazette*, 30 October 1846.

[47] From an advetisement in the St. Joseph *Commercial Cycle*, 26 August 1853.
[48] Rutt, *Daily News History of Buchanan County*, 174.

[49] Ibid., 175.

[50] Ibid., 174. Also see Eaton, *Southern Civilization*, 117.

[51] From an advertisement in the St. Joseph *Gazette*, 20 October 1848. Also see Eaton, *Southern Civilization*, 117.

[52] St. Joseph *Commercial Cycle*, 24 June 1853.

[53] Rutt, *Daily News History of Buchanan County*, 176.

[54] St. Joseph's people modeled the type and style of entertainment similar in most southern towns and cities as described in Eaton, *Southern Civilization*, 261-265.

[55] St. Joseph *Gazette*, 10 October 1845.

[56] St. Joseph *Commercial Cycle*, 24 June 1853.

[57] St. Joseph *Gazette*, 9 June 1848.

[58] Besides advertisments in the period newspapers, see Elbert R. Bowen, "Amusements and Entertainments in Early Missouri," 47 *Missouri Historical Review* (July 1953): 307-317. Also see Eaton, *Southern Civilzation*, 264.

CHAPTER 5 NOTES

[1] *St.Joseph Free Democrat*, 24 November 1860.

[2] William Parrish, *A History of Missouri 1860-1875* (Columbia: University of Missouri Press, 1973), 3.

[3] Ibid.

[4] Excerpt from Jackson's inaugural address, City of Kansas *Western Journal of Commerce*, 10

January 1861. Also see Parrish, *A History of Missouri*, 4.

[5] For Thompson's war record and his attempt to receive a confederate commission, see Stephen Davis, "Jeff Thompson's Unsuccessful Quest For a Confederate Generalship," *Missouri Historical Review* 85 (October 1990): 53-65.

[6] *History of Buchanan County*, 328.

[7] Rutt, *Daily News History*, 374.

[8] *History of Buchanan County*, 460.

[9] Ibid., 940-941.

[10] General Order No. 5. Printed in the St. Joseph *Morning Herald*, 15 February 1862.
[11] General Order No. 4. Ibid., 12 February 1862.

[12] Special Order. Ibid., 22 April 1862.

[13] Special Order No. 368. Ibid., 12-13 August, 1862.

[14] Special Orders Nos. 373 and 374. Ibid., 18 August 1862.

[15] Ibid., 15 February 1862.

[16] Ibid., 7 March 1862.

[17] Ibid., 26 March 1862.

[18] Excerpt from the complete speech printed in the, *Morning Herald*, 2 March 1862.

[19] Ibid., 26 March 1862.

[20] Kansas City *Weekly Journal of Commerce*, 4 July 1863.

[21] Ibid., 16 May 1863.

[22] St. Joseph *Morning Herald*, 9 September 1862.

[23] Kansas City *Weekly Journal of Commerce*, 24 October 1863.

[24] Ibid.

[25] Ibid., 7 November 1863.

[26] St. Joseph *Morning Herald*, 5 June 1862.

[27] Ibid., 22 June 1862.

[28] Johnson and Supple, *Boston Capitalist*, 196.

[25] St. Joseph *Morning Herald*, 27 June 1862.

[26] Glaab, *Kansas City*, 110.

[27] St. Joseph *Morning Herald*, 25 July 1862.

[28] Johnson and Supple, *Boston Capitalist*, 230-231.

[29] Kansas City *Weekly Journal of Commerce*, 12 December 1863. Also see Glaab and Brown, *Urban America*, 115-116.

[30] Glaab, *Kansas City*, 124-125.

[31] Kansas City *Weekly Journal of Commerce*, 19 December 1863.

[32] Ibid. Also see Glaab, *Kansas City*, 126-127.

[33] Ibid., 13 February 1864.

[34] St. Joseph *Morning Daily Herald*, 2 April 1868.

[35] Ibid., 28 March 1868.

[36] Parrish, *History of Missouri*, 219-221.

[37] St. Joseph *Morning Herald*, 29 March 1868.

[38] Ibid., 2 May 1868.

[39] Ibid., 29 April 1868.

[40] Kansas City *Weekly Journal of Commerce*, 12 August 1865.

[41] Glaab, *Kansas City*, 157.

[42] See earlier references to the influence of the Forbes group and the Hannibal and St. Joseph Railroad in Chapter 3 of this work. See Johnson and Supple, *Boston Capitalists*, 226-227. Also see Glaab, *Kansas City*, 156-159.

[43] Ibid. Joy had arranged for the Hannibal and St. Joseph to assume control of the Cameron line when local Kansas City investors could not raise the money to finish it themselves. Also see Larsen, *The Urban West*, 101-102, and Parrish, *History of Missouri*, 219-221.

[44] St. Joseph *Morning Herald*, 3 July 1869.

[45] Ibid., 4 July 1869.

[46] Parrish, *History of Missouri*, 219.

[47] St. Joseph *Morning Herald*, 28 May 1868.

⁴⁸ Joy's strategy had been to develop a railroad loop which connected Chicago, St. Louis, Kansas City, and Council Bluffs/Omaha. His primary focus involved creating north-south lines, like the Kansas City, Council Bluffs route through St. Joseph. However, the strength of the east-west routes, running directly to Chicago from the Great Plains region eventually doomed his strategy. See Johnson and Supple, *Boston Capitalists*, 229-239. Also see Glaab, *Kansas City*, 161-172.

⁴⁹ St. Joseph *Morning Herald*, 29 July 1868.

⁵⁰ Ibid.

⁵¹ Ibid., 30 July 1868.

⁵² Figures from a population table in, Bureau of Statistics, *Statistical Abstract of the United States, 1907*, 56-57.
⁵³ St. Joseph *Morning Herald*, 28 May 1868.

⁵⁴ Ibid., 29 May 1868.

CHAPTER 6 NOTES

¹ The stories about large numbers of millionaires residing in St. Joseph appear to have been partially propagated by the local press and the early published histories of the city, possibly as part of the overall plan of civic promotion. The later examination of some financial records of men who were reported to be millionaires proves otherwise, while for others, their millionaire status existed only as financial paper rather than accumulated cash. The files of the Boder Collection contain some such records. County and city assessment books only give an estimate of real property values. An article in an 1886 St. Louis paper, the *Globe-Democrat*, 17 April 1886, listed only one millionaire in St. Joseph at that time. For an example of the public promotion of the millionaire story, see *History of Buchanan County*, 592.

² Historians, sociologists, and political scientists have explored the concept of who exercises community power, or control over a city's destiny, in numerous, excellent quantitative and qualitative studies. Many, but not all, of those studies suggest that the wealthy, socio-economic upper class, have nearly always exercised community power and direction, for good or bad. The classic work in the field is still considered to be that done by Robert and Helen Lynd during the 1920s and 1930s. See, *Middletown* (New York, Harcourt, Brace & World, 1929) and *Middletown in Transition* (New York: Harcourt, Brace & World, 1937) by those authors.

³ Schlesinger is often attributed with creating the urban thesis of America's development as a modern nation. His landmark work, published in 1933, provides many insights into how the nation was transformed from a population of farmers into a population of city dwellers, beginning in the late nineteenth century. See Arthur Meier Schlesinger, *The Rise of the City 1878-1898* (New York: The Macmillan Company, 1933), 53-57.

⁴ Minutes of the Board of Trade meeting were published in the St. Joseph *Morning Herald*, 15 March 1870.

⁵ Ibid., 31 December 1870. The list of names of bridge company directors was published numerous times in the local paper and lists of city officials can be found published in both the city directory for the year 1870 and in the *History of Buchanan County*, 440-457. The city

ordinance authorizing the stock subscription was also published in the local newspaper.

6 The vote tally for the bond election was published in the St. Joseph *Morning Herald*, 26 January 1871.

7 Ibid., 17 December 1871.

8 Ibid., 1 January 1873.

9 Ibid., 1 June 1873.

10 Ibid.

11 Figures taken from yearly totals for 1874, published in the St. Joseph *Morning Herald*, 1 January 1875.

12 Ibid., 31 December 1871. Profiles of St. Joseph's business leaders were often published in the year end editions of the *Herald*. Those editions are also an excellent source of figures for yearly trade.

13 Table taken from the *Morning Herald*, 1 January 1874.

14 Figures compiled from year end totals published in the *Morning Herald*. 1 January 1871 through 1879.

15 Ibid., 3 January 1879.

16 Figures compiled from *Compendium of the Eleventh Census: 1890*, Part II (Washington: Government Printing Office, 1894), 968-969.

17 St. Joseph *Morning Herald*, 3 January 1880.

18 Ibid.

19 Ibid., 1 January 1881.

20 Ibid.

21 A brief history of the Board of Trade can be found in the new years editions of the *Herald*, each year through the 1880's and 1890's. Also see *History of Buchanan County*, 588-591.

22 St. Joseph *Morning Herald*, 17 December 1871. For a good biograhical sketch of Tootle see Bartlett Boder, "Milton Tootle The First," *Museum Graphics* (winter 1963): 7-8.

23 Ibid., 1 January 1877.

24 An original probate court document listing the financial status of the Milton Tootle estate can be found in the extensive collection of personal papers of John Lemon, one of Tootle's administrators and a partner, in file 734, Boder Collection. An article in the St.Louis *Globe-Democrat*, 17 April 1886, which listed the richest men in St. Joseph for that year, estimated his fortune at $3,500,000.

25 St. Joseph *Weekly Gazette*, 12 June 1873.

26 St. Joseph *Morning Herald*, 1 January 1875.

27 Ibid., 1 January 1874.

28 Ibid., 31 December 1879. For an excellent oveview of Chicago's dominance of the meatpacking industry which ultimately affected development of that industry in St. Joseph, see Cronon, *Nature's Metropolis*, 225-247.

29 Frank S. Popplewell, "St. Joseph, Missouri as a Center of the Cattle Trade," *Missouri Historical Review* 32 (July 1938): 443-457.

30 Ibid.

31 St. Joseph *Daily Herald*, 1 January 1889.

32 St. Joseph *Daily Herald*, 1 October 1889.

33 St. Joseph *Weekly Herald*, 29 October 1891.

34 Between 1870 and 1900, three significant economic downturns occurred in American history. Those downturns were often referred to as panics. See Raymond A. Mohl, *The New City: Urban America in the Industrial Age, 1860-1920* (Wheeling, Illinois: Harlan Davidson, 1985), 147-148.

35 St. Joseph *Daily Herald*, 22 September 1895.

36 Ibid., 29 November 1895.

37 Ibid., 10 August 1899.

38 One of the first major steps in Chicago's rise to dominance of the Midwest was its success in developing its grain trade through the creation of extensive grain elevators, connected by rail from its hinterland, and a grain exchange. See Cronon, *Natures Metropolis,* 109-142.

39 St. Joseph *Daily Gazette*, 15 July 1873.

40 Figures published in St. Joseph *Morning Herald*, 1 January 1875.

41 Ibid., 1 January, 1876.

42 Rutt, *Daily News History*, 542-543.

43 Ibid., 544.

44 Ibid., 288.

45 St. Joseph *Morning Herald*, 1 January 1877.

46 Ibid.

[47] Ibid., 13 October 1885.

[48] That opinion of the Burnes brothers was widely circulated in a flier titled in 1875. "Public Opinion," 6 April 1875, file 464, Boder Collection. Also see Rutt, *Daily News History*, 141-142.

[49] From an original partnership agreement between Tootle, Lemon, Nave, and McCord, dated June 24, 1896, found in the personal papers of John S. Lemon, file 645, Boder Collection.

[50] Ibid. From an original partnership agreement between Tootle, Lemon, and Lacy, dated January 1, 1898.

[51] Figures compiled from bank and clearing house statements in the St. Joseph *Herald, Morning Herald,* and *Daily Herald,* years 1870-1900.
[52] The figure is from an original accounting statement in the personal papers of John S. Lemon, file 714, Boder Collection. A general biographical sketch of Lemon can be found in the biographical sections of any of the published 19th century general histories of the city, including *The History of Buchanan County,* 807-808, and Rutt, *Daily News History,* 356.

[53] A large number, but likely not all of Lemon's personal stock certificates, are found in file 644, Boder Collection.

[54] Found in Lemon's personal papers are a number of receipts for the trade of pure breed Jersey stock, both cows and bulls, certified by the American Jersey Association in New York. Also in the his papers are receipts from milk sales for certain years from the farm. Files 642-643, Boder Collection.

[55] For correspondence regarding the sale of stock in St. Louis banks see file 743, Boder Collection.

[56] Lemon's notebook of woolen prices can be found in file 640 while a trust agreement for the control of Buell manufacturing can be found in file 677. The document granting Lemon power of attorney for John J. Tootle, is dated April 26, 1895. See file 739, Boder Collection.

[57] Ibid., file 678.

[58] Ibid., file 645.

[59] Ibid., files 646,647, 648.

CHAPTER 7 NOTES

[1] Schlesinger, *Rise of the City,* 64-65. See also Mohl, *The New City,* 61.

[2] Mohl, *The New City,* 53-55.

[3] Schlesinger, *Rise of the City,* 80. John Garraty also provides an excellent overview of urbanization during the latter part of the nineteenth century in his work, *The New Commonwealth 1877-1890* (New York: Harper & Row, 1968), 179-219.

4 George Waring Jr., compiler, *Report on the Social Statistics of Cities, Tenth Census of the United States, 1880, Part II* (Washington: Government Printing Office, 1887), volume 19:563.

5 Ibid.

6 Department of Commerce and Labor, Bureau of the Census, Bulletin 20, *Statistics of Cities Having a Population of Over 25,000, 1902-1903* (Washington: Government Printing Office, 1905), 109.

7 Waring, *Social Statistics*, 563.

8 *Statistics of Cities*, 1902-1903, 109. Also see Rutt, *Daily News History*, 146.

9 Waring, *Social Statistics*, 563. Also see *History of Buchanan County*, 598, and Rutt, *Daily News History*, 141-142.
10 Rutt, *Daily News History*, 143-144.

11 Rutt, *Daily News History*, 143. Also see Schlesinger, *Rise of the City*, 100-102.

12 The development of St. Joseph's early telephone system is covered in Rutt, *Daily News History*, 144-145. The impact of the telephone on urban development is discussed in Schlesinger, *Rise of the City*, 94-97.

13 Waring, *Social Statistics*, 565.

14 St. Joseph *Daily Herald*, 6 January 1900.

15 Waring, *Social Statistics*, 563.

16 Ibid., 565.

17 St. Joseph *Daily Herald*, 13 October 1885.

18 St. Joseph *Gazette*, 12 December 1878.

19 Waring, *Social Statistics*, 564.

20 Ibid., 564.

21 Rutt, *Daily News History*, 238.

22 Ibid., 156-157.

23 Waring, *Social Statistics*, 564.

24 *Statistics of Cities*, 78-79.

25 Waring, *Social Statistics*, 565. Also see, Bartlett Buder, "Jesse James of St. Joseph" Museum Graphics 9 (Spring, 1957): 13-22.

26 The metropolitan system was widely adopted by many cities during the late nineteenth

211

century as a way to hopefully end corruption in local departments. The system called for independent police commissioners to oversee the forces. See. Schlesinger, *Rise of the City*, 116.

27 Bartlett Boder, "The Tootle Opera House" 15 *Museum Graphics* (winter 1963): 4-7.

28 St. Joseph *Morning Herald*, 10 December 1872. Also ses Boder, "The Tootle Opera House," 4-7.

29 Ibid.

30 Ibid.

31 For the life and accomplishments of Edmund J. Eckel, see Toni M. Prawl, "E. J. Eckel The Education of a Beaux-Arts Architect and His Practice in Missouri" (Ph.D. diss., University of Missouri, 1994). Also see a brief biography and photograph in Rutt, *Daily News History*, 393.

32 St. Joseph *Daily Herald*, 8 May 1892.

33 Ibid.

34 Tootle wedding announcement in the St. Joseph *Gazette*, 13 November 1892, and in reference to the Krugs, 19 June 1892.

35 Ibid., 30 December 1894.

36 John S. Lemon was a charter member of the Benton Club, and in his personal papers can be found some membership information and an original stock certificate from the club, file 644, Boder Collection. The preamble of the Benton Club was published in the centennial edition of the St. Joseph *News-Press*, 25 July 1943.

37 For further reading and early photographs of the Lotus Club see Clyde Weeks, *Lake Contrary: Days of Glory, 1880-1964* (St. Joseph: Blacksnake Creek Press, 1992), 41-43. Also see an article on the club in the centennial edition of the St. Joseph *News-Press*, 25 July 1943.

38 An overview of the problems of working class Americans can be found in Garraty, *The New Commonwealth*, 128-178.

39 St. Joseph *Daily Herald*, 26 July 1893.

40 Wage figures from a table published in the St. Joseph *Morning Herald*, 1 January 1875.

41 For a complete discription of the park and excellent early photographs, see Clyde Weeks, *Krug Park: St. Joseph Crown Jewel* (St. Joseph: Blacksnake Creek Press, 1993). For a brief overview of the importance of parks in the urban setting see Glaab and Brown, *Urban America*, 178-179.

42 For reports on the exposition see the St. Joseph *Daily Herald*, 3 September 1889, through 3 October 1889.

43 Advertisements for the Tootle Opera House ran daily in the papers. Admission prices taken

from the St. Joseph *Daily Herald*, 2 January 1881.

44 St. Joseph *Daily Herald*, 26 July 1868. For an overview of baseball's influence on city life during the period see Schlesinger, *Rise of the City*, 311-313.

45 Ibid., 10 June 1893. By the beginning of the 1890s, the *Herald* ran a daily sports section of at least three columns, with baseball scores, reports on boxing matches, and horse racing.

46 Ibid., 2 February 1900.

47 Ibid., 25 February 1900. Beside the Donovan Hotel Alley the St. Joseph city directory for 1900, listed the Monarch alleys as being located under the Monarch Saloon.

48 Schlesinger, *Rise of the City*, 288.

49 *Directory of St. Joseph* (St. Joseph: Combe Printing Company, 1899).

50 Ibid.

51 Schlesinger, *Rise of the City*, 289.

52 From the secret society listing in the St. Joseph *Daily Herald*, 10 August 1899.

53 St. Joseph *Morning Herald*, 22 April 1868.

54 *Directory of St. Joseph, 1890* (St. Joseph: Combe Printing Co., 1890), 684. *Directory of St. Joseph, 1900* (St. Joseph: Combe Printing Co., 1900), 768.

55 Schlesinger, *Rise of the City*, 389.

56 Ibid., 390. For further discussion of city bosses also see Mohl, *The New City*, 83-100, and Garraty, *The New Commonwealth*, 216-219.

57 Excerpted from the flier, "Public Opinion," 6 April 1875. An original copy of the flier can be found in file 464, Boder Collection.

58 Mohl, *The New City*, 100-107.

59 The chart of presidential elections and the vote patterns of city wards have been compiled by the author from the official election results published in various editions of the St. Joseph *Morning Herald, Daily Herald, and Gazette-Herald* between 1872 and 1900.

60 The vote counts of city wards have been compiled by the author from the official election results published in the St. Joseph *Daily Herald*, 9 November 1888 and *Gazette-Herald*, 9 November 1900.

61 Definitions of "political boss" vary, but a good interpretation has been put forward by sociologist Robert Merton, who said, "The key structural function of the boss was to organize, centralize, and maintain in good working condition the fragments of power dispersed throughout the city's political structure." From a quotation cited in Mohl, *The New City*, 107.

[62] Ibid., 103.

[63] St.Joseph *Daily Herald*, 2 February 1900.

[64] Rutt, *Daily News History*, 104.

[65] A photograph of St. Joseph script can be found in Rutt, *Daily News History*, 105.

[66] St. Joseph *Daily Herald*, 27 March 1900.

[67] William Riordon, *Plunkitt of Tammany Hall* (New York: E. P. Dutton & Company, 1963), 3.

[68] See the study of city government in Lynd, *Middletown*, 413-434.

CHAPTER 8 NOTES

[1] St. Joseph *Daily Herald*, 8 February 1900.

[2] Ibid.

[3] Ibid., 28 March 1900. For further reading on the conflict between city, county, and state government see, Glaab and Brown, *Urban America*, 167-199.

[4] Ibid., 29 March 1900.

[5] Ibid.

[6] Ibid., 8 June 1900.

[7] Ibid., 12 June 1900.

[8] Ibid., 15 June 1900.

[9] The population of Los Angeles grew from 50,395 in 1890 to 102, 479 in 1900, representing a percentage increase of 104%. Portland grew from 46,385 to 90,426, an increase of 95%. St. Joseph had a growth rate of nearly 97 %. See Department of Commerce and Labor, Bureau of the Census, Bulletin 20, *Statistics of Cities Having a Population of Over 25,000, 1902 and 1903* (Washington: Government Printing Office, 1905), 65.

[10] St. Joseph *Gazette-Herald*, 28 September 1900.

[11] Ibid.

[12] Ibid.

[13] Ibid., 29 September 1900.

[14] Ibid., 30 September 1900.

[15] The local account is attributed to longtime St. Joseph newspaperman and editor Frederick W. Slater. He recounted the story in an editorial in the St. Joseph *News-Press*, 19 August

1983, and in a personal conversation with the author. His comment was that he believed the story was basically true although the part about the telegram had been embellished over time. Frederick W. Slater, interviewed by author, St. Joseph, Missouri, 12 November 1996.

[16] Department of Commerce and Labor, Bureau of the Census, Bulletin 50, *Statistics of Cities Having a Population of Over 30,000, 1904* (Washington: Government Printing Office, 1906), 41.

[17] *Statistics of Cities, 1902-1903*, 71.

[18] Ibid., 78.

[19] Ibid., 98.

[20] Ibid., 133. St. Joseph did issue more building permits that all other cities in her population class except Los Angeles and Memphis, however the other cities in the class were older and did not have so dramatic percentages of population increase as proported for St. Joseph.

[21] Ibid., 166.

[22] Ibid., 142.

[23] Bureau of Statistics, *Statistical Abstract of the United States, 1912* (Washington D. C.: Government Printing Office, 1914), 38-39.

[24] Schlesinger, *Rise of the City*, 421.

BIBLIOGRAPHY

The following listings do not represent a complete bibliography for the history of St. Joseph, Missouri. They do represent a list of works or publications either cited or consulted by the author for this text. Newspapers and the dates consulted are listed first, followed by all other sources in alphabetical order.

NEWSPAPERS

The Kansas City *Weekly Journal of Commerce*, May 1863 to December 1869.

The St. Joseph *Adventure*, May 1848 to April 1852.

The St. Joseph *Commercial Cycle*, April 1853 to January 1858.

The St. Joseph *Daily Herald*, October 1876 to July 1900.

The St. Joseph *Free Democrat*, August 1859 to April 1861.

The St. Joseph *Gazette*, weekly, April 1845 to December 1898.

The St. Joseph *Gazette*, daily, July 1868 to January 1899.

The St. Joseph *Gazette-Herald*, July to October, 1900.

The St. Joseph *Morning Daily Herald*, July 1866 to October 1876.

The St. Joseph *Morning Herald*, February 1862 to October 1864.

The St. Joseph *Morning Herald & Daily Tribune*, October 1864 to July 1866.

The St. Joseph *Weekly Herald*, March 1862 to December 1899.

The St. Joseph *Weekly West*, May 1859 to April 1860

OTHER SOURCES

Billington, Ray Allen. *The Far Western Frontier, 1830-1869.* New York: Harper & Row, 1956.

___. *Westward Expansion: A History of the American Frontier.* New York: Macmillan Company, 1967.

Boder, Bartlett. "Missouri and the Latter-Day Saints." *Museum Graphics* 9 (Fall 1957): 4-6.

___. "Old St. Jo." *Museum Graphics* 6 (Spring 1954): 3-6.

___. "Captain Thomas H. Brierly." *Museum Graphics* 7 (Fall 1955): 4-6.

___. "The Railroad is Built." *Museum Graphics* 10 (Summer 1958): 8-9.

___. "Arrival in St. Joseph." *Museum Graphics* 7 (Spring 1955): 18-20.

___. "Milton Tootle The First." *Museum Graphics* 15 (Winter 1963):7-8.

___. "The Tootle Opera House." *Museum Graphics* 15 (Winter 1963): 5-7.

Boutros, David. "The West Illustrated: Meyer's Views of Missouri River Towns." *Missouri Historical Review* 80 (April 1986): 304-320.

Bowen, Elbert R.. "Amusements and Entertainments in Early Missouri." *Missouri Historical Review* 47 (July 1953): 307-317.

"Brothers Robidoux, The." *The Santa Fean* 6 (April 1978): 38-40.

Buchanan County, Missouri, *Records of the Buchanan County Court*, Books 1-4.

Bureau of Statistics Bulletin No. 30. *Statistical Abstract of the United States, 1907.* Washington: Government Printing Office, 1908.

Campbell's Gazeteer of Missouri. St. Louis: R. A. Campbell, Publisher, 1874.

City of St. Joseph, Missouri. *Notes From the Board of Trustee Meetings, 1845-1851.*

City of St. Joseph, Missouri. *Incorporation and Ordinance Book, 1845-1851.*

City of St. Joseph, Missouri. *Ordinance Book, 1851-1857.*

Clevenger, Homer. "The Building of the Hannibal and St. Joseph Railroad." *Missouri Historical Review* 36 (October 1941): 32-47.

Compendium of the Eleventh Census: 1890, Part II. Washington: Government Printing Office, 1894.

Coy, Roy. "The Early Years." *Museum Graphics* 17 (Spring 1965): 6-7.

Cronon, William. *Nature's Metropolis-Chicago and the Great West.* New York: W.W. Norton, 1991.

Davis, Stephen. "Jeff Thompson's Unsuccessful Quest For a Confederate Generalship." *Missouri Historical Review* 85 (October 1990): 53-65.

Department of Commerce and Labor, Bureau of the Census, Bulletin 20, *Statistics of Cities Having a Population of Over 25,000, 1902 and 1903.* Washington: Government Printing Office, 1905.

Department of Commerce and Labor, Bureau of the Census, Bulletin 50, *Statistics of Cities Having a Population of Over 30,000, 1904.* Washington: Government Printing Office, 1906.

Eaton, Clement. *The Growth of Southern Civilization, 1790 to 1860.* New York: Harper & Brothers, 1961.

Finch, Frank. *Cartoons of St. Joe Boys.* St. Joseph: 1905.

Foley, William. *A History of Missouri, Volume I, 1673-1820.* Columbia: University of Missouri Press, 1971.

Garraty, John. *The New Commonwealth, 1877-1890.* New York: Harper & Row, 1968.

Gates, Paul. "The Railroads of Missouri, 1850-1870." *Missouri Historical Review* 26 (October 1931): 126-141.

Glaab, Charles N.. *Kansas City and the Railroads, Community Policy in the Growth of a Regional Metropolis.* Madison: The State Historical Society of Wisconsin, 1962.

Glaab, Charles, and Theodore A. Brown. *A History of Urban America.* New York: Macmillan Company, 1967.

Grant, H. Roger. "Courting the Great Western Railway: An Episode of Town Rivalry." *Missouri Historical Review* 76 (July 1982): 405-421.

Greeley, Horace. *An Overland Journey, From NewYork to San Francisco.* New York: C. M. Saxton, Barker & Co., 1860.

Gregg, Kate. "Missourians in the Gold Rush." *Missouri Historical Review* 39 (January 1945): 137-154.

Grenier, Mildred. *St. Joseph: A Pictoral History.* Virginia Beach, Virginia: Donning Company, 1981.

Hagen, Olaf. "The Pony Express Starts From St. Joseph." *Missouri Historical Review* 43, (October 1948): 1-17.

Hewitt, J.N.B., ed.. *Journal of Rudolph Friedrich Kurz.* Bureau of American Ethology Bulletin 115. Washington: Government Printing Office, 1937.
History of Buchanan County, Missouri. (1881 reprint) Cassville, Missouri: Litho Printers & Bindery, 1973.

Holt, Edgar. "Missouri River Transportation in the Expansion of the West." *Missouri Historical Review* 20 (March 1926): 361-381.

Johnson, Arthur M. and Barry Supple. *Boston Capitalists and Western Railroads: A Study in the Nineteenth-Century Railroad Investment Process.* Cambridge: Harvard University Press, 1967.

Larsen, Lawrence H.. *The Urban West at the End of the Frontier.* Lawrence, Kansas: The

Regents Press of Kansas, 1978.

Laws of the State of Missouri, 14th General Assembly, 1st Session, 1846-47.

Laws of the State of Missouri, 16th General Assembly, 1850-1851.

Lewis, Meriwether. *Lewis and Clark Expedition.* 1814 Edition, Unabridged. 3 vols. Philadelphia: J. B. Lippencott, 1961.

Logan, Sheridan. *Old Saint Jo.* John Sublett Logan Foundation, 1979.

Lynd, Robert and Helen Lynd. *Middletown.* New York: Harcourt, Brace & World, 1929.

Mahoney, Timothy. *River Towns in the Great West.* Cambridge: Cambridge University Press, 1990.

March, David. *History of Missouri.* New York: Lewis Historical Publishing Co., 1967.

Mattes, Merrill J.. "Joseph Robidoux." In *The Moutain Men and the Fur Trade of the Far West,* edited by LeRoy Hafen. 10 vols. Glendale, California: Arthur H. Clark Company, 1965.

Maxmillian, Prince of Wied. *Travels in the Interior of North America, 1832-1834,* reprinted in *Early Western Travels,* edited by Rueben Gold Thwaites. 32 vols. Cleveland: Arthur H. Clark Company, 1906.

McCandless, Perry. *A History of Missouri, Volume II, 1820-1860.* Columbia: University of Missouri Press, 1972.

McDonald, E. L. and W. S. King, eds.. *History of Buchanan County and St. Joseph, Missouri.* St. Joseph: Midland Printing Co., 1915.

McKee, Howard. "The Platte Purchase." *Missouri Historical Review* 32 (January 1938): 129-147.

McReynolds, Edwin. *Missouri: A History of the Crossroads State.* Norman: University of Oklahoma Press, 1962.

Meinig, D. W.. *The Shaping of America: A Geographical Perspective on 500 Years of History, Volume 2, Continental America, 1800-1867.* New Haven: Yale University Press, 1993.

Merk, Frederick. *History of the Westward Movement.* New York: Alfred A. Knopf, 1978.

Mohl, Raymond A.. *The New City: Urban America in the Industrial Age, 1860-1920.* Wheeling, Illinois: Harlan Davidson, 1985.

Morgan, Dale L. ed.. *The West of William Ashley, 1822-1838.* Denver: The Old West Publishing Company, 1964.

Ohman, Marian. *History of Missouri's Counties, County Seats, and Courthouse Squares.* Columbia: University of Missouri Press, 1983.

Oster, Donald B.. "The Hannibal and St. Joseph Railroad, Government and Town Founding, 1846-1861." *Missouri Historical Review,* 87 (July 1993): 403-421.

Overton, Richard. *Burlington Route: A History of the Burlington Lines.* New York: Alfred A. Knopf, 1965.

Palmer, Joel. *Journal of Travels Over the Rocky Mountains,* reprinted in *Early Western Travels,* edited by Rueben Gold Thwaites. 32 vols. Cleveland: Arthur H. Clark Company, 1906.

Parrish, William. *A History of Missouri, Volume III, 1860-1875.* Columbia: University of Missouri Press, 1973.

Piott, Steven. "Missouri and the Beef Trust:Consumer Action and Investigation." *Missouri Historical Review* 76 (October 1981): 31-52.

Popplewell, Frank S.. "St. Joseph, Missouri as a Center of the Cattle Trade." *Missouri Historical Review* 32 (July 1938): 443-457.

Prawl, Toni M.. "E. J. Eckel: The Education of a Beaux-Arts Architect and His Practice in Missouri." Ph.D. diss., University of Missouri, 1994.

Pumphrey, Frederic. "The Old St. Jo Gazette." *Missouri Historical Review* 38 (October 1943): 33-43.

Revised Statutes of Missouri, 1835.

Reps, John. *The Making of Urban America: A History of City Planning in the United States.* Princeton: Princeton University Press, 1965.

Rogers, Ann. *Lewis and Clark in Missouri.* St. Louis: Meredco, 1981.

Robidoux, Orrel Messmore. *Memorial to the Robidoux Brothers.* Kansas City: Smith Grieves Company, 1924.

Rutt, Christian. *The Daily News History of Buchanan County and St. Joseph, Missouri.* St. Joseph: St. Joseph Publishing Company, 1898.

_____ ed.. *History of Buchanan County and the City of St. Joseph and Representative Citizens, 1826-1904.* Chicago: Biographical Publishing Co., 1904.

St. Joseph Cathedral Parish, Our Story, 1845-1995. Marceline, Missouri: Wadsworth Publishing Company, 1995.

Schlesinger, Arthur Meier. *The Rise of the City 1878-1898.* New York: The Macmillan Company, 1933.

Settle, Raymond W., and Mary Lund Settle. *War Drums and Wagon Wheels, The Story of Russell, Majors and Waddell.* Lincoln: University of Nebraska Press, 1966.

Shoemaker, Floyd. "The Pony Express: Comemoration, Stables, and Museum." *Missouri Historical Review* 44 (July 1950): 343-363.

221

____. "Missouri's Proslavery Fight for Kansas." *Missouri Historical Review* 48 (July 1950): 218-236.

Slater, Harold, and George Sherman. *Behind the Headlines.* Loose Creek, Missouri: The Westphalia Press, 1989.

Tracy, W. P.. *Men Who Made St. Joseph.* St. Joseph: Combe Printing Co., 1920.

Waring, George Jr., compiler. *Report on the Social Statistics of Cities, Tenth Census of the United States, 1880, Part II.* Washington: Government Printing Office, 1887.

Weeks, Clyde. *Krug Park: St. Joseph Crown Jewel.* St. Joseph: Blacksnake Creek Press, 1993.

____. *Lake Contrary: Days of Glory, 1880-1964.* St. Joseph: Blacksnake Creek Press, 1992.

Williams, Walter. *History of Northwest Missouri.* 3 vols. Chicago: Lewis Publishing Co., 1915.

Williams, Walter, and Floyd Shoemaker, *Missouri, Mother of the West.* Chicago: American Historical Society, 1930.

Williamson, Hugh. "One Who Went West." *Missouri Historical Review* 57 (April 1963): 368-378.

INDEX